THE WEALTH OF WIVES

The Other Voice in Early Modern Europe:
The Toronto Series, 42

MEDIEVAL AND RENAISSANCE
TEXTS AND STUDIES

VOLUME 485

The Other Voice in
Early Modern Europe:
The Toronto Series

SERIES EDITORS Margaret L. King *and* Albert Rabil, Jr.
SERIES EDITOR, ENGLISH TEXTS Elizabeth H. Hageman

Previous Publications in the Series

The Other Voice in Early Modern Europe: The Toronto Series

SERIES EDITORS Margaret L. King *and* Albert Rabil, Jr.
SERIES EDITOR, ENGLISH TEXTS Elizabeth H. Hageman

Previous Publications in the Series

The Other Voice in Early Modern Europe: The Toronto Series

SERIES EDITORS Margaret L. King *and* Albert Rabil, Jr.
SERIES EDITOR, ENGLISH TEXTS Elizabeth H. Hageman

Previous Publications in the Series

The Other Voice in Early Modern Europe: The Toronto Series

SERIES EDITORS Margaret L. King *and* Albert Rabil, Jr.
SERIES EDITOR, ENGLISH TEXTS Elizabeth H. Hageman

Previous Publications in the Series

The Other Voice in
Early Modern Europe:
The Toronto Series

SERIES EDITORS Margaret L. King *and* Albert Rabil, Jr.
SERIES EDITOR, ENGLISH TEXTS Elizabeth H. Hageman

Previous Publications in the Series

FRANCESCO BARBARO

The Wealth of Wives:
A Fifteenth-Century Marriage Manual

◦~

Edited and translated by
MARGARET L. KING

Iter Academic Press
Toronto, Ontario

Arizona Center for Medieval and Renaissance Studies
Tempe, Arizona

2015

Iter Academic Press
Tel: 416/978-7074   Email: iter@utoronto.ca
Fax: 416/978-1668   Web: www.itergateway.org

Arizona Center for Medieval and Renaissance Studies
Tel: 480/965-5900   Email: mrts@acmrs.org
Fax: 480/965-1681   Web: acmrs.org

Library of Congress Cataloging-in-Publication Data

Barbaro, Francesco, 1390-1454, author.
[De re uxoria. English]
The wealth of wives : a fifteenth-century marriage manual / Francesco Barbaro ; edited and translated by Margaret L. King.
        pages cm -- (The other voice in early modern Europe ; 42) (Medieval and renaissance texts and studies ; volume 485)
    ISBN 978-0-86698-540-6 (alk. paper)
1. Marriage--Early works to 1800. I. King, Margaret L., 1947- II. Title. III. Series: Other voice in early modern Europe ; 42. IV. Series: Medieval & Renaissance Texts & Studies (Series) ; v. 485.
    HQ731.B2413 2015
    306.8109'01--dc23

                                                    2015027681

Cover illustration:
Licinio, Bernardino (c.1489–before 1565), *Portrait of the Family of the Artist's Brother*. Galleria Borghese, Rome, Italy. Scala / Art Resource, NY. ART28297.

Cover design:
Maureen Morin, Information Technology Services, University of Toronto Libraries.

Typesetting and production:
Iter Inc.

For Albert Rabil, Jr.

Contents

Acknowledgments

Francesco Barbaro's *De re uxoria*—its title properly translated at last as *The Wealth of Wives* in the volume now in your hands—was one of the first works of Venetian humanism I encountered when doing my dissertation research in 1970–1972. It was a building-block of my eventual analysis of Venetian humanism published in 1986. By that date, I had also described the work in a widely-cited article discussing the works of three Venetian humanists on marriage and the family. After 1986, I continued to draw on Barbaro's work in my studies of the role of mothers in the transmission of culture. Over the years, I drew on the insights of many colleagues and students in my continued meditation on this pioneering work. Now nearly fifty years later, in 2015, I acknowledge all of their comments and criticism. Thank you, all of you.

Working as I necessarily have in isolation, though situated in a world metropolis, but employed at a public university where humanistic scholarship was not a top priority, I am immensely grateful for the support of those without whom no intellectual endeavor may succeed: librarians. The support of the Brooklyn College library has been constant and is deeply appreciated. More recently, I have benefited from the unfailing energy and resourcefulness of William R. Bowen, Director of Iter at the University of Toronto Libraries, and Margaret English-Haskin and Anabela Piersol, his capable lieutenants.

In my labors over the years, three scholars have been a source of inspiration and assistance: Paul Oskar Kristeller (1905-1999), Paul F. Grendler, and Albert Rabil, Jr. At this time, I especially want to acknowledge Al Rabil's importance, as I dedicate to him this volume in the Other Voice series that he and I launched in 1995.

Our association has been long, predating that event by more than twenty years, and it has continued ever since. I shall claim the honor of having first envisioned the Other Voice series, sketching out an initial set of ten or twelve volumes giving voice to the assertion of women's moral and intellectual equality with men. The first volume of the series, Al's translation of Henricus Cornelius Agrippa's *Declamation on the Nobility and Preeminence of the Female Sex*, appeared in 1996.

Although the initial plan may have been mine, Al quickly took the ball and ran with it. Over the next twenty years, he developed a huge list of projects in conversations with scholars, most of them women, and many of them participants in a series of NEH-funded summer institutes that he ran in New York City and later, in retirement, in Chapel Hill, NC. The projects kept coming: works in Latin, Italian, French, Spanish, German, Russian, and Polish; in verse and in prose; fiction and non-fiction. Long-forgotten was the original focus on works explicitly addressing the issue of female equality. In Al's mind, any work written by a woman in this period, or by a man on related issues, was ipso facto an assertion of female power.

And so the list grew: beyond the 60 volumes published by the University of Chicago Press, and the 100 or so that migrated to a new Canadian home provided by Iter Inc. and the Centre for Reformation and Renaissance Studies at the University of Toronto, and that now is published jointly by Iter Academic Press and the Arizona Center for Medieval and Renaissance Studies. In 2015, the 100th volume of the Other Voice series will be published, followed soon after, in 2015 or 2016, by the 50th of the Toronto series. My guess is that the series will close in the early 2020s—best that it come to a graceful conclusion before its time, and ours, is past—having engendered some 150 volumes.

This achievement is not minor, although it is not yet widely recognized. Individual books have been published and positively reviewed; many have received prizes. But there is no apprehension as yet of the collective effect of a mass of work, culminating in some 150 books, concretizing not only the contribution of women (and their male supporters) to European culture, but the claim of women to intellectual equality and participation in that cultural realm.

Yet in time, I am confident, the Other Voice series will be duly recognized, as one participant in a recent conference noted, as transformational. In Western Europe between the fourteenth and eighteenth centuries, women participated at an accelerating rate in mainstream culture at a time when that mainstream was itself at a zenith of achievement. They wrote wherever they were: as nuns, as princesses, as housewives, as coerced brides, as widows; they wrote lyric, dramatic and epic verse, pastoral, romance, and satire, history and scientific and medical treatises, and many, many letters that open windows not only on their lives but on the textured fabric of the society they inhabited. And they were joined by a few men—one participant in that same conference called them "fellow travelers"—who without hesitation or restraint acclaimed the intellectual and spiritual capacity of women writers and thinkers.

This massive entry of women into mainstream intellectual life is unique in the history of the world. From it all else comes. For those who complain that the composition by women of Petrarchan sonnets, or of accounts of their mystical visions, is irrelevant to the later struggles women waged for social and political power willfully resist the significance of those achievements: those sonnets, those visions, were the first shots fired in a long and continuing battle. The Other Voice series has highlighted more than any other project of our generation the importance of the intellectual activity of women in the early modern era. By the time the last volume is published, it will have changed the way the history of that era is written.

This achievement is due primarily to Al Rabil's enthusiasm, commitment, material support, and unceasing labor—labor from which he has now decided to rest, as I have taken over the mission of achieving the goal that was once mine, then his, but always ours. To him I dedicate this work that has been at the center of my thoughts as long as I have known him, and that I proudly include in the series that is our mutual endeavor.

Introduction

The Other Voice

In 1415, the young and still unmarried Francesco Barbaro (1390–1454) wrote the revolutionary treatise *The Wealth of Wives (De re uxoria)* that posits the value a wife contributes to a marriage as the mother of offspring.[1] It is revolutionary because it identifies the mother—a woman, not a man; an interloper in the household, not its patriarch—as the critical figure for the rearing of the young and, consequently, for the social and cultural reproduction of the noble family. It is the mother, not the father, Barbaro argues, who transmits her own mental and moral characteristics to her offspring in the processes of gestation and lactation,

1. Barbaro would be married in 1419 to the noblewoman Maria, daughter of the eminent Pietro Loredan, procurator of San Marco, and would father one son, the humanist Zaccaria Barbaro, and four daughters. For Barbaro, see especially Margaret L. King, *Venetian Humanism in an Age of Patrician Dominance* (Princeton: Princeton University Press, 1986), 323–25, and studies there cited; and Francesco Barbaro, *Epistolario*, ed. Claudio Griggio, 2 vols. (Florence: L.S. Olschki, 1991, 1999). For the *De re uxoria*, see Attilio Gnesotto, ed., *De re uxoria liber, in partes duas*, in *Atti e Memorie della R. Accademia di Scienze, Lettere ed Arti in Padova*, n.s. 32 (1915–1916), 6–105 (offprint, Padua: Randi, 1915), Introduction, vii–xx; Percy Gothein, ed. and trans., *Das Buch von der Ehe: De re uxoria* (Berlin: Verlag die Runde, 1933), Vorrede, 9–10, and Nachwort, 85–88; and Benjamin G. Kohl, "Introduction" to "On Wifely Duties," a partial translation of *De re uxoria*, in Kohl and Ronald G. Witt, eds., *The Earthly Republic: Italian Humanists on Government and Society* (Philadelphia: University of Pennsylvania Press, 1978), 177–228, at 177–88. See also studies of the *De re uxoria* by Carole Collier Frick, "The Downcast Eyes of the Women of the Upper Class in Francesco Barbaro's *De re uxoria*," *UCLA Historical Journal* 9 (1989), online at http://escholarship.org/uc/item/8cm5t90d; Frick, "Francesco Barbaro's *De re uxoria*: A Silent Dialogue for a Young Medici Bride," in *Printed Voices: The Renaissance Culture of Dialogue,* ed. Dorothea B. Heitsch and Jean-François Vallée (Toronto: University of Toronto Press, 2004), 193–205; Percy Gothein, *Francesco Barbaro: Früh-Humanismus und Staatskunst in Venedig* (Berlin: Verlag die Runde, 1932), chapter 4: "De re uxoria und ihr Verfasser: Ideen- und literargeschichtliche Zusammenhänge," 61–99; King, "Caldiera and the Barbaros on Marriage and the Family: Humanist Reflections of Venetian Realities," *Journal of Medieval and Renaissance Studies* 6, no. 1 (1976): 19–50, rpt. in King, *Humanism, Venice, and Women: Essays on the Italian Renaissance* (Aldershot, UK: Ashgate, 2005), V; Manfred Lentzen, "Frühhumanistische Auffassungen über Ehe und Familie (Francesco Barbaro—Matteo Palmieri—Leon Battista Alberti)," in *Saeculum tamquam aureum: Internationales Symposion zur italienischen Renaissance des 14.–16. Jahrhunderts (am 17./18. September 1996 in Mainz)*, ed. Ute Ecker and Clemens Zintzen (Hildesheim: G. Olms, 1997), 379–94; Alberto Tenenti, "La *res uxoria* tra Francesco Barbaro e Leon Battista Alberti," in *Una famiglia veneziana nella storia: i Barbaro: Atti del convegno di studi in occasione del quinto centenario della morte dell'umanista Ermolao, Venezia, 4–6 novembre 1993*, ed. Michela Marangoni and Manlio Pastore Stocchi (Venice: Istituto veneto di scienze, lettere ed arti, 1996), 43–66; and the chapter on Barbaro in Sister Prudence Allen's *The Concept of Woman*, vol. 2: *The Early Humanist Reformation, 1250–1500* (Grand Rapids, MI: Wm. B. Eerdmans, 2002), 712–31.

and who further guides her child's religious and intellectual development during the first years of life. Barbaro's elevation of the role of women in the formation of future generations is unprecedented in the classical or Christian traditions. Ironically, it is a man of the highest social rank in the imperial city of Venice, who will during his career exercise enormous political power, and who makes no apology for his position of social and political privilege, who becomes the first champion of maternal capacity in the domain of the family, and an advocate of the other voice.

Barbaro: Humanist and Statesman

Francesco Barbaro was twenty-five years old when he wrote *The Wealth of Wives*, having just finished his studies: Latin, Greek, philosophical, and legal. Unmarried and, as was typical of elite men in their mid-twenties during the Italian Renaissance, with as yet no political or professional role, he would soon embark on marriage and career, and enter the vortex at the center of Venetian public life. But for the moment, he was poised on the verge of that future, and engaged above all in a season of cultural exhilaration, as the intellectual movement of humanism gained full force and, in Venice, converged with a new political mission.

In Venice, humanism begins with the great Italian poet and Latin scholar Petrarch (Francesco Petrarca, 1304–1374).[2] In 1351, some four decades before Barbaro's birth, Petrarch came to Venice as an emissary of Milan, and bonded with the Doge of Venice Andrea Dandolo (1306–1354), a prodigy of learning as well as of politics. Petrarch returned to his wanderings and Dandolo soon died. But Petrarch had planted the seed of humanism in Dandolo's coterie of bureaucrats and secretaries, who subsequently invited him back to Venice to take up permanent residence. He came in 1361, and there resided until 1367, the lodestone of Venetian intellectual life at a critical juncture. Three years later, he left in a huff over an academic squabble.[3] At about that time, Zaccaria Trevisan (c. 1370–1414) was born, the inheritor of the Petrarchan legacy in Venice and the prototypical figure of Venetian humanism.[4]

Like most of the Venetian humanists who followed him, Trevisan was a nobleman. He had not been born noble, however. His family was one of thirty

2. Humanism has earlier origins in the northern Italian communes, as has been exhaustively demonstrated by Ronald G. Witt: *In the Footsteps of the Ancients: The Origins of Humanism from Lovato to Bruni* (Leiden: Brill, 2000); *The Two Latin Cultures and the Foundation of Renaissance Humanism in Medieval Italy* (Cambridge: Cambridge University Press, 2012).

3. One of immense significance, as documented fully in Petrarch's *De sui ipsius et multorum aliorum ignorantia*, trans. and ed. Hans Nachod as *On His Own Ignorance and That of Many Others*, in Ernst Cassirer, Paul Oskar Kristeller, and John Herman Randall, Jr., eds., *The Renaissance Philosophy of Man: Selections in Translation* (Chicago: University of Chicago Press, 1948), 47–133.

4. For Zaccaria Trevisan, see King, *Venetian Humanism*, 436–37, and sources there cited.

wealthy commoner families granted nobility—the last time noble status would be granted to anyone before the seventeenth century—in recognition of their sacrificial service. That service was performed in 1381 during the epochal Chioggian war, in which Venice was nearly destroyed but rallied to defeat Genoa, its longtime commercial rival. It is likely that the prize of noble status, so rare and so valuable, was one that Trevisan cherished profoundly. It is certain that he developed important contacts with older patrician families, including the Marcellos and the Barbaros. In 1395, he married the noblewoman Caterina di Giovanni Marcello, and he would in 1413 deliver a celebratory oration in honor of the doctorate at the University of Padua of her kinsman Pietro Marcello, that city's bishop—one whom Francesco Barbaro, then a student, no doubt heard *viva voce*. In the 1390s, even as he pursued his university studies in canon and civil law, Trevisan likely visited the Barbaro household, when Francesco was a boy. In 1412 and 1413, when he held the position of Captain of Padua (one of the two executive positions held by Venetian noblemen in their mainland subject cities), the two were close. Barbaro records that intimacy in the dedicatory preface of *The Wealth of Wives*, and again in its culminating paragraph when he recalls Trevisan as "a man worthy of the highest praise—whose memory I celebrate."[5]

Zaccaria Trevisan embodied the tendencies of Venetian intellectual culture that would come to typify that majority (about two-thirds) of the Venetian humanists who were of noble origin. His humanism was passionate and genuine—but it was infused by the disciplines of philosophy and law taught at the university of Padua, a neighboring city that became subject to Venice in 1405; and it was enlisted in the service of Venetian political interests. Francesco Barbaro would follow Trevisan's example. His treatise *The Wealth of Wives* is an early manifestation of that complex and distinctively Venetian form of humanism, and is the first major work of the Venetian humanist tradition.

Prior to 1407, Barbaro studied with the humanist Giovanni Conversini da Ravenna, resident in Padua from 1392 to 1405 and in Venice in 1405–1406,[6] who numbered among his pupils Pier Paolo Vergerio the Elder (1370–1444/1445) and Guarino Veronese, later Barbaro's instructor in Greek, of whom more below. From 1405 to 1408, under Conversini's tutelage, Barbaro began his formal education in the *studia humanitatis*—those disciplines that formed the core of the humanist program, including grammar (Latin and, sometimes, Greek), rhetoric, poetry, moral philosophy, and history. He then continued his studies under Gasparino Barzizza (1360–1431), who, after a sojourn in Venice in 1407, when he made

---

5. See below, 124. Subsequent citations of Barbaro's *Wealth of Wives* will be given within parentheses in the text.

6. Conversini has been extensively studied by Benjamin G. Kohl; see the convenient collection of his studies in *Culture and Politics in Early Renaissance Padua* (Aldershot, UK: Ashgate, 2001).

contact with the Barbaro family, moved to Padua in 1408.[7] There Barzizza taught at the university until 1421, while at the same time maintaining in his home a school with a resident group of adolescents, Francesco Barbaro among them.[8] In Padua, Barbaro mastered Latin prose on the Ciceronian model, in which Barzizza was the leading expert, and read the essential Latin classics—including Cicero's *De officiis* (On Duties), a humanist favorite, whose pages richly inform Barbaro's own work. Through Barzizza, as well, Barbaro likely came to know Pier Paolo Vergerio's *De ingenuis moribus et liberalibus studiis adulescentiae* (The Character and Studies Befitting a Free-Born Youth, 1402/1403),[9] to which he would allude in his *The Wealth of Wives*, written not long afterward. Vergerio's prescriptions, indeed, for the education of the heir apparent of the Carrara dynasty then ruling Padua very likely approximated that which Barbaro was receiving at that time and not far away, in Venice.

Remaining in Padua, Barbaro pursued the university program of studies in philosophy and law, and received on October 1, 1412, at the age of twenty-two, his doctorate in civil and canon law, the degree most commonly sought by the Venetian noble humanists. By this time, Zaccaria Trevisan had taken up his office as Captain of Padua, making possible the discussions between Barbaro and Trevisan that are fundamental to Barbaro's conceptualization of marriage.

There remained, to prepare Barbaro for the intellectual labors evidenced in *The Wealth of Wives*, the acquisition of Greek. Barbaro began his study of Greek with Guarino Veronese (1374–1460) in July 1414, when—after a four-year stint in Florence—Guarino had returned to Venice and residied in the Barbaro

7. For Barzizza, see Guido Martellotti's profile in the *Dizionario biografico degli italiani*, vol. 7 (1970), online at http://www.treccani.it/enciclopedia/gasperino-barzizza_%28Dizionario_Biografico%29/, as well as Lucia Gualdo Rosa, ed., *Gasparino Barzizza e la Rinascita degli studi classici: fra continuità e rinnovamento: Atti del seminario di studi, Napoli, Palazzo Sforza, 11 Aprile 1997* (Naples: Istituto universitario orientale, 1999).

8. For the lively household school Barzizza maintained while carrying on his university teaching, see R.G.G. Mercer, *The Teaching of Gasparino Barzizza: With Special Reference to His Place in Paduan Humanism* (London: Modern Humanities Research Association, 1979).

9. *Petri Pauli Vergerii De ingenuis moribus et liberalibus studiis adulescentiae*, ed. Attilio Gnesotto, *Atti e memorie della R. Accademia di Scienze, Lettere ed Arti in Padova*, n.s. 34, no. 2 (1917–1918): 75–157 (offprint, Padua: Randi, 1918); see also the bilingual edition and translation by Craig Kallendorf in *Humanist Educational Treatises*, ed. Kallendorf (Cambridge, MA: Harvard University Press, 2002), 2–91. For Vergerio, see the introduction of Michael Katchmer to his *Pier Paolo Vergerio and the Paulus, a Latin Comedy* (New York: P. Lang, 1998), 1–88; John M. McManamon, *Pierpaolo Vergerio the Elder: The Humanist as Orator* (Tempe, AZ: Medieval and Renaissance Texts and Studies, 1996); David Robey, "Humanism and Education in the Early Quattrocento: The *De ingenuis moribus* of Pier Paolo Vergerio," *Bibliothèque d'Humanisme et Renaissance* 42, no. 1 (1980): 27–58; Robey, "Pier Paolo Vergerio the Elder: Republicanism and Civic Values in the Work of an Early Humanist," *Past and Present* 58 (1973): 3–37; and the critical edition of Vergerio's letters by Leonardo Smith: *Epistolario di Pier Paolo Vergerio* (Rome: Tipografia del Senato, 1934).

household.[10] Guarino's prior acquaintance with Barbaro is documented by his 1408 letter from Constantinople—one of the earliest extant of his correspondence—to his "dearly loved brother" Francesco, then an adolescent enthusiast of classical studies.[11] In Constantinople from 1403 to 1408, Guarino studied Greek with the great scholar and statesman Manuel Chrysoloras, becoming one of the first Italian masters of that language and literature. Now in 1414–1415, he in turn instructed Francesco Barbaro. In a single year (his "anno del greco," as Attilio Gnesotto writes in some stupefaction at the speed of his progress[12]), Barbaro digested a huge corpus of Greek classics, including the many that he cites in *The Wealth of Wives*, as he declares in the final paragraph of the work:

> Having been immersed in these Greek studies for only a few months, yet I have managed already to extract from them rich and delightful fruit. In this task I have been empowered by the mind and soul of the eminent and erudite Guarino Veronese, my teacher and most devoted of friends. (Barbaro, 125)

Guarino's tutelage provided Barbaro with a rich harvest of insights and anecdotes that illustrate every turn of his argument. Plutarch reigns supreme in Barbaro's repertoire: the *Lives*, naturally—one of Barbaro's first literary ventures was a translation of Plutarch's life of Marcus Porcius Cato the Elder—but also, and principally, the essays of the *Moralia*, especially the *Conjugalia praecepta* (Advice to Married Couples), *De amore prolis* (On the Love for Offpsring), and the *De liberis educandis* (On the Education of Children). He was demonstrably familiar, as well, with works of Homer, Herodotus, Xenophon, Isocrates, Demosthenes, Plato, and Aristotle, among other Greek authors. This Greek library augmented his already solid Latin one, which included Cicero, above all, the anthologies of

---

10. Guarino Guarini da Verona, or Guarino Veronese, as he is referred to here to distinguish him from the later architect Guarino Guarini (1624–1683). For Guarino, see the many works of Remigio Sabbadini, of which two, *La vita di Guarino Veronese* (orig. 1891) and *La scuola e gli studi di Guarino Veronese* (1896), are reprinted in the single volume *Guariniana*, ed. Mario Sancipriano (Turin: Bottega d'Erasmo, 1964); Sabbadini, ed., *Epistolario di Guarino Veronese*, 3 vols. (Venice: A spese della Società di storia veneta, 1915–1919); and the bibliography by Craig Kallendorf, "Guarino da Verona," in *Oxford Bibliographies Online: Renaissance and Reformation*, http://www.oxfordbibliographies.com/view/document/obo-9780195399301/obo-9780195399301-0084.xml.

11. In Sabbadini, *Epistolario*, 1:7–11, letter 4, "to my dearly loved brother Francesco Barbaro, glorious in literature as in nobility" (*fratri meo amantissimo Francisci Barbari literatura pariter ac nobilitate*), 1:11. For Barbaro's relations with Guarino, see also Claudio Griggio, "Senofonte, Guarino, Francesco e Ermolao Barbaro, Alberti," *Filologia e critica* 31 (2006): 161–76, and Antonio Rollo, "Dalla biblioteca di Guarino a quella di Francesco Barbaro," *Studi medievali e umanistici* 3 (2005): 9–40.

12. Gnesotto, ed., *De re uxoria*, Introduction, x.

Aulus Gellius and Valerius Maximus, and works of law and theology (as his familiarity with Saint Augustine attests).

Saturated with this new Greek learning, Barbaro journeyed in the summer of 1415 to Florence, where he spent some time as a guest of the Medici family.[13] The two brothers Cosimo (1389–1464) and Lorenzo (c. 1395–1440),[14] sons of the great banker Giovanni di Bicci (c. 1360–1429), were roughly his contemporaries, and products, like Barbaro, of a humanist education. Both, but especially Cosimo, the first Medici ruler of Florence, later became proponents and patrons of humanism and the arts.

Barbaro was close at hand, therefore, for the engagement in 1415 of Lorenzo de' Medici to Ginevra Cavalcanti (to whom he would be married in early 1416), the triggering event for the composition of *The Wealth of Wives*. Fresh from the study of Greek, and shortly before that, the study of law, and in between these two experiences, protracted discussions on the topic with Zaccaria Trevisan, Barbaro needed only the prospect of the marriage of a contemporary to launch him on the project of a humanist treatise on marriage. Written by the scion of one of the wealthiest and most powerful noble clans of Venice to the scion of one of the wealthiest families of Florence, one destined soon to reach the apex of political power in that city, it identifies marriage as the pivotal social institution for the Renaissance patriciate, requiring a discussion of its philosophical, legal, moral, and historical ramifications.

Barbaro likely finished *The Wealth of Wives* by the end of 1415, and dispatched it as a wedding gift to Lorenzo—Barbaro opining that Lorenzo would prefer a gift "from his Francesco" to one from his "fortune": "I see that a gift would be more welcome and pleasing to you if it came not from Francesco's fortune, but from your friend Francesco." (Barbaro, 65) Now twenty-five, he was still, in the thinking of the day, an adolescent: for patrician youths did not enter upon careers until they were almost thirty, and many did not marry until that time, allowing them a long span of years during which to acquire an education and pursue an array of amusements. Barbaro remained in contact with humanist friends during this time, which was, coincidentally, the moment when several of them were gathered in the Swiss Alps at the Council of Constance (Konstanz, modern Germany). That ecclesiastical convention met from 1414 to 1418, with the mission of ending

13. For this venture, see Remigio Sabbadini, "La gita di Francesco Barbaro a Firenze," in *Miscellanea di studi in onore di Attilio Hortis*, 2 vols. (Trieste: Stabilimento artistico tipografico G. Caprin, 1910), 2:615–27, reprinted in Sabbadini, *Storia e critica di testi latini*, 2nd ed., ed. Eugene and Myriam Billanovich (Padua: Antenore, 1971), 25–35.

14. This Lorenzo is designated "the Elder" to distinguish him from Cosimo's grandson Lorenzo (1449–1492), the third Medici ruler of Florence, known as "the Magnificent." For the Medici family, see the annotated bibliography of Stella Fletcher in *Oxford Bibliographies Online: Renaissance and Reformation*, http://www.oxfordbibliographies.com/view/document/obo-9780195399301/obo-9780195399301-0260.xml.

the schism of the church (the papal see at this point having three claimants) and, collaterally, the settlement of the Wycliffite and Hussite heresies. Among the throng of bureaucrats and secretaries who accompanied the dignitaries were humanists whose eyes were set on a prize: the books said to be found in the nearby abbey of St. Gallen, an early medieval foundation whose monks, over the years, had copied a multitude of manuscripts and stored them in a long-neglected library. In the last months of 1416, a group of papal secretaries went on an outing to investigate this treasure trove. It proved, in fact, to be full of fine copies of Latin books, including a few priceless titles that had been lost to view—notably Quintilian's *Institutio oratoria*, a rhetorical handbook of first importance, known to have existed but not prior to this moment recovered.

The jubilant book-hunters announced their finds to the humanists back home in a flurry of letters, including one by Poggio Bracciolini (1380–1459) to Guarino Veronese, from whom Barbaro learned of the find.[15] Barbaro responded with a letter of his own to Poggio, congratulating him on his triumph.[16]

> ... I have thought it proper, on account of the bond of literature which ties us particularly together, to thank you and not to pass over in silence the tremendous service you did for mankind, by sending us a list of those books which by your effort and diligence you have recovered for us and for posterity .... For no news could have been brought us that was more joyful and welcome than that which relates both to your glory ... and to the expansion of culture in the highest degree.[17]

And in the same letter, in commenting on the great contribution the Constance discoveries had made to the world of learning, Barbaro coined a phrase that would become universal currency over the next three centuries, used to describe the international community of the learned: the *respublica litterarum*, the "republic of letters."[18] How fitting that a man about to enter upon a career as leading figure in the *respublica venetorum*, the "Venetian Republic," would have republics on his mind, and define as a "republic" a group of men bounded by no geographical or political frontiers, sharing only their commitment to the life of the mind.

---

15. See Phyllis W.G. Gordan, ed. and trans., *Two Renaissance Book Hunters: The Letters of Poggius Bracciolini to Nicolaus de Niccolis* (New York: Columbia University Press, 1974), Appendix, 187–206, for the eight letters related to the Constance discoveries, including the letter to Guarino (dated December 15, 1416) at 193–96.

16. Gordan, *Two Renaissance Book Hunters*, 196–203, letter dated July 6, 1417.

17. Gordan, *Two Renaissance Book Hunters*, 196.

18. Gordan, *Two Renaissance Book Hunters*, 199.

The moment at which he penned those words, in 1417, is the last time that Barbaro will be seen as a humanist among humanists. He would become a patron of humanists[19] more than an active participant in their circles—their *respublica*—although he continued his classical studies throughout his life and wrote in a fine humanist Latin, besides some orations, an enormous quantity of letters. But now in his late twenties, he assumed the responsibilities of a Venetian nobleman. He married the noblewoman Maria Loredan in 1419, and named his eldest son, born 1422, Zaccaria—a commemoration not only of his elder brother of that name, but also of the mentor of his youth, Zaccaria Trevisan. In that year, as well, he assumed his first major political office, that of podestà, or governor, of Treviso. That position was followed by an unbroken series of high-level appointments as, repeatedly, provincial governor (*rettore*) or captain (*capitano*), "great sage" (*savio grande*) or "sage of the terraferma"(*savio di terraferma*), ducal councilor or member of the Council of Ten, and eventually, in 1452, the highest office short of the dogeship itself, Procurator of San Marco.

For Barbaro belonged to that set of about 100 patricians who, at any time, dominated the political machinery of Venice. Moreover, the arc of his career, from 1422 until his death in 1454, corresponds almost precisely to the *dogado* of Francesco Foscari, from 1423 to 1457, the architect of Venice's imperial expansion onto the Italian mainland—the *terraferma*.[20] It was a venture in which Barbaro was fully engaged, as is witnessed by, among other documents, his nearly 100 letters written from Brescia during the period 1437–1440, when, as captain of that provincial city and protector of its population, he withstood a desperate three-year siege.[21] Barbaro lived not quite a year after the fall of Constantinople in 1453, the consequences of which would strain the political fortunes of his beloved city. The humanist Filippo Morandi da Rimini (c. 1407–1497) had written from nearby Corfù, where he was stationed as Venetian chancellor, and dedicated to Barbaro, his patron, an account of that tragedy soon after it occurred; in 1454, Morandi delivered Barbaro's funeral oration.[22]

Wives and the Venetian Nobility

Barbaro was evidently a committed and engaged member of the Venetian nobility, in origin and by definition the city's ruling class. And it is as a nobleman, fully

19. Notably of the historian Flavio Biondo, and the Greek immigrant rhetorician George of Trebizond.

20. For Foscari, see Dennis Romano, *The Likeness of Venice: A Life of Doge Francesco Foscari, 1373–1457* (New Haven, CT: Yale University Press, 2007).

21. Francesco Barbaro, *Epistolario*, 2:167–360, letters 70–164, which span the period of Barbaro's captaincy in Brescia; most of these are by Barbaro, written from Brescia, with a few by correspondents elsewhere addressed to him.

22. King, *Venetian Humanism*, 75–76.

conscious of looming demographic challenges, that he writes *The Wealth of Wives*. The work addresses a critical issue: that to continue its sovereignty, the Venetian nobility must reproduce itself, and worthily; and that to do so, it must rely on the women who would bear and rear their offspring. These nobles were dependent upon the fertility, the fortitude, the character, and the intelligence of their wives.

This context requires, it follows, that the Venetian nobleman who writes a treatise on marriage be himself unmarried—however much he otherwise had participated in the vibrant sexual underworld of Renaissance Italy, along with others of his contemporaries who boasted of their Christian or humanist virtue. It was urgently important to reach these young men, so as to convince them not only to marry, but to choose as a wife a woman who would be the best mother for their offspring.

Barbaro targets this audience of young nobles, his contemporaries and his peers, in two ways: first, by dedicating the work to a young man of equivalent status, although a Florentine and not a Venetian, who was himself imminently to marry a woman who was a paragon of desired qualities; and second, by addressing through this intermediary others of their acquaintance and set. In the dedication, Barbaro writes that he did not compose his treatise to instruct Lorenzo in particular, "but so that through you I might reach many of our generation." (Barbaro, 66) Later, he chides those young men who seek either beauty or wealth in a wife, rather than all-important moral and intellectual qualities. Of the former, he asks: "What kind of a wife will she be, if she who should be joined to us by dignity and friendliness is tied to us only by beauty?" (Barbaro, 84) As for those seeking wealth, he grumbles that they "have been from their childhood so infused and imbued with the love of gain that they will perform any labor and expend any effort to acquire and achieve it, not neglecting any path by which they think they may satisfy their avarice." (Barbaro, 86) In closing his treatise, Barbaro calls on the young to follow the example of Lorenzo de' Medici in choosing a wife worthy of their noble status: "Your peers, therefore, my Lorenzo, should be inspired to imitate you and eagerly follow your path, who have chosen as your wife Ginevra, who ... is the most splendid young woman anywhere to be found." (Barbaro, 124)

At first sight, the critical importance that Barbaro ascribes to wives seems to contradict what we have learned over recent decades about the real situation of women in Renaissance Italy. Even women who were members of respectable households suffered constraints—setting aside for the moment the misery of prostitutes or the vulnerability of young servant girls or the differential death by infanticide or neglect of female infants. Before marriage, girls were held to a stern requirement of virginity, since even the appearance of impropriety threatened their status and dishonored their family. That family determined the marital destinies of these young women, and their non-marital destinies as well: for parents often determined that their daughters would not marry, but live out their lives in a convent, whether or not they had embraced a religious vocation. Married women brought to their husbands a dowry, constituting that portion of their father's wealth they were to inherit—but control of dowry wealth was exercised entirely by their husbands, on whose death it reverted, in most cases, to a woman's natal family, or that of her subsequent spouse. While wives could own private property, they could not normally engage in financial or legal agreements; and, naturally, unless they were as consorts or regents the surrogates of rulers, they could not exercise political power. Widows, perhaps, suffered the fewest constraints. But their actions, too, were circumscribed, and in the absence of protection by other family members, they often descended into irremediable poverty.

In Venice, the condition of women was better than in some other settings, and certainly better than in Florence.[23] Prostitutes reportedly numbering in the thousands—working women even if compelled by circumstances—certainly had ample opportunities to earn an income in the thriving and cosmopolitan port city of Venice. Of loftier rank were the courtesans, famous throughout Europe, of whom those denoted as "honest courtesans" were proficient conversationalists, musicians, and poets. Beyond the sex trades, married and lone women worked at a variety of skilled and unskilled trades, including as assistants in the thriving shops of their husbands. Women in abusive marriages could seek justice in Venetian ecclesiastical courts, and apparently obtained it. Numerous places of refuge existed for specifically female victims of circumstance: orphans, for instance, and former prostitutes. In Venice, too, however, despite a general level of freedom and opportunity greater than that in many other European settings, the dowry system—and especially the wild dowry inflation of the Renaissance centuries—resulted in the forced monachation of many women, although we cannot know what portion of the total of professed women these unhappy nuns represented.

More pertinent to Barbaro's theme, and distinctive of Venice, is the relatively great prominence enjoyed by noblewomen.[24] Like women of the elites everywhere

23. For women in Venice, see Monica Chojnacka, *Working Women of Early Modern Venice* (Baltimore: Johns Hopkins University Press, 2001); Stanley Chojnacki, *Women and Men in Renaissance Venice: Twelve Essays on Patrician Society* (Baltimore: Johns Hopkins University Press, 2000); Alexander Cowan, *Marriage, Manners and Mobility in Early Modern Venice* (Aldershot, UK: Ashgate, 2007); Cecilia Cristellon, *La carità e l'eros: il matrimonio, la chiesa, i suoi giudici nella Venezia del Rinascimento, 1420–1545* (Bologna: Società Editrice Il Mulino, 2010); Joanne M. Ferraro, *Marriage Wars in Late Renaissance Venice* (Oxford: Oxford University Press, 2001); Daniela Hacke, *Women, Sex, and Marriage in Early Modern Venice* (Aldershot, UK: Ashgate, 2004); Jutta G. Sperling, *Convents and the Body Politic in Late Renaissance Venice* (Chicago: University of Chicago Press, 1999); and three essays from Eric Dursteler, ed., *A Companion to Venetian History, 1400–1797* (Leiden: Brill, 2013): Anna Bellavitis, "Family and Society," 319–52; Cecilia Cristellon and Silvana Seidel Menchi, "Religious Life," 379–420; and Anne Jacobson Schutte, "Society and the Sexes in the Venetian Republic," 353–78.

24. A complex and comprehensive understanding of the condition of noblewomen in Venice is provided by the many essays of Stanley Chojnacki, of which twelve are collected in his *Women and Men,*

in Europe at this time, their sexual lives were exceedingly constricted, as were their opportunities to appear in public settings and participate in political affairs. But they had other and not negligible liberties. They could own personal property acquired as gifts from their kin. Their dowry wealth was their property, too; and although its management was ceded to their husbands so long as the latter lived, women reclaimed their dowries as widows, from which they could make gifts while alive and bequests at their deaths benefiting both their marital and natal kin. Thus they were benefactors not only of their sons and daughters, but also of other kin, as well as female servants and friends.[25]

Most striking, however, is the authority enjoyed by noblewomen as the mothers of their sons. These they reared in the absences of their husbands—and their husbands were often absent, for months or even years at a time, on commercial ventures, as provincial officials, or as ambassadors to distant courts—and very often as widows, choosing to remain in the marital household for decades while their children reached maturity. Acting in their husbands' stead, they had the capacity to present their sons at age eighteen (after 1497, age twenty) to the Avogaria di Comun, an august body of state attorneys, to present proof of their registration as legitimate descendants of a noble clan and thus as eligible to enter the political offices of the Republic.[26] Beyond this exceptional privilege, their high prestige in Venetian society is manifested in many ways, as it is to some extent in the exalted status accorded the *dogaressa*, the wife of the Doge.[27]

The extraordinary position of Venetian noblewomen is the consequence of the exceptional nature of the Venetian nobility. Elsewhere in Italy and northern Europe, nobles were mounted soldiers, and the horse was virtually the synecdoche of nobility, reflected in the terms used for that elite in the western European languages (*cavaliere, chevalier, cavalier, caballero, Ritter*). But Venetian nobles were not horsemen, and while they did do battle at sea, neither they nor their subordinates fought on land, employing mercenary forces in their conquests of *terraferma*. The Venetian nobility was not a warrior class, therefore, but a network of extended families whose wealth and status derived from maritime ventures, at least before 1500, rather than agricultural production or territorial aggrandizement. Although composed of merchants, who were often viewed as upstarts and newcomers, the Venetian nobility was very old—ancient, in fact, as several of the

---

and which provide much of the material reviewed in this section.

25. For their role as patronesses, disposing of this wealth, to women of their household, courtyard, and neighborhood, see Dennis Romano, *Patricians and* Popolani: *The Social Foundations of the Venetian Renaissance State* (Baltimore: Johns Hopkins University Press, 1987), 131–40.

26. A role frequently noted by Chojnacki, but see especially his essay "Kinship Ties and Young Patricians" (orig. 1985) in *Women and Men*, 206–26.

27. Holly S. Hurlburt, *The Dogaressa of Venice, 1200–1500: Wife and Icon* (New York: Palgrave Macmillan, 2006).

old noble clans had migrated to the Adriatic lagoons on which Venice arose during the last centuries of the Roman era. It was indeed, as Ronnie Ferguson terms it, "Europe's oldest mercantile aristocracy."[28]

Furthermore, although this noble stratum evolved over time, with newer families joining and sometimes surpassing older ones, it was at one particular moment—actually a number of decades, beginning in the 1290s—that its identity became fixed. That moment, or process, known as the *serrata del Gran Consiglio* ("closing of the Great Council"), resulted in the permanent definition of the noble class as those belonging to, or descending from, those families which then were members of the principal Venetian governing council. Where other nobilities, however legitimate might be their claims to high status, had a shifting composition, rarely established by any record of origin, with unclear and often contested claims to authority, the Venetian nobility was created by legislative act and constituted a legally-defined class uniquely entitled to participate in government. And so it was until 1797, when Napoleon Bonaparte put an end to the Republic, with two exceptions: in 1381, when thirty wealthy commoner families (including Trevisan's) were admitted to the nobility in recognition of their sacrificial contributions to Venetian coffers, and in the seventeenth century, when demographic and fiscal stress prompted the Republic to open the rolls of nobility to those who were willing to pay to be inscribed.

The closure of the nobility entailed necessarily the high valuation of women. An elite that one entered only by birth necessarily assigned to women, in their roles as mothers, responsibility for the reproduction of the class. The quality of those women became, in consequence, an issue. In 1420, although the women chosen as wives by members of the patriciate could come from foreign or commoner origins, it was required that they be of legitimate birth.[29] In 1422, it was further required that sons of patricians who had married women of low origins would be denied noble status—thus making "maternity," as Stanley Chojnacki comments, "a determinant of nobility."[30] In 1506, it was decreed that women marrying patricians must themselves be of noble birth, so that the nobility of sons now depended on the noble status of both paternal and maternal lineages. Here is the origin of the famous *Libri d'oro*, or "golden books," the registers in which were inscribed the names of these illustrious progenitors of the next generation of noble sons.[31] In 1526, it was further ruled, to accentuate these requirements and

28. Ronnie Ferguson, "Venetian Language," in Dursteler, ed., *Companion to Venetian History*, 929–57, at 932.

29. Chojnacki, "Marriage Regulation in Venice, 1420–1535" (orig. 1998), in *Women and Men*, 53–75, at 56–57.

30. Chojnacki, "Marriage Regulation," 56, 63–64; "The Power of Love: Wives and Husbands" (orig. 1988), in *Women and Men*, 153–68, at 156–57n15 (302).

31. Chojnacki, "Marriage Regulation," 63.

guarantee their fulfillment, that as a condition of holding political office, the marriages of noblemen be officially registered.[32] Finally, in 1535, it was required that the marriage contracts detailing the identities of both spouses be read aloud in the presence of the Doge and at least four of the six ducal councillors.[33] The wives who married Venetian noblemen, in short, were to possess the highest social valuation, so as to ensure the genuine nobility of their male issue. Oddly, then, in this situation, the patriarchy was dependent on a matriarchy.

The requirement of high-value wives drove dowry prices higher. The dowry was a nearly universal phenomenon in Europe.[34] It consisted of a quantity of wealth transferred from a bride's natal family to that of her spouse, considered to be her share of her father's patrimony, utilized in theory for her maintenance during the marriage and intended in the end, in most cases, to promote the welfare of her children. Dowry inflation was characteristic of the Renaissance era, and was by no means specific to Venice. But rates of dowry inflation in Venice were exceptional. The average patrician dowry (net of trousseau, a gift to the groom) rose from 873 ducats in the period 1361–1390 to 1,230 ducats in the period 1466–1477, to 1,732 ducats in the period 1505–1507.[35] The Republic attempted to stem the tide of dowry increases, which had the undesirable consequence of creating a privileged subgroup of the nobility capable of demanding, and supplying, such huge sums. In 1420, it set a cap to patrician dowries of 1,600 ducats, which was raised to 3,000 in 1505 and to 4,000 in 1535.[36] Despite the imposition of this ladder of caps on dowry expenditure, the limits were circumvented (in the fifteenth century) in about half the cases,[37] and continued to be flouted after 1505.[38]

---

32. Chojnacki, "Marriage Regulation," 65. Despite this legislation, a very few women of high social status but of foreign or commoner birth were, by special petition, allowed to marry Venetian noblemen: see Cowan, *Marriage, Manners and Mobility.*

33. Chojnacki, "Marriage Regulation," 72.

34. See the annotated bibliography of Alexander Cowan, "Marriage and Dowry," in *Oxford Bibliographies Online: Renaissance and Reformation,* http://www.oxfordbibliographies.com/view/document/obo-9780195399301/obo-9780195399301-0014.xml.

35. Chojnacki, "Gender and the Early Renaissance State" (orig. 1998), 27–52, at 44; "Getting Back the Dowry" (orig. 1999), in *Women and Men,* 95–111, at 97. These figures are for nobles. To compare, in the mid-fifteenth century, the median patrician dowry was five times as large as the median dowry for commoner families: Chojnacki, Introduction, 1–24, at 9. For the dowry in Venice, see also Anna Bellavitis, "La dote a Venezia tra medioevo e prima età moderna," in *Spazi, poteri, diritti delle donne a Venezia in età moderna,* ed. Anna Bellavitis, Nadia Maria Filippini, and Tiziana Plebani (Verona: QuiEdit, 2012), 5–20.

36. Chojnacki, "Gender and the Early Renaissance State," 45, 48, 52; "Marriage Regulation," 56–57, 67, 71.

37. Chojnacki, "Gender and the Early Renaissance State," 46.

38. Chojnacki, "Marriage Regulation," 70.

Other consequences flowed from soaring dowry costs. Fewer women married, because the huge dowry one daughter required meant that another could not be funded, and would be dispatched instead to a convent, whether or not she had a religious vocation.[39] At the same time, fewer men married, both because fewer women were available, but also because families came to designate one son to carry on the lineage, while the others, as bachelors, resorted to concubinage or other alternatives for sexual expression amply available in Venice. More pertinent to Barbaro's theme, however, is that those few women on whom dowry wealth was lavished often acquired considerable power through their capacity to dispense wealth in life and, by testament, in death.[40] In the end, they distributed their riches in roughly equal parts: one-half to their marital family (their sons and daughters), and one-half to their natal family (their brothers, sisters, and other kin).[41] In so doing, they created a second system of inheritance, parallel to but unlike the patrimonial system, whereby wealth among the nobility descended only in the male line. Moreover, they won the interest and loyalty of their kinsmen, who could look forward to splendid gifts from their mothers, aunts, grandmothers, and sisters, to augment their inheritance from their fathers. Dowries tended to reduce wives to a quantity of wealth, but wives who were free to manage their dowry and other personal possessions themselves became wealthy.

Thus did the distinctive nature of the Venetian nobility impel it to exalt the position of the noble matron and mother. And such is the social context for a cultural phenomenon otherwise inexplicable: the authorship of a treatise on marriage focused on the capacity and responsibility of the wife by a young bachelor on the verge of his career as a member of a unique political class. Writing in 1415, Barbaro could have observed only the first stages of this evolution of marital ideology and practice characteristic of the Venetian Renaissance. Yet he anticipates the effects of its full development over the next 150 years,[42] grasping with uncanny foresight how the obsession with dowry would corrupt noblemen in search of a bride, and jeopardize the essential project, if Venice were to prevail, of the biological and cultural reproduction of the noble class. This threat he confronts with the force of his classical learning, displayed in his disciplined and persuasive prose. In

39. Chojnacki, "Measuring Adulthood: Adolescence and Gender" (orig. 1992), in *Women and Men*, 185–205, at 199; "Subaltern Patriarchs: Patrician Bachelors" (orig. 1994), in *Women and Men*, 244–56.

40. Chojnacki, "Patrician Women in Early Renaissance Venice" (orig. 1974), in *Women and Men*, 115–31, at 126–31; "Dowries and Kinsmen" (orig. 1975), 132–52, at 143. For the accumulation of dowry wealth by English wives in this era, see also Barbara A. Hanawalt, *The Wealth of Wives: Women, Law, and Economy in Late Medieval London* (Oxford: Oxford University Press, 2007).

41. Chojnacki, "Patrician Women," 118, 125.

42. A point Chojnacki often makes, citing Barbaro in text and notes: see, for instance, his "Marriage Regulation," 59; "The Power of Love," 156–57; "'The Most Serious Duty': Motherhood, Gender, and Patrician Culture" (orig. 1991), in *Women and Men*, 169–82, at 169; "Measuring Adulthood: Adolescence and Gender," 187; and "Subaltern Patriarchs," 247–48.

the history of culture, there are few cases so explicit of the intersection of theory and practice as this one of a young nobleman and precocious humanist engaging the system of marriage and dowry, the major engine of social interaction within the ruling elite.

Why De re uxoria?

It is now apparent why Francesco Barbaro wrote the treatise *De re uxoria*, a phrase translated here as *The Wealth of Wives*. But whence this title? And why this translation?

Barbaro's work has often been referred to as a work "on marriage," including by the present author.[43] The German classicist Percy Gothein, likewise, its major twentieth-century translator, entitled it *Das Buch von der Ehe* (The Book on Marriage, 1933).[44] Earlier, in 1536, the earlier German translator Erasmus Alber had named his version of the work *Eyn güt büch von der Ehe* (A Good Book about Marriage); in 1667, the French translator Claude Joly opted for *L'estat du mariage* (The Condition of Marriage); and in 1677, the anonymous English translator expanded the title to *Directions for Love and Marriage*. But if Barbaro had wished to write a treatise "on marriage," he had better titles readily at hand. He could have written *De nuptiis, De coniugio, De matrimonio* (all three mean On Marriage), or even, following Saint Augustine, *De bono coniugali* (On the Good of Marriage), a work he knew well. But this was not his intent. He is concerned not with marriage *per se*, but with the contribution of wives to the family, as critical participants in family formation and continuity.

So we return to the exact words of Barbaro's title: *De re uxoria*. Literal translations might include *On the Wifely Matter*—since *uxoria*, the adjective modifying the noun *res* ("thing" or "matter"), stems from the noun *uxor*, meaning "wife"—or possibly *On the Matter of Wives*. But these titles do not clearly convey the nature of the project Barbaro has undertaken. Nor would the titles *De uxoribus* (On Wives) or *De officio uxoris* (On the Duties of a Wife), although the latter, appearing in the earliest manuscripts of the work, is the title of its second part—a match to the first part, entitled *De delectu uxoris* (On the Selection of a Wife). The title of the first part alone, to complicate the matter, is assigned to the whole work by Italian translator Alberto Lollio in 1548: *La elettion della moglie* (The Selection of

---

43. In King, "Caldiera and the Barbaros," 31–35; "The School of Infancy: The Emergence of Mother as Teacher in Early Modern Times," in *The Renaissance in the Streets, Schools, and Studies: Essays in Honour of Paul F. Grendler*, ed. Konrad Eisenbichler and Nicholas Terpstra (Toronto: Centre for Reformation and Renaissance Studies, 2008), 41–86 (hereinafter cited as "The Emergence of Mother as Teacher"), at 59–61; *Venetian Humanism*, 92–98.

44. Gothein, ed., *Das Buch von der Ehe*. For the remaining titles named here, see the Bibliography, "*De re uxoria*: Editions and Translations."

the Wife), changed to *La scelta della moglie* (The Choice of the Wife) in the revised edition of Lollio's translation published in 1778 and subsequently. [45]

At this point, it should be recalled that in 1412, Barbaro received his doctorate in both laws at the University of Padua. There he was steeped in the language of the *Corpus iuris civilis* (The Body of Civil Law) composed from 529 to 534 by the committee of legal experts delegated by Emperor Justinian I to codify not merely the laws, but the books of laws, and thus the legal theory of ancient Rome—arguably that civilization's greatest achievement, and the foundation, as well, of European legal thought. In those legal texts, too, Barbaro would have encountered many times over the term *res*, meaning not just "thing," but in the legal universe—then as now—the "matter" or case under discussion. He was also likely aware that the second-century CE Roman jurist Gaius had written the textbook *De re uxoria,* and he certainly knew that the phrase *res uxoria* made a substantial appearance in Justinian's *Codex,* one of the four sections of the sixth-century *Corpus iuris civilis,* in Liber V, especially Titulus XIII, among other scattered references.[46] In these legal writings, the phrase *res uxoria* was concerned with the dowry and related property issues, and thus not with the wife but with that portion of her father's wealth that she brought to her marital family. In this sense, as well, the phrase appears in two works with which Barbaro was also thoroughly familiar: Cicero's *De officiis* (On Duties), and, with a slightly broader intonation, the *Noctes atticae* (Attic Nights) of Aulus Gellius.[47]

In sum: Barbaro does not intend a treatise "on marriage" or on "wives," simply put, but something else. He wishes, in fact, to discuss precisely what he says: the *res uxoria,* the wealth the wife brings as a dowry from her father's household to her husband's, intended to pass ultimately to the children of the marriage. The dowry was a matter of resounding importance in the society of Renaissance Italy, as evident in accelerating dowry values, and important for no one more than the young men who hoped to benefit from the immense sums that they could acquire by an advantageous marriage. But it is the worth of dotal wealth in this sense, the most commonplace and consensual sense, that Barbaro rejects. His treatise *De re uxoria* envisions, in fact, a very different kind of marital wealth: that consisting

---

45. For Lollio's translation of 1548 and its subsequent reprintings, see the Bibliography, "*De re uxoria*: Editions and Translations."

46. For Gaius's *De re uxoria,* see *ad vocem* Gaius in *A Dictionary of Greek and Roman Biography and Mythology,* ed. William Smith (London: John Murray, 1902), online at http://www.perseus.tufts.edu/hopper/text?doc=Perseus:text:1999.04.0104:entry=gaius-bio-2. Liber V, Titulus XIII of Justinian's *Codex* is online at (among other sites) http://www.thelatinlibrary.com/justinian/codex5.shtml.

47. Cicero, *De officiis* 3:15; Aulus Gellius, *Noctes atticae* 1.6.3, quoting the orator Quintus Metellus, who speaks of the perturbations of having a wife: "non oportuisse de molestia incommodisque perpetuis rei uxoriae confiteri ...." A reference to legal issues concerning the dowry is also found in Quintilian, *Institutio oratoria* 7.4.11, but Barbaro could not have known this passage at this time. These passages are identified by Gothein in *Buch von der Ehe,* 89.

of the moral and intellectual qualities of the wife. It is these, not the conventional dowry, which will enrich the family, and secure the continuation of the lineage by ensuring the robust health and mental and spiritual characteristics of its progeny.

Consequently, the title *De re uxoria* is translated here as *The Wealth of Wives*, so as to capture Barbaro's principal argument: that a young man should marry a wife who brings with her a real endowment of moral and intellectual qualities, and not a false and delusory dowry measured in ducats and trinkets. It is a deliberately allusive phrase, for the "wealth of wives" suggests not only the gifts made to their husbands, but the gifts of mind and soul that are inherently theirs and never given away, employed for the benefit of the family. That allusiveness matches the allusiveness of the original Latin title, which seems to announce what Barbaro will denigrate, the conventional dowry, but signifies an altogether different kind of wifely wealth. With the phrase *de re uxoria*, Barbaro summons up the rhetoric of the law courts, but in the treatise that follows, he erodes and inverts the significance of the legal principle. The Latin title, *De re uxoria*, is in fact a trick, a riddle, a clever pun.

But if Barbaro plays with his readers—and those to whom he addressed himself would have had, unlike ourselves, an instant recognition of the dissonance between his title, read superficially, and his message—his object is not to amuse, but rather, loftily, to instruct. For although he refers at times to his treatise with some deprecation, calling it "this brief commentary," or "these few notes," or "these jottings of mine," in a somber tone he also articulates plainly, at one key point, the larger claim that animates the whole. That statement is found in the dedicatory letter to Lorenzo, in which Barbaro tells how his mentor Zaccaria Trevisan "gravely expounded to me nearly the whole of the elegant science of marriage as taught by the ancients."[48] (Barbaro, 66) The vision of marriage Barbaro presents is in his own mind no small manual of wise precepts, but in itself a branch of philosophy, a "science," as it was understood in his day, although not in ours.

Barbaro paints with a broad brush in his treatise on *The Wealth of Wives* because of the immeasurable importance of what he has to say to the young men of his generation, aristocrats like himself, on the verge of marriages that will result either in worthy descendants who will bring honor to the family and distinguish the lineage—or, should they fail in their marital responsibility, unworthy offspring who will hasten the deterioration and eventual annihilation of the clans whose ancestors had built and sustained their world.

---

48. The phrase "science of marriage" is used to translate Barbaro's very elusive *ratio uxoria*, a term also used at a later point to describe Lorenzo's deep understanding of marriage: "sic cum ad praeceptionem meam tua quoque uxoria ratio accesserit …." Gnesotto, *De re uxoria*, 99 (77). In both cases, the Latin phrase describes a profound knowledge of the nature of marriage, but especially as concerning the *uxor*, the wife.

The Dedication to Lorenzo de' Medici

One such young aristocrat, and the particular dedicatee of Barbaro's work, was the scion of a patrician family just engaged to be married to the daughter of another. The Medici were the richest bankers in Florence, and enjoyed the powerful connections that went with mercantile wealth—connections that would allow Lorenzo's brother Cosimo, less than twenty years after Barbaro's 1415 visit, to rise to become covert lord of the city. The Cavalcanti clan, whose daughter Ginevra was espoused to Lorenzo, was of equivalent stature, and could boast as ancestor Guido Cavalcanti (1250/1259–1300), pioneer of the poetic *dolce stil nuovo* (sweet new style) and friend of Dante Alighieri.

Barbaro was certainly not of lesser social rank than his Medici hosts—not at all. His own family was one of the inner circle of the Venetian nobility, whose origins were mercantile, like those of the Florentine patricians, but who had acquired an addendum of luster from their legally-prescribed privilege and permanent membership in a political elite. In wealth, in cultural refinement, in political importance, Barbaro's family matched or exceeded the claims of the Medici clan at this stage of its evolution.

Over the next decades, however, the Medici would become the foremost patrons in Italy of Renaissance art and ideas. In 1415, they were already on the road to that eminence. As Barbaro recounts in his dedication to Lorenzo, the humanist Roberto de' Rossi, Lorenzo's teacher, was in attendance at the Medici gatherings.[49] Lorenzo had his Rossi just as Barbaro had his Barzizza and his Guarino. Also in attendance were two more prominent members of the vibrant Florentine humanist circle that orbited about the Medici: the orator and later chancellor of Florence Leonardo Bruni (c. 1370–1444), and the wealthy bibliophile Niccolò Niccoli (1364–1437).[50]

So these young noblemen were peers, amid a generation of others like themselves, who would make splendid marriages so as to accumulate wealth,

49. The humanist Roberto de' Rossi had studied Greek with Manuel Chrysoloras in Florence during the latter's stay in Florence from 1397 to 1400. He was, as teacher of Cosimo and Lorenzo, a major figure of the Medici circle and, as colleague of Leonardo Bruni and Niccolò Niccoli, of early Florentine humanism. See Lauro Martines, *The Social World of the Florentine Humanists, 1390–1460* (Princeton: Princeton University Press, 1963; reprint Toronto: University of Toronto Press for the Renaissance Society of America, 2011), 108–10.

50. Leonardo Bruni was the most eminent of the early Florentine humanists, chancellor of the Florentine republic (1410–1411, 1427–1444), and author of enormously important rhetorical works, translations from the Greek, and the first humanist history of Florence. Niccolò Niccoli was a wealthy patron, bibliophile, and collector. For these figures, see the annotated bibliographies by Craig Kallendorf in *Oxford Bibliographies Online: Renaissance and Reformation*, at (respectively) http://www.oxfordbibliographies.com/view/document/obo-9780195399301/obo-9780195399301-0069.xml and http://www.oxfordbibliographies.com/view/document/obo-9780195399301/obo-9780195399301-0175.xml.

consolidate alliances, and above all, with the births of sons, continue the lineages from which their own social amplitude derived. It is to these young men, through Lorenzo, that Barbaro will speak—"so that through you I might reach many of our generation" (Barbaro, 66)—to alert them to their most serious responsibilities and the need to consider in their calculations the true wealth of wives.

Barbaro wishes to reach wider circles of the young elite because, as he points out, Lorenzo himself does not require instruction: he has already learned the sage truths that Barbaro offers from the wise elders of his family: "For you imitate that excellent man, your father Giovanni, and your illustrious brother Cosimo, with the stores of whose authority, wisdom, and counsel you have been amply supplied." (Barbaro, 66) And in his marriage to Ginevra Cavalcanti, a young woman of incomparable worth, he himself exemplifies the principles that Barbaro will expound: "What more luminous, what more worthy example could I put forward than yours?" (Barbaro, 124)

Yet, though Lorenzo does not require Barbaro's instruction, Barbaro will bestow his treatise upon him as a gift: a wedding present. In this, he is an early practitioner, if not the originator, of an Italian custom that endured into modern times: the presentation of a literary gift *per nozze,* on the occasion of a marriage—sometimes a brief work illuminating the history of the families thus united, sometimes an extensive and important work of scholarship. At the outset, Barbaro explains: "Our ancestors … used to give gifts to those who were joined together in marriage, so that the token they gave of their love and support would be not only a pledge but also an ornament." (Barbaro, 65) He will not give a rich gift, however, a superfluous show to one who is already rich, but rather, a gift not from his fortune but of his friendship: a work of his own hand, a "brief commentary on the wealth of wives," which will be useful because it comes at "this moment of your own nuptials," and will be recognized "as the sign of our good will and firm friendship." (Barbaro, 67) In closing the dedicatory letter, he reinforces his message: "May you hear me with kind and attentive ears, and receive this work, such as it is, for the sake of our friendship, and in lieu of a glittering gift, on the occasion of your nuptials." (Barbaro, 67)

Although Lorenzo de' Medici, inarguably, is the focus of Barbaro's dedication, he is not the only figure to whom Barbaro offers lavish tribute. For here appears, as well, Zaccaria Trevisan, the Venetian nobleman and pioneering humanist who had long mentored Barbaro, especially in the period 1412 to 1413, after the younger man had completed his formal university studies and before the elder's death. Barbaro describes Trevisan's contribution to his work: "… I have for the most part followed [the precepts] I learned from Zaccaria Trevisan—that illustrious citizen of Venice, a man peerless in our age for his intellect, wisdom, justice, deep knowledge, and great deeds, and tightly bound to me by the law of friendship—in conversations about this matter we had from time to time. In these he gravely expounded to me nearly the whole of the elegant science of marriage as taught by the ancients." (Barbaro, 66) Whatever the other intellectual influences on the young student Barbaro, Trevisan must have impressed upon him, at a philosophical level, the importance of marriage, and the real wealth of wives.

What Marriage Is

Having presented his commentary on *The Wealth of Wives* to Lorenzo de' Medici "in lieu of a glittering gift," Barbaro moves on to a preliminary discussion, in a separate prologue, of the nature of marriage. And so it is entitled *Quid sit coniugium*: what sort of thing is marriage? "Before I discuss the choice of a wife and her responsibilities, I first wish to define here what marriage is ...." (Barbaro, 67) Here the discussion is not about the wealth of wives, but the institution itself, the conjoining of male and female.

Barbaro explains that he will draw on the works of "learned men," both Greco-Roman and Christian—and indeed, as his editor Gnesotto remarks, Barbaro's discussion relies on a "collaboration and fusion" of the two civilizations,[51] cycling between them in the same way that he ambles from historical to literary to biological to theological theorizations. He begins with Rome, alluding to the Augustan legislation (unsuccessful, in the event) to encourage marriage and childbearing among the elites by rewarding mothers of multiple children and penalizing celibate males. From there he turns to animals, in every species of whom nature "has instilled ... a desire for coition for the sake of procreation, and a belief that its success consists in having reproduced." Nor are animals driven merely to reproduce; some care for their young much as humans do, like birds whose nesting instinct "provides for both the birthing and the nourishment of their young." (Barbaro, 68)

What marriage is for Barbaro, then, as his first paragraphs declare, is procreative: its goal is the reproduction and rearing of the young. He illustrates his point with anecdotes about the Spartans, the Persians, and the Romans again, acceding that "[t]he list would be endless if I enumerated the philosophers, historians, poets, kings, and princes of cities, who jump forth from the pages of the monuments of letters like the warriors who poured out of the belly of the Trojan horse, who celebrate this institution that binds two people in love and piety." (Barbaro, 70) He will largely refrain from adducing more examples from classical antiquity, but cannot resist, at the end, commending Cyrus's deference to the judgment of his parents on the suitability of a spouse.

Turning to the Christian view of marriage—"whose weight," he states most dutifully, "is so great that even without the aid of reasoned argument, its authority prevails" (Barbaro, 70)—Barbaro follows Saint Augustine's prescriptions closely. A marriage is valid forever: "man and wife are joined by a law, a pact, a force so

---

51. Gnesotto, ed., *De re uxoria*, 28 (6) n3.

strong that no kind of separation can sever that union." (Barbaro, 70) It has two compelling benefits: the progeny that result from sexual union, which is in marriage free of "all sin of incontinence," even for the barren and the elderly who have no further hope of children; and the companionship of male and female. On the last point, Barbaro expatiates broadly and well beyond the recommendations of Augustine or other Christian or Greco-Roman authorities:

> ... [W]hat is more pleasant than to share our thoughts with our wives, and so resolve domestic cares? And to be wed to a prudent wife who in both good and bad is partner, companion, and friend? To whom you may confide your innermost thoughts about things that lie within her province, to whom you may entrust the little children that you bear together? To whom in sweet conversation you may unburden your cares and sorrows? Whom you so love, that your own hope of happiness depends in some measure on her well-being? (Barbaro, 69)

This high valuation of companionship in marriage is striking and novel—can we detect here the hand of Zaccaria Trevisan?

Still, even as he introduces this alluring ideal of a companionate marriage, it is the birth of children that is central for Barbaro, in whose ears apparently rings the word of God in Genesis 9:7: *crescete et multiplicamini*—in the Vulgate Latin translation then in use, "increase and multiply." God's command is to the whole human community, but for Barbaro, it specifically addresses the members of his caste. That is why he also highlights the quality of legitimacy: the object is not merely the birth of children, but of legitimate children, who will inherit the mantle of rule prepared for them by their forebears. In general, children born legitimately "are more inclined to honor, are more responsibly reared, and ultimately make better citizens," Barbaro explains, than those born out of wedlock who are "conceived in lust," and "are for the most part violent and dishonest and inclined to all that is base." Among the legitimates, those "born honorably"—that is, to the elevated social caste to which Barbaro himself belongs—are compelled by the example of their ancestors to achieve great things, and to become the defenders of their city and its way of life:

> But the splendor of their ancestors demands that those born honorably achieve excellence: they know that the glories of their forefathers will be more of a burden than a blessing unless by their own merit they match those forebears in dignity and eminence. For they realize that all eyes will be turned on them in expectation that they will in some way reiterate in their own lives the virtue they have inherited

from their ancestors. So we may call those born thus honorably "the walls of the city."[52] (Barbaro, 69)

What, then, is marriage for Barbaro? It exists for the procreation of children, as both the ancients and Christians agree. A collateral benefit is the pleasant relationship of man and wife. But the ultimate goal is the reproduction of a leadership class, generation after generation of children who will be worthy successors of their parents and equal or exceed those forebears in the social, cultural, and political skills that ruling the state requires.

Now that he has established that the core value of marriage is the procreation of worthy children, Barbaro may proceed to his main theme: the importance of wives, who are essential for the conception, birthing, and rearing of exceptional children. First, he will define how the ideal wife is to be chosen, a discussion forming part of a larger discussion: "a full analysis of the role of the wife, which to my knowledge was never undertaken by ancient authorities." (Barbaro, 71) What a bold claim—echoing that in his dedicatory letter to Lorenzo, where he proposes to elucidate the whole "elegant science" of marriage as constructed by the ancients. This, in his first major work, will be his unprecedented contribution to learning, and to the modern understanding of women's role as mothers.

On Choosing a Wife

Following the brief dedicatory letter to Lorenzo, and the prologue exploring the nature of marriage, Barbaro's treatise now unfolds in two main parts: the first offering guidance on choosing a wife, the second instructing the wife in her duties. Both offer surprising advice.

The surprise in the first part—the second to be discussed in its place—is that Barbaro staunchly opposes the criteria for selecting a wife that were commonplace in his city and his century. She is not to be chosen for her wealth, nor even for her beauty, but for her virtue. The reason is self-evident. As the previous discussion has already explained, her main role in marriage is as the mother of progeny on whom the welfare of the family and the state depends. Their mother's good character is crucial to the children's success; her wealth and her beauty are irrelevant.

The primacy of a wife's moral character is not only the general theme of the first part of the treatise, but of its first chapter as well. Barbaro begins by naming the series of qualities—character, age, descent, beauty, and wealth—that the ancients tagged as essential in a wife: and "if any of these is neglected, we will certainly bring dishonor and sorrow to our families, and often grief to ourselves; but if we attend to them diligently, we win honor for our family, and for ourselves,

52. The trope of the citizens forming "the walls of the city" is ancient; see below, note 16.

reputation and enduring joy." (Barbaro, 71) But immediately afterward, he asserts that one of these qualities is more valuable than the others: "Virtue ... is the preeminent requirement, whose power and worth is so great that, even if other qualities are lacking, yet the marriage should be considered a good one; and if it is present, then without doubt, the marriage will be successful." Even the requirement that a wife be a good domestic manager is satisfied when a wife of good character is chosen, for those tasks will not be managed well "unless the woman in charge guides, governs, and orders them with prudence, diligence, and industry." (Barbaro, 71)

As is his usual method, Barbaro provides classical examples to support his contention. Based on Plutarch's life of Cato the Elder (234–149 BCE), which Barbaro had translated into Latin as the proof piece of his Greek studies, the case of the famous Roman censor is discussed at some length. Cato chose for his second wife a virtuous woman of no wealth or rank, the daughter of his own subordinate. Less attention is given to Peisistratus, the Athenian tyrant (from 561 to 527 BCE), who chose as his second wife a woman of "exceptional modesty, since the great virtue of his sons increased in him daily the desire to procreate more of them." (Barbaro, 73) Both of these men had grown sons when they chose these second wives, and so each introduced into his household a stepmother and potential mother of rival offspring—a stressor both in antiquity and in Barbaro's own day, and a circumstance that may help illuminate the special importance of the new spouse's benign character.

That same issue arises in the next two examples that Barbaro offers, the most remarkable in his treatise: for they feature contemporary figures, drawn from Barbaro's own city, his elite circle, and indeed, in the case of the first, his own clan. His ancestor Andrea Barbaro had asked Lucia Viara to marry him on account of her "remarkable and conspicuous probity ... setting aside any consideration of wealth." (Barbaro, 73) The success of the marriage was measured by her performance as a stepmother: for "she cherished his children with such concern and piety that no greater harmony or peace could be desired than prevailed in their household." (Barbaro, 73) Andrea Barbaro's marriage served as a model, some years later, for another nobleman of advanced years, Giusto Contarini, who, "having ascertained the moderation, modesty, and exceptional beauty of Francesca, the daughter of Pantaleone Barbo," a third nobleman in this anecdotal sequence, asked the father's permission to marry her. Upon consulting his circle of kin, Barbo agreed, and so Contarini took his bride "although she brought a very small dowry, as the family's circumstances dictated." Yet it was a successful marriage, as measured by her care of his children: for "she treated the children of Giusto's former wife with such kindness and generosity that in their daily life, many of the stepchildren found that other than the name, she was in no way like a stepmother." (Barbaro, 73)

It is most unusual in humanist literature to find colloquial moments of this sort, with recollections of nearly current happenings among the author's social equals. Here again, one suspects that Zaccaria Trevisan prompted the discussion, purveying to his young protégé examples drawn from their close circle. Also striking in these cases, as in the classical examples earlier, is the exemplary performance of these women as stepmothers, which is taken as proof of their exceptional virtue, despite poverty or modesty of circumstances. Their poverty, as well, calls for comment. Neither in Greco-Roman society nor in the wealthy mercantile cities of the Italian Renaissance—outside of the sermons of mendicant preachers—was poverty generally viewed as a recommended or even tolerable state of being.

And yet Barbaro presses the point: virtue in a wife must trump wealth: " ... we consider virtue in a wife of such great importance that, if our fortune permits, we should either pay no attention to the size of her dowry, or settle for a very small one, in order to obtain domestic honor and harmony." He continues: "This quality by itself brings us greater glory than if we marry a wife laden with gold, but devoid of probity." (Barbaro, 74) Turning to Lorenzo, Barbaro observes that his friend, too, must be aware that one must marry a wife of good character, "without which what hope domestic life may hold for us, I cannot imagine." (Barbaro, 74)

Barbaro sends his message that virtue in a wife is preferable to dowry wealth—that virtue is, in effect, the true wealth that wives bring to marriage—early in a century marked by opportunistic marriage-making. The obsession with the dowry worked to the harm of women and children, denying many women, even from elite families, the opportunity to marry, and building marriages on mercenary foundations to such an extent that the corruption of family relationships was the likely result. Barbaro saw these mechanisms at work before they reached their full crescendo, and recognized their threat to the successful reproduction of the noble caste to which he unashamedly belonged.

The second chapter of the first part, while it is focused on the smaller question of the ideal age of a wife, reprises some of the concerns of the first. A young wife, Barbaro maintains, is preferable to an older one, because her character, as yet unformed, can be shaped to the preferences of her (implicitly, older) husband: "For we can easily imprint images in soft wax, while those impressed on surfaces that are hard and unyielding are difficult to erase." (Barbaro, 75) She should, as well, be a virgin, not a widow—an alternate way of saying she should be young, for young women were expected to be virginal, and great care was expended to make sure that they were. Widows, in general, were somewhat older, and given their sexual experience with another man, even if not advanced in years, by definition something tougher than soft wax. Indeed, their previous sexual experience implies not only less pliability, but the prior indulgence in sin, a meaning suggested here, as Barbaro switches from household to horticultural metaphors: "For who will hope to straighten vines that are now old if they were allowed to grow wild at the start?" (Barbaro, 75) For Barbaro, youth implies innocence and therefore virtue; widowhood signals sexual experience and, on that account, wilful resistance to a new husband's wishes. In the same way that virtue is to be preferred to wealth, youth is to be preferred to experience.

But if virtue even though coupled with poverty, and youth that promises malleability, were desiderata for Barbaro, he does not abandon the assumption conventional for his class of the high importance of family origin. The third chapter of the first part is entitled, in the Latin, *Quo genere*, which can mean many things: Of what origin? Of what family? Of what race? Given the Venetian social context, it plainly asks, "From what lineage should a wife come?" To which the response is: from a noble one.

As Barbaro uses the word *genus* (from which derives his title, *quo genere?*), it means "lineage," and so contains within itself the preference for the aristocratic that Barbaro displays. That is clearly his intent when he opens the chapter with an aside to Lorenzo, his friend and peer, that he would like to treat the whole issue of lineage at length, since it is so neglected at the present moment: "certainly I would argue forcefully that our ancestral heritage should be valued most highly, as I believe, rather than, as is the custom, of allowing it daily to decay." (Barbaro, 78) In a city ruled by a hereditary nobility, Barbaro finds that insufficient honor is accorded noble descent! But he has not the space to address the matter, and so proceeds to the immediately pressing matter: the importance of noble lineage in a wife—not quite so important, perhaps, but almost as important as moral character.[53]

To make his point, Barbaro turns "to nature itself," and specifically to agriculture:

> A flourishing pasture, planted and sown, is a strong argument to us that for the sake of our offspring, we should marry women of noble birth. For seeds are better or worse according to their origins; and the best seed bears the finest fruits. And we know that many, and indeed the finest kinds of berries, nuts, and fruits, if they are not planted in proper and suitable soil, will not bear fruit; and if they are transplanted to an ignoble field, they lose their noble spirit ...; while fine young shoots, if they are grafted to weak branches, yield inferior buds. (Barbaro, 78)

53. Barbaro's strong advocacy here of the notion of the biological transmission of noble character enters him into the ongoing humanist debate on the nature of nobility, for which see Albert Rabil, Jr., ed. and trans., *Knowledge, Goodness, and Power: The Debate over Nobility among Quattrocento Italian Humanists* (Binghamton, NY: Medieval and Renaissance Texts and Studies, 1991), and Claudio Donati, *L'idea di nobiltà in Italia: secoli XIV–XVII* (Rome: Laterza, 1988), 3–28.

In these three sentences, Barbaro compares the woman who gives birth, in turn, to a pasture, to a seed, and to a branch. She is a "flourishing pasture," whose "proper and suitable soil" can nourish the finest "berries, nuts, and fruits"; but she is also a "best seed" that "bears the finest fruits"; and she is, as well, a "young [shoot]," which will yield only "inferior buds" if it is grafted to a weak branch, but presumably will thrive and bear superior ones if grafted to a strong one. In all three readings, the woman is seen as genetrix, the one who bears a child who is only as fine, noble, or superior to the extent that his mother—whether field, seed, or shoot—possesses those qualities.

What confusion! The whole of Greco-Roman thought, social, legal, and medical, which was absorbed by European civilization, supported the notion that nobility is transmitted by the male to his descendants; but here it is the female! Seed, moreover—in Latin, semen, the same word that denoted the male genera-tive sperm-bearing fluid called *semen*, as well, in English—was overwhelmingly viewed as male, self-evidently masculine. The generative power of the male is also implicit in the two main ancient theories of conception, derived respectively from Aristotle and Galen, although more in the first than in the second.[54] In the earlier, Aristotelian view, the spermatic material was the creative entity, and the womb, the female contribution to conception, a passive vehicle for the gestation of the fetus—a view entirely at odds, in this case, with Barbaro's, although Barbaro is generally an uncritical Aristotelian. In the alternate, Galenic view, both sperm and womb contribute to the creation of a new life. But even if Barbaro may seem more Galenist than Aristotelian, he is in the end neither one nor the other, for in his view of conception, and the transmission of nobility, a "superior" nature, or "fineness" to new generations, there is no role for the male at all.

Barbaro expands further on the maternal role in the shaping of progeny, for among humans, as among vegetables, "worthier offspring" can be anticipated "from women of greater worth." (Barbaro, 79) Confirmation of the mother's par-ticular role is found in Roman law, which decrees that the child's legal status is determined by the mother's condition: thus the child of a freeborn mother is free, even if the father is a slave. Furthermore, the ancient poets considered the sons of goddesses to be divine, although their fathers were ordinary men: "The day is not long enough for me to name them all; but Achilles, Aeneas, and Orpheus were considered to possess divinity precisely on this basis." (Barbaro, 79) The maternal role is critical in the rearing of children, as well as in their birthing—a point to

54. For an overview of the different views on conception of Aristotle and Galen, see Margaret L. King and Albert Rabil, Jr., "The Old Voice and the Other Voice: Introduction to the Series," reprinted in every volume of the first 60 volumes of the series The Other Voice in Early Modern Europe (University of Chicago Press), 1996–2010, now online at http://www.othervoiceineme.com/othervoice.html. The Galenic view was foreshadowed to some extent by the twelfth-century Saint Hildegard of Bingen; see Joan Cadden, *Meanings of Sex Difference in the Middle Ages: Medicine, Science, and Culture* (Cambridge: Cambridge University Press, 1993), 70–88.

which Barbaro will return for full development in the final chapter of his treatise: "Who is so ignorant that he does not perceive the great influence that mothers exert on the children they bear?" (Barbaro, 79)

Having argued the preeminence of mothers, remarkably, relative to fathers in the determination of the nature of their offspring—as indeed he seems to have done—Barbaro now shifts to a more modest but still bold claim: that noble progeny will inherit (biologically) and (culturally) replicate and even surpass the nobility of their progenitors, female as well as male: "With nobly-born mothers, it is far more likely that the splendor of the parents will shine forth with even greater brightness in their offspring ...." (Barbaro, 79) How does this accumulation of splendor occur? Both by accident of birth and by personal endeavor: for those nobly-born will "strive with their own particular virtue that accrues to them as though by the laws of nature ..., knowing "that if this innate virtue is not realized in action, they will be judged harshly by all, and know that they have degenerated from the ancestral standard." (Barbaro, 79) By these means, Barbaro explains, both biological and cultural, by descent and by the exertion of will, nobility is reproduced.

In choosing a wife of noble birth, in sum, a man of noble rank not only upholds his own dignity, but ensures that the quality of nobility, transmitted through the body of a woman, will be conveyed to his children, making them "more powerful and resplendent." (Barbaro, 80) Barbaro concludes his vision of the generational transmission of nobility, conditional on the correct selection of a wife, by turning to his counterpart Lorenzo:

> Therefore let us take noble wives—just as you, Lorenzo, have most wisely done—so that ..., having acquired sons ennobled both by nature and by nurture, and having prepared them for glory by the example of their forebears, we may abundantly bestow upon them honor and power.... so that the merit that they acquire not only from their father, but also from their mother, they may piously and righteously transmit, as though an inheritance, to their own descendants. (Barbaro, 81)

In the first three chapters just discussed of the first part of *The Wealth of Wives*, Barbaro establishes two interrelated principles: that the foremost criterion for the choice of a wife is virtue (best nurtured if she is married when young), but that virtue is a quality coterminous with nobility—the moral dimension of the social condition, inextricably linked, both essential in a wife suitable for a young man of the elite circle to which Barbaro and Lorenzo belonged.

In the next two chapters, Barbaro deals with two characteristics of wifely candidates that most men—but not he—consider essential: beauty and wealth.

Beauty is, he will grant, pleasing, but it should only be valued if it accompanies other, more important assets. Wealth—in an argument already forecast in the earlier discussion of the requirement of virtue—is not to be sought; its allure must be resisted, and it must be superseded as a consideration by fundamentally more significant qualities.

As he opens the fourth chapter, Barbaro highlights the contrast between the criterion of beauty in the selection of a wife with the criteria he had considered in the previous three: "Now it is time for me to approach that issue with which the discussion of marriage usually begins, by those who would have omitted all that has been said above." (Barbaro, 81) For many men, beauty is the principal quality desired in a wife—or perhaps beauty after only wealth, as will soon be seen. Barbaro empathizes, recognizing the power of beauty, and lingering a bit on the compelling power of a woman's hair: for Homer, he suggests, it was from "her lovely hair" that Helen's fateful beauty derived. (Barbaro, 82) And to Lorenzo, referring to the famous dalliance between two of the ancient deities, he notes that "if Mars had seen Venus shorn of her hair, the ardor that possessed that bellicose god would have vanished posthaste ...." (Barbaro, 82)

Other aspects of female beauty Barbaro mentions in passing: eyes, neck, hands, and stature—those of small stature being dismissed as promising little in terms of procreation. And beauty in general is acknowledged to be seen by many "as divine and worthy of many honors," while for some men it is "the sole or the most important requirement in a wife," and others not only choose beautiful wives but "would even die" for them. Nor is love of beauty the same as lust, which is despicable; but beauty fosters both child-bearing and companionship, "the joyful friendliness of a shared life." (Barbaro, 83) The affective force of beauty in women is undeniable: "We must accordingly value beauty in wives, or any fool will know that I am telling a silly tale." (Barbaro, 83)

Barbaro is no puritan. But while he does not censure beauty in wives, he remains firm on his crucial point—that beauty is a fine adjunct to the qualities to be sought in a wife, but it is not in itself sufficient:

> ... [I]f beauty be joined to noble character and other admirable qualities, I would value it highly; but apart from these, I would in no way praise it.... What kind of a wife will she be, if she who should be joined to us by dignity and friendliness is tied to us only by beauty? .... Let us love beautiful women, if they possess the other qualities necessary to make marriage delightful for us, and honorable and advantageous for our progeny. (Barbaro, 83)

The criterion of beauty in a wife, though understandable, must be secondary, subordinated to other goods. The criterion of wealth, in contrast, must be annihilated.

For those who chase after the specious lure of dowry wealth, Barbaro explains in the next chapter, will be denied both the joy of companionship and the prize of worthy offspring who will in their own lives replicate, and surpass, the nobility of their progenitors.

Barbaro does not deny the value of wealth any more than he does of beauty. Its fruits are "gratitude, liberality, and magnificence" (Barbaro, 96): three classical virtues. By exercising these, he explains, we show our gratitude to those who have bestowed a benefit on us; demonstrate our generosity to those who are worthy, including our own children; and display in the abundance of our possessions the honor and reputation of our family. Gifts made to our children are especially useful, especially if these contribute to their education in the liberal arts,[55] for children thus educated are further equipped to embody and enhance the nobility first embodied by their forbears: "Endowed with these benefits [that accrue from liberal studies], these offspring may be worthy of those honorable men, their fathers, and render their ancestors still more illustrious." (Barbaro, 85) The purpose of wealth, that is to say, is not our own "ease and comfort" (Barbaro, 85) but the enhancement of the lineage.

There exists, however, another form of wealth that, for Barbaro, is pernicious: the wealth that is sought for pleasure and indulgence, and, specifically, the dowry wealth that young men seek to advance their own interests. This kind of wealth is inherently immoral, for it is acquired not to benefit the lineage, the household, or its progeny, but for selfish ends. Barbaro's condemnation is strong:

> I wish that we lived in that age long ago when young people could be taught, and not misled as they are now, that they should not too greatly esteem wealth and possessions in marriage: truly that would have better served the interests of the human community. But most young men have been from their childhood so infused and imbued with the love of gain that they will perform any labor and expend any effort to acquire and achieve it, not neglecting any path by which they think they may satisfy their avarice. (Barbaro, 86)

Young suitors should consider not gain, but "the other factors I have written about here" that are truly of weight in choosing a wife: indeed, Barbaro "cannot accuse those enough, who however wealthy they may be themselves, still zealously seek wives who possess in no way the qualities necessary in a wife." Granted, there are many men, both among the ancients and at the present time, who did not measure their wives by their dowries, "with whose praise, like a galaxy of stars, history sparkles." But there are even more whose appetite for more cannot be satisfied, although they possess grand estates and luxurious furnishings, and

---

55. *In egregiis studiis et artibus* ("excellent studies and arts"); 16.

who, "since they are impoverished in the midst of great wealth, so they desire not more worthy, but more lucrative marriages." (Barbaro, 87)

> And just as those untrained in the equestrian art make much of horses with splendid equipage; and those ignorant of the military art vaunt their golden helmets; and those without learning display their worthless books—useless, dull, and full of lies, though bound with gilded covers; so most men seek out wives whose coffers are full—not coffers, in truth, but glittering coffins, as my learned and beloved mentor Guarino[56] used to say. For inside these, while their ornamented surface is encrusted with a variety of adornments, there is within nothing worthy, but rather the greatest filth, fetor, even de-filement, and many other such horrors that only the dead can bear. (Barbaro, 87)

A mighty indictment of what was the prevalent practice among his very class and generation! Barbaro knows his views are out of sync with the times, but still he will speak: "I fear I shall be criticized for saying this; yet I must say what I believe." (Barbaro, 86)

The diminution of the role of the dowry in spousal choice is so crucial for Barbaro that he even proposes imitating the Spartans in adopting the reverse dowry—the bridegift that is the custom in many societies, as it was in Europe before the twelfth-century triumph of the dowry system. In that alternate scenario, the husband would bring a gift to the bride, or rather her family. Barbaro urges the reinstatement of this custom, which would eliminate dowry-chasing, and acknowledge the great value a wife brings to the groom and his household. "For if we pay farmers and laborers to cultivate our fields," he argues, "so that we may spend the profit in turn on things that are useful to us, why should we not also do so for a wife, from whom we expect such necessary, and such sweet fruit?" (Barbaro, 88) The real wealth of wives, after all, is their capacity to conceive, give birth to, and rear the offspring of their husbands' lineage.

Young men must renounce their quest for the pernicious form of wealth constituted by the dowry, and "free [themselves] from pleasure, that seductive tyrant, and cast away the precious garments and fripperies befitting a lecher, and the other supposed necessities [they] do not really need, and quell that desire that is content with no limit … lest for the sake of money, or in the hope of gain, they make themselves slaves to a dowry, and so kindle a domestic fire that cannot easily be put out." (Barbaro, 88)

In his frontal assault on the dowry system that lures young men into choos-ing wives not for their enduring virtue but for their illusory and deceptive wealth,

---

56. Guarino Veronese, who had been Barbaro's instructor in Greek; see above, 3, 4–6.

Barbaro has reached the climax of the first part of *The Wealth of Wives*. He is eager to move on to the second part, where he will discuss what wives must do, but first addresses in the sixth and seventh chapters possible objections to his program and the proper celebration of the wedding.

Evidently written in response to some criticism of his earlier chapters, which had perhaps been circulated in draft or had been reviewed in conversation, Barbaro's sixth chapter, with the accommodating title "for what causes it may be necessary to alter these precepts," softens the demands that earlier ones had laid on young men in search of wives. The objection was raised that some suitors could not afford to dispense entirely with dowry calculations in selecting a future bride. Barbaro concedes the difficulty, but responds with a touch of hauteur:

> I would greatly prefer that these jottings of mine could be equally useful for all. But if there is someone who cannot follow my advice, either because of lowliness of birth or lack of funds, let him rage at his misfortune, not my precepts. (Barbaro, 88)

It was likewise objected that Barbaro's bar had been placed too high: not all would be able to attain a wife with all the requisites named. In response, Barbaro concedes, comparing these unfortunate but striving suitors to his Florentine friend: that "indeed, they cannot all be Lorenzos, to whom, superbly endowed in soul, body, and fortune, wives of every sort and every rank are available." (Barbaro, 89) They must do as well as they can, like the suitors of Penelope, who, when finally rebuffed, turned to her handmaidens:

> [S]o if we cannot win as wives the most excellent of women, let us, to the extent that our dignity allows, take those whom we can .... Regarding which that old saying comes to mind ...: equals are best suited to equals. For what could be more pleasant, what more comfortable, what more easy, than to take as a wife a woman equal to oneself? (Barbaro, 89)

Above all, these young suitors should remember that character is the foremost consideration: "Nor do I wish to burden the men of our generation with so many prerequisites for a wife—for all that I wish and desire is difficult and nearly infinite, yet I require all of it; but let them demand virtue, and with it, they may be confident that all else will follow." (Barbaro, 91)

In chapter 7, while still impatient to move on to the second section of his work, Barbaro will first discuss marriage customs and the wedding ceremony itself—for in these, after all, culminate the choice of the ideal wife. To do so, he will turn again to the books of the ancients:

It remains for me to speak of wifely duties, about which there is such fullness of joy, sweetness, loveliness, and all that is in every way so beautiful to behold, that, overwhelmed by the force of ideas, I almost neglected one thing that must first be presented here. For surely, before I come to the second part of this work, I must say a few words about the wedding ceremony itself, which, though they are now forgotten and nearly obliterated, I shall recover from the records of antiquity. (Barbaro, 91)

For the Greeks and the Romans, as in Barbaro's own society, the wedding took place in the sight of God, who affirms the profound emotional bond that will join man and wife. Barbaro briefly notes mostly Roman marriage customs: the strewing of greenery; the placing of a ring on the finger of the left hand from which a nerve runs directly to the heart; the bride's touching vessels of water and fire placed before her that "demonstrat[e] her responsibility for the procreation of children"; the lifting of the bride over the threshold of her husband's house, recalling a prior association of marriage with rape; and various approved and prohibited dates and times for the celebration of the nuptials.

If resources allow, the wedding celebration may be splendid, "lest we be denied this kind of honor." (Barbaro, 94) While some have condemned this kind of display, many authorities, including the towering Aristotle, permit a lavish show on this occasion for those of high rank. Barbaro recounts here a charming anecdote about Manuel Chrysoloras (c. 1355–1415), the great Byzantine statesman and scholar with whom Guarino had studied, on the occasion of the nuptials of his nephew John. Guarino was likely Barbaro's source.

The respected and renowned philosopher Manuel Chrysoloras chose a wife for his nephew John, a learned and upstanding man of the equestrian order, whose wedding was celebrated with a most splendid show; and when one of his companions charged that the display diminished the dignity of that grave philosopher, he replied, "God preserve us! It is permitted us on joyous occasions to have magnificent celebrations; and for the honor of our family, so long as we do no injury to our neighbors, this kind of splendor is never prohibited." (Barbaro, 94)

From the wedding ceremony, Barbaro proceeds to the nuptial event, the culmination of the preceding courtship. The veiled bride enters the chamber "to perform her marital duty," and "her husband embraces her as his spouse"; and then, as Barbaro coyly describes it in the words of the poet Virgil, "nestled in her bosom, languor spreads through all his limbs."[57] (Barbaro, 95) Outside, the celebrants scatter nuts, "so that over the clamor of children collecting them, the sounds the newlywed emits due either to pain or lost innocence might not be heard by the crowd gathered outside." (Barbaro, 95)

With this flourish of eroticism, now Barbaro will say no more, lest he offend Lorenzo's ears with unchaste remarks: for "now that you have devoted your soul, concern, and passion to these divine humanities, [they] should be greeted by nothing but pure speech and a grave and learned message." (Barbaro, 95) Here again, as in the dedicatory letter, Barbaro alludes to the bond between him and the Florentine, sealed as it is for them, as for many of the young men of their circle, by a common schooling in the new humanist curriculum of the liberal arts. He encourages that audience to acknowledge their debt to "those ancient authors," the source not only of the wisdom that enriches the soul, but of guidance in matrimonial matters: for from these "in long nights of study, if they do not fail in the task, they will not only improve themselves, but also win wives of sharper wit, and celebrate more splendid nuptials." (Barbaro, 96)

And now, Barbaro comments in closing, "[w]e come to greater things" (Barbaro, 96): to the second part of his treatise, devoted to the duties of a wife.

On Wifely Duties

The symmetry of Barbaro's treatise is now clear: a wife is chosen in the first part, and performs her responsibilities in the second—and if she has been properly chosen, she will properly perform. But the two halves of the treatise differ in texture. The first part, though systematic in structure, is startling: Barbaro counters the reader's expectations, ranking the chosen woman's moral and intellectual character ahead of both wealth and beauty. The second part, until its last section, is more predictable. It begins with seven brief chapters on wifely behavior, delivering a sternly patriarchal message: the wife, who is wholly subordinate to her husband, must show him obedience and, indeed, love, while strictly regulating her own behavior according to norms that are both Christian and Greco-Roman. It then shifts, in an eighth chapter, to the wife's role as domestic manager, where she is depicted as directing the household system, making important decisions and acting with some autonomy.

After these routine and prescriptive messages, in the expansive ninth chapter, Barbaro comes to the culminating message of *The Wealth of Wives*—a message as surprising as was that conveyed in the first part of the treatise. Here he describes the wife's responsibility for the crucial and interrelated tasks of the gestation, parturition, lactation, and education of children. For in these offices consist, as seen in the first part of the treatise, the wealth that is sought in a wife:

---

57. Virgil, *Aeneid* 8.405–406. My translation.

the capacity to engender in the next generation the qualities of mind and soul that animate the parents who give it birth.

The first seven chapters of the second book, then, are concerned with the regulation of the wife's behavior: her own self-regulation, and her regulation by her husband. The first quality required of her is obedience to her husband: "than which nothing is more pleasing, nothing more desirable." (Barbaro, 96) Barbaro advises the wife to adjust her behavior to her husband's needs. If he is angry, she should endure the storm; but if he is troubled, she should intercede to comfort and advise. She should avoid wearing garments that annoy her husband, and avoid repeating things she has overheard so as not to provoke his wrath. She must give no cause for his ill-temper, but endure it when it comes—and not leave his bed during these times of unease, for the bedroom is the ideal site of reconciliation. Barbaro concludes: "If [a wife] is to perform her duty of maintaining and securing peace and quiet in her marriage, then nothing should more occupy her mind than the need in all matters to assent to her husband." (Barbaro, 99)

The following chapter, on marital love, sketches in even more rapturous tones the theme of harmony between the spouses. A wife should "love her husband with such earnestness, faithfulness, and delight that nothing is lacking in concern, attentiveness, or good will." (Barbaro, 99) Conjugal love has such "extraordinary force and unmatched dignity" that it poses a "model of perfect friendship," in which the souls of husband and wife are "somehow intermingled," so that, as Pythagoras had wished, "the two become one." (Barbaro, 100) Many ancient authors had celebrated marital love of this kind, Barbaro points out, and he himself provides a number of examples: among them Pantheia, the wife of the king of Susa, a friend of the Persian king Cyrus, who slew herself on her husband's dead body; Thesta, the sister of Dionysius the tyrant of Syracuse, who joined her husband, his enemy, in exile; Andromache, Hector's wife as depicted by Homer, crazed by the death of her beloved husband; and, at length, the Galatian princess Camma, who willingly drank poison in order to poison the man who had murdered her husband. Beyond these, Barbaro writes, are also many other such stories that, addressing his educated audience, "are readily available to all of those who have any familiarity with history." (Barbaro, 103)

These classical anecdotes, which Barbaro dwells on and then dismisses, reveal a dimension of his thoughts on conjugal love possibly troubling to some modern readers. They suggest that the love required in a loyal wife is not only wholehearted and solicitous, but also sacrificial and self-negating. A wife is to be celebrated when she denies her own interests for those of her husband; and ultimately, as in the cases of Pantheia and Camma, when she destroys herself as the expression of that love.

After this resounding if complicated affirmation of conjugal affection, Barbaro moves on to five chapters decidedly repressive in intent. They define the ways in which a wife must not merely regulate her behavior, but seemingly suppress normal energies and emotions in order to meet the marital ideal. The first of these, the third of the second part, deals with the quality of moderation—"in which enduring love between husband and wife is often rooted"—that serves as an umbrella for the others to follow. Moderation is displayed, first of all, in the motions of face and body. The face, "the surest image of the mind," and "found in no living creature except man," should exhibit modesty and temperance, for here is "plainly declare[d] with what kind of passions the soul may be affected." (Barbaro, 104) The motions of the body, likewise, must "preserve balance and constancy":

> For the wandering of the eyes, a hasty walk, too much movement of the hands or other parts of the body are always indecorous, and betray an underlying levity or vanity .... Diligence in this matter will bring them joy and honor, while negligence will result in anguish and censure. (Barbaro, 104)

Barbaro presents, in his usual pattern, classical examples of such restraint, culminating in the requirement of Greek rhetor Gorgias that wives remain strictly confined to the house, and of the historian Thucydides, who recommended that the wife be completely invisible, the cause of neither praise nor blame. (Barbaro, 105) These recommendations the Venetian finds too stern, saying that his own contemporaries afford their wives greater latitude: "For we do not require wives to be bound in chains, as it were, but permit them to walk out openly in public, this indulgence shown them serving as a testimony to their virtue and probity." (Barbaro, 105) In fifteenth-century Venice, married women were in fact permitted to leave their homes—though under close supervision.

The fourth chapter discusses restraint in speech to complement the restraint in facial and bodily expression just presented. Loquacity in wives is to be avoided, and silence commended: "Let them respond modestly when called by those close to them, report on their health, and when the place and occasion permits, speak briefly, so that they seem to have been provoked to speech, rather than to provoke it." (Barbaro, 106) In dress, likewise, discussed in the following chapter, they should observe decorum. The violation of this norm, indeed, threatens not only the marriage (*matrimonium*), but also household wealth (the *patrimonium*) (Barbaro, 107), for excessive dress is expensive, and may dishonor the husband of the inappropriately bedecked wife: "For surely a plethora of precious clothing is of little use to husbands, but rather often painful, while it always provides pleasure to lovers, for whose sake such fripperies are created." (Barbaro, 108) Of course, Barbaro allows that a woman of high rank should be appropriately costumed, and he encourages wives to adorn themselves "with gold, gems, and pearls": for these "declare the amplitude of her husband rather than amuse the eyes of lovers." (Barbaro, 109)

Wives must not only temper their movements, their speech, and their apparel, but also restrain, as set forth in chapters 6 and 7, their physical indulgence both in the seemingly innocent pleasures of food and drink, and the more dangerous ones of sex. Restraint in both areas of bodily self-indulgence has, for Barbaro, a broadly moral dimension. The "delicacies" that "the multitude believes affords us the good life" do not merely plump our bellies and muddle our minds, but "tear at and shatter the sinews of virtue." (Barbaro, 109) Wives must, accordingly, "diligently abstain from these things that arouse, implant, and increase the craving for pleasure." They must do so not only for themselves, but for their children, "for whom they must do all things," "whose welfare is the point of all that is said in this commentary"—here Barbaro glances ahead to what will be the culminating argument of his book—and who will never, if they are coddled and overfed in their early years, "achieve in adulthood a semblance of moderation or of good morals." (Barbaro, 110)

In sex, equally, wives must show restraint; "for sexual intercourse, too, must follow the path of right living, as a tender chick follows after its mother." (Barbaro, 112) Sex in marriage, Barbaro reminds readers, is for the purpose of procreation, the goal of the marriage relationship cherished by the husband. For that reason, husbands actually prefer that a wife be "loving and lovable" in sexual relations, "but neither shameless nor impudent"—such forward behavior making a wife "less desirable to their husbands," even though they may not audibly complain about it. (Barbaro, 113) Barbaro follows up his discussion, characteristically, with a string of anecdotes, ending with the obscure story of Brasilla of Durazzo, told at some length: herein the heroine averts rape by her captor by, having convinced him that the act would ensure his invincibility, enticing him to behead her in an ultimate "demonstration of determined chastity." (Barbaro, 114)

The eighth chapter of the second book turns from the steamy topic of marital sex to the safer one of household management, developed largely from pertinent works of Xenophon and Aristotle.[58] The wife is to manage the three main engines driving the domestic project: its possessions, its servants, and its children. Reserving the last and most important of these for the next and final chapter of his treatise, Barbaro treats the first two here, which, "unless they have been ordered by the precepts and guidance of the wife, they lack all foundation, and are prone to collapse and fail." (Barbaro, 115) Wives must exercise constant diligence in the management of household stores, for "[t]o what end is wealth brought into the home, unless once within its walls, a wife guards, preserves, and distributes it?" (Barbaro, 115) It is of first importance that everything be maintained in order, so that nothing goes amiss in the pantry or storerooms of oil and wine. Everything

---

58. Xenophon's *Oeconomicus* and Aristotle's *Politics*, to some extent, but more often the very popular pseudo-Aristotelian *Economics*. For Barbaro's use of Xenophon, see Griggio, "Senofonte," and Rollo, "Dalla biblioteca di Guarino," 25–26.

must be regularly counted, lest a wife "discover to [her] shame that what should be sufficient for a year proves to be scarcely enough for a month." (Barbaro, 116)

The supervision of servants requires the same kind of diligence. They should be taught the tasks they must perform, and not be angrily rebuked unless they fail to do something about which they had been amply instructed. It is best that they be assigned specific tasks, the accomplishment of which can be readily measured and noted. They must be fed sufficiently to support the labor required of them, clothed appropriately, and cared for when sick: "For this compassion and generosity will make servants loyal and well-disposed to the welfare of the household." (Barbaro, 118) In the management of both household goods and staff, the wife acts like the queen bee. The queen resides in the hive while teams of energetic and well-organized workers, delighted to do her bidding, bring in supplies; and there she rests stationary, a benign presiding force, while the honey enriches and matures. Thus humans and things, when properly ordered under a wife's supervision, "will work together for the splendor and utility and delight of the household." (Barbaro, 119)

Just as a wife must care for her husband's possessions and servant staff, so too, and this above all, she must bear, nurture, and rear his children—for, as Barbaro reminded his readers earlier, it is they "whose welfare is the point of all that is said in this commentary" (Barbaro, 111) and for whom the household comes into existence. In chapter 9, the final and the longest of his work, Barbaro writes of "that most important and rewarding of a wife's responsibilities," the education of her children. As established in the prologue and reiterated thereafter, marriage exists for the sake of the procreation of children rather than to satisfy any personal ambitions of the two spouses. It is the children who are to inherit the wealth that the householder has patiently accumulated, with the aid of his wife; and to these progenitors, they will be indebted for their care and instruction, absent which "they would be utterly abandoned and forlorn." How much greater will be the debt if those benefactors "also provide a liberal education and the precepts of moral living"! Barbaro here describes a circle of giving, where goods flow from parents to children, and gratitude from children to parents, locked in an intergenerational exchange. (Barbaro, 119)

Yet though he speaks of two parents in the terms just presented, he proceeds to focus next on mothers, on whom alone falls the inescapable burden of caregiving and early training—as nature has decreed: for "if you reflect deeply with all your mind and soul, you will conclude that if mothers are not bereft of natural instinct, the duty of educating their children is so incumbent upon them, that they cannot refuse it without imperiling their ability to function at all: for in every way nature signifies that the love for offspring is innate, and can in no way be denied." (Barbaro, 119) Both maternal love and maternal duty are rooted, Barbaro argues, in biology.

What follows is Barbaro's presentation of an understanding of human gestation inherited from antiquity and widely accepted during the Middle Ages. These
ideas circulated in medical books, the property of a limited circle of university-
trained professionals, and were not often introduced, as Barbaro does, in works
intended for a broader readership. Accordingly, he expresses some hesitation at
the outset: time does not permit a full explanation, "and nature has so positioned
those parts of the body in such secret places that they cannot be observed without shame, and hardly spoken of with honor." But he will forge on nonetheless:
"[W]hat cannot be left unsaid, I shall set forth." (Barbaro, 119)

For Barbaro, the maternal nurture of a child cycles between the poles constituted by two fluids, seen as inherently female, identical in essence, but opposite
in function as they are in appearance: blood and milk.[59] Although men evidently
bleed when an injury ruptures skin or organ, women bleed every month of their
fertile maturity, except, notably, during pregnancy, in a pattern of mystifying reg-
ularity that stamps the substance as female. The effluence of milk is even more distinctively female, for men do not lactate; and it is equally regular, responding, in
normal circumstances, not to a monthly trigger but to each incident of childbirth,
a liquid bounty both mystifying and joyous: for it supports life, as birth bestows
it. In the process of gestation, the blood normally expelled each month is retained
by the woman's body to support the *conceptus,* also substantially formed of that
same blood. During lactation, that same fluid is transformed into its counterpart,
the milk that nourishes the infant after birth as maternal blood had nourished the
fetus during pregnancy.

The maternal nurturance provided by the two fluids of blood and milk,
thus dialectically related in the female body, would continue after weaning in the
further process of education. For both fluids, in Barbaro's explanation of this sequence of care, had partaken of the maternal soul, and had transmitted spiritual
characteristics to the child *in utero* and at the breast; subsequently, that task would
be completed by the mother's spiritual, moral, and intellectual teaching.

The foregoing is a précis of the story Barbaro tells about the biological
processes, as he understood them, that determine maternal activity. It cannot
convey the fervor with which he tells it. Once the fetus is born, in his words,
"... nature supplies milk as nourishment, and fills the breasts from which, as
from welling fountains, the infant drinks, so that gradually his members grow
and he thrives." (Barbaro, 120) Indeed, women are supplied with two breasts,
so as to nurse, if needed, two infants at one time; and, by the "particular care
and diligence of nature," her nipples are planted on her bosom—not, as with
other animals, on her underbelly—so that she may embrace them as they drink.
For these mechanics are meaningless if they are not accompanied by the human
ingredient of love: "While these things are arranged in this manner by divine

59. For the blood-milk complex, see King, "The Emergence of Mother as Teacher," 52.

providence, it would have been done in vain, if nature had not also instilled in the mother an exceptional love and warmth towards those she has brought into the world." (Barbaro, 120) The maternal body is equipped to conceive, carry, bear, and nourish the child; but all of those functions are completed by an out-pouring of spirit: "So nature has assigned to mothers the office of birthing and educating their children not only as a necessary burden, but as an expression of exceptional love and kindness." Mothers must not abandon their children to "live only for themselves," therefore, but "should provide for their children in body and in soul." (Barbaro, 120)

Doing so—exerting both body and soul—means that a mother should herself suckle her children with her own milk, "[f]or there exists no more suitable or salutary nourishment to be offered to the infant as a familiar and trusted food than that very blood, aglow with natural warmth and vigor." (Barbaro, 121) In doing so, she fulfills the implied promise of conception and gestation[60]:

> Let [mothers] feed [their infants], offering their breasts, so that those whom they nourished with their own blood when they were yet unknown, now that they have come forth into the light, now that they are human, now that they are known, now that they are loved, let them rear those who now cry out for them, performing in every way they can the role not merely of nurse, but the office of mother. (Barbaro, 121)

Along with her milk, as Barbaro believes in concert with the consensus of the learned, a mother transmits to her infant traits of mind and character.[61] That belief underlies a principal argument against non-maternal nursing, during which the infant is infused with alien and possibly inferior dispositions. In those rare cases where a mother cannot nurse her own child, surrogates must be carefully chosen who will not "act from false or mercenary motives":

> ... [N]urses should be sought who may substitute for [mothers] in that office—not servants, nor foreigners, nor drunks or whores, but well-born and well-bred women commanding proper speech. Otherwise the tender infant can be corrupted by vulgar words and behavior, and by drinking in error, impurity, and disease along with

---

60. Barbaro here adds his voice to those of a host of physicians, theologians, preachers, and moralists; for an overview of this tradition, see King, "The Emergence of Mother as Teacher," 50–54.

61. Cicero, for example, had complained that our ignorance is so natural that we must have sucked in error with our mother's milk: *Tusculan Disputations*, 3.1.2. See also Suzanne Dixon, *The Roman Mother* (Norman: University of Oklahoma Press, 1988), 115, and Valerie Fildes, *Breasts, Bottles and Babies: A History of Infant Feeding* (Edinburgh: Edinburgh University Press, 1986), 30.

the very milk, be infected by a pernicious contagion, and degenerate in both body and soul. For in the same way that the limbs of the infant can easily be guided and formed, so also from infancy, its character may be aptly and harmoniously composed. (Barbaro, 121)

From conception through gestation, parturition, and lactation, mothers are for Barbaro the key agents in the shaping of the next generation in body, mind, and spirit. That role continues even after infancy—and here Barbaro is completely original and, in his era, unique. The transposition of maternal responsibility from infancy to childhood is crucial: for now it is not through bodily fluids, those shifting components that manifest themselves in the dialectically matched entities of blood and milk, but through her own qualities of mind, character, and soul— those powered not by physiological changes but acts of will—that a mother shapes her child. So Barbaro indicates: "Once their children have grown past infancy, mothers will need to commit much thought, care, and energy to guide them to excel in qualities of mind and body." (Barbaro, 122)

That guidance includes religious and moral instruction, instruction in manners, and preparation for intellectual developments to follow at a later age.[62] First, mothers must teach children "to revere Almighty God," establishing the "habit of piety" that underlies all other acquisitions of virtue. Those virtues are learned from imitation, so in the presence of their children (presumably, at all other times as well!), mothers must "avoid anger, avarice, and lust, for these sins deplete virtue." In this way, children will from their earliest youth learn to "despise, reject, and hate these despotic vices." They must especially be taught to "shudder" at blasphemy and revere what is sacred: for who will not scorn those who, at such a tender age, "despise what is holy?" (Barbaro, 123)

The moral restraint required of these little ones extends to social obligations and behaviors that make for worldly success. They must learn to "honor their parents, respect their elders, love their peers, and cherish those younger than they": that is, to participate in the social networks pertaining to their rank—which is, for children, their age. To these persons they should show an "open countenance and friendly words, especially seeking to know the best of them." Only children who master these relationships "will give grounds for hope." (Barbaro, 122) Even at this early age, moreover, they should be temperate in eating and drinking,

62. In 1400/1405, not long before Barbaro wrote the *De re uxoria*, the Florentine Dominican friar (and later cardinal) Giovanni Dominici (1346–1419) wrote a guide for a widowed patrician mother on the moral upbringing of her children, showing that such a role was a known and accepted one. See his *Regola del governo di cura familiare, compilata dal beato Giovanni Dominici, fiorentino*, ed. Donato Salvi (Florence: A. Garinei, 1860); part 4 in English translation by Arthur Basil Coté: *Regola del governo di cura familiare, parte quarta, on the Education of Children* (Washington, DC: Catholic University of America, 1927). For Dominici's *Regola*, see also Giuseppina Battista, *L'educazione dei figli nella regola di Giovanni Dominici, 1355/6–1419* (Florence: Pagnini e Martinelli, 2002).

initiating "the lifelong practice of moderation." They should not laugh too much, or speak excessively or about improper things: "Mothers should forbid filthy or disrespectful language," and, harshly, respond to it "not with a smile or a kiss, but a whip." Mothers should teach their children, as well, to refrain from belittling others for misfortunes of chance, and encourage them to develop bodily strength in physical exercise:

> They should teach their children, further, never to mock others for their poverty, or their humble ancestry, or other such calamities, by which behavior they arouse enmities that do not go away, and acquire, besides, the habit of arrogance. They should have their children engage in sports, in which they willingly exert themselves so that, if the need occur, they will be able to tolerate more stressful challenges. (Barbaro, 123)

If children acquire these postures and principles from their mothers at an early age, they will be prepared to occupy the social niche prepared for them, achieving "the gravity and rectitude of their parents." They will be readied as well to "apply their mind and soul to those studies that will be to them in later years honorable, useful, and pleasurable," and "as youths they will more easily and solidly acquire the benefits of learning." (Barbaro, 122) All this is the mother's task, before the child—presumably the son—is handed to a male tutor for academic instruction.

This, then, is the real wealth that a wife contributes to the household that she joins through marriage: not the material dowry that she brings from her own patrimony, but the nurture of her husband's children by means bodily, mental, and spiritual, thus achieving the successful reproduction, cultural as well as biological, of his family and his class. The duties named earlier in the second part of Barbaro's treatise—those of self-restraint in thought and action, and prudent management of the domestic establishment—are evidently subordinate to the greater and culminating ones of childbirth and childrearing. For she is no servant or subordinate, in Barbaro's view, but triumphant and regal—truly a queen bee—however much she operates to support the interests of the male lineage. The prominence accorded the wife is uniquely Barbaro's, even as virtually every other dimension of his argument rests on the foundation of Greek moral and philosophical sources and Roman legal traditions.

Now Barbaro closes his treatise, returning to the point from which his discourse began: to his princely Florentine friend Lorenzo, whose own marriage is lauded as a paradigm of the principles that the Venetian has unfolded in what is at once his book and his gift—"you now have, instead of a present, my treatise on the wealth of wives." (Barbaro, 124)

So be pleased now to take this wifely necklace, then, if I may so call it, on the occasion of your nuptials. You will treasure it, I know, either because it is the kind of gift that cannot, like other necklaces, be broken and worn by use, or because it comes to you in all sincerity from a soul that is entirely yours. (Barbaro, 125)

Legacy

Francesco Barbaro's treatise *De re uxoria: The Wealth of Wives*[63] was an immediate success in Italian humanist circles, winning the commendation of Ambrogio Traversari in his letter of June 1, 1416,[64] and reaching the small fraternity gathered, as seen earlier, in Constance. From there, two humanists dispatched letters commending Barbaro's work: on December 31, 1416, Poggio Bracciolini, in a letter to Guarino; and on April 3, 1417, Pier Paolo Vergerio, in a letter to the Venetian physician and humanist Niccolò Leonardi.[65] Guarino had sent Poggio a copy of the book, and Poggio, after thanking him, jokes that it would have been more useful to him if he were about to marry; but further reports that after a first hasty reading, and then a more sustained one, he finds much to commend. Besides "the novelty of the subject," he notes—a comment testifying to his close reading of the work—"the order and sweetness of the discourse," which was "so methodically ordered, that nothing could be more methodical."[66] To Leonardi, an older member of Barbaro's circle, Vergerio pronounces the work "elegant indeed,

63. The work will be referred to by its Latin title, *De re uxoria*, in the analysis that follows of its reception by a European audience.

64. Ambrogio Traversari, *Aliorumque ad ipsum, et ad alios de eodem Ambrosio latinae epistolae*, ordered by Petrus Cannetus, ed. Laurentius Mehus, 2 vols. (Florence: ex typographi Caesareo, 1759; reprint Bologna: Forni, 1968), 2, ep. VI, 15. Traversari had read the work "quasi certamente" in the house of his patron, Cosimo de' Medici: see Claudio Griggio, "Copisti ed editori del *De re uxoria* di Francesco Barbaro," in *Filologia umanistica per Gianvito Resta*, ed. Vincenzo Fera and Giacomo Ferraú, 3 vols. (Padua: Antenore, 1997), 2:1033–55, at 1034.

65. The letters of Poggio and Vergerio from Constance to, respectively, Guarino Veronese and Nicholaos Leontinus (actually Niccolò Leonardi), appear on pages 181–84 (dated at end) and 185–88 (dated at end) of the Amsterdam 1639 edition of *De re uxoria* (Typis Ioannis Ianssonii), as they do in many manuscript and most other printed versions. Poggio's letter is also read in the nineteenth-century edition of his *Epistulae* by Thomas de Tonellis, reprinted as vol. 3 of Poggio Bracciolini, *Opera omnia*, ed. Riccardo Fubini, 4 vols. (Turin: Bottega d'Erasmo, 1963–1969), at 3:20–21. Vergerio's letter is also found in the modern edition of his *Epistolario*, ed. Leonardo Smith, 360–62. For the dating, and the identification of Vergerio's correspondent as Leonardi, see also Griggio, "Copisti ed editori," 1045. For Leonardi, see King, *Venetian Humanism*, 387–89.

66. Poggio, ed. Tonellis, 20–21: "… cum primum mihi redditus est liber ita avide eum legi, ductus tum novititate materiae, tum ordine ac suavitate dicendi, ut universum transcurrerim uno die, postea vero maturius relegerim. Res quidem jucunda ac suavis et plurimis ornate exemplis. Ita vero in ordinem digesta, ut nihil ordinatius dici queat."

excelling both in the charm of its prose, and in the abundance of fine precepts and apt examples gathered from all of Greek and Latin history."[67] Most remarkably, "that a young man as yet unmarried has written with such erudition and eloquence about marriage, and knows so well in theory what he knows not from experience, that I must exceedingly admire."[68] These two letters circulated widely, like twins, often appearing as a pair appended to the *De re uxoria* in manuscript and print versions, to which attention will turn shortly.

Thus blessed by these two humanist masters, the *De re uxoria* made its splendid debut in the *respublica litterarum*. Thereafter it circulated widely in Italian humanist circles and, in due course, beyond the Alps. Its success was known to its author: responding on December 10, 1447, to a letter praising the work, 32 years after its publication, he noted with pride that "this treatise, composed at the beginning of my studies, is approved by many learned and outstanding men."[69] Indeed, with over 100 manuscript copies extant, it should be ranked among the most popular works of Italian humanism.[70] Those manuscripts are distributed in at least 24 different Italian collections; in other European centers including Paris, Amsterdam, Hamburg, Madrid, and London; and beyond Europe in Australia (Sydney) and the United States (including nine in the Beinecke, Houghton, Newberry, and Pierpont Morgan collections). The manuscript diffusion of *De re uxoria* approaches or surpasses those of other widely-circulated titles, such as Pier Paolo Vergerio's *De ingenuis moribus et liberalibus adulescentiae studiis* (The Character

---

67. Vergerio, ed. Smith, 360: "… elegantem quidem et ut venustate sermonis praeclarum, ita praeceptis optimis, et exemplis uberrimis, ex omni Graeca Latinaque historia collectis redundantem."

68. Vergerio, ed. Smith, 361: "Quod vero nunc de re uxoria, tam erudite copioseque juvenis inexpertusque nuptiarum scripserit, idque tam bene sciat, quod nescit, hoc est, quod ego non magnopere admirari non potui."

69. Barbaro, *Epistolario*, 2:559–60, letter 273, to the learned Venetian nobleman Ludovico Barozzi, at 559; trans. by Kohl, *The Earthly Republic*, 186.

70. Griggio, "Copisti ed editori," 1038. Of these, 88 are found through searches of the online edition of Paul Oskar Kristeller, *Iter Italicum: A Finding List of Uncatalogued or Incompletely Catalogued Humanistic Manuscripts of the Renaissance in Italian and other Libraries*, 7 vols. in 9 (London: Warburg Institute; Leiden: E.J. Brill, 1963–1992), accessible at Iter Gateway to the Middle Ages and Renaissance (University of Toronto Libraries), http://cf.itergateway.org/italicum/. Gnesotto names 19 manuscripts of the work in his introduction to the *De re uxoria* at 18–20; of these, 13 duplicate manuscripts named by Kristeller. See also Gnesotto's two preliminary articles on manuscripts of the *De re uxoria*: "Dei Mediceo-Laurenziani e del codice padovano del 'De re uxoria' di Francesco Barbaro," in *Atti e Memorie della R. Accademia di scienze, lettere ed arti in Padova*, n.s. 30 (1913–1914), 281–94; and "I codici Marciani del 'De re uxoria' di Francesco Barbaro," in *Atti e Memorie della R. Accademia di scienze, lettere ed arti in Padova*, n.s. 30 (1913–1914), 105–28. The electronic catalog WorldCat describes eight manuscripts, all of which correspond to manuscripts named by Kristeller. At 1039–47, Griggio closely studies four early manuscripts of the *De re uxoria*, three of which (Laurenziana 78.25 and 78.24; Marc. Lat. Zan. 473 [=1592]) were known to Gnesotto; the fourth, in the Boston Public Library (cod q. Med. 24 [G. 38. 34]) is named by Kristeller and described in WorldCat.

and Studies Befitting a Free-Born Youth) with over 120; Giovanni Boccaccio's *De mulieribus claris* (On Famous Women) with over 100; Leonardo Bruni's *De studiis et litteris* (On Studies and Literature) with over 60; Lorenzo Valla's *De donatione Constantini* (On the Donation of Constantine) with over 40; and Leon Battista Alberti's *De pictura* (On Painting) with over 30.[71]

Many of the Barbaro manuscripts are elegant productions, with the *De re uxoria* the sole or principal work. Some are illuminated, or associated with elite owners; twenty-two, to this author's knowledge, are dated by their copyists or buyers.[72] Other manuscripts are miscellanies, where the *De re uxoria* appears in the company of other works, principally those having to do with childrearing and education: Vergerio's *De ingenuis moribus*, or Guarino's translation (from Greek to Latin) of Plutarch's *De liberis educandis* (On the Education of Children), or Leonardo Bruni's translation (from Greek to Latin) of St. Basil of Caesarea's *De legendis antiquorum libris* (On the Benefit to be Gained from the Study of Greek Literature). It sometimes also appeared with the treatises *De nobilitate* (On Nobility) of Poggio Bracciolini or Buonaccorso da Montemagno—like education, a theme related to Barbaro's own—or, more rarely, with other works of Francesco Barbaro.

The four early manuscripts meticulously described by Claudio Griggio are of exceptional importance.[73] One (early 1416) is the dedication copy to Lorenzo de' Medici, and a second was copied from the first a few months later (May 24, 1416), having been commissioned by Cosimo de' Medici. Both of these appear in the 1418 inventory of Cosimo's books. The first of these and the final two were all written (in 1417 and c. 1434, respectively) by the same scribe, Michele Salvatico

---

71. Based on searches of the online edition of Kristeller's *Iter Italicum*. For Vergerio, see also Robey, "Humanism and Education," 56–57, which notes that there exist "well over a hundred extant fifteenth and sixteenth-century manuscripts of the text in Italian libraries alone," in addition to 30 Italian printed editions before 1500; for Boccaccio, the edition of Virginia Brown, *Famous Women* (Cambridge, MA: Harvard University Press, 2003), xii; for Bruni, Hans Baron, ed. and trans., *Leonardo Bruni Aretino: Humanistisch-philosophische Schriften mit einer Chronologie seiner Werke und Briefe* (Leipzig: B.G. Teubner, 1928; rpt. Wiesbaden: Dr. Martin Sändig, 1969), 5–6n, analyzing the six principal manuscripts; for Valla, the edition of Wolfram Setz of *De falso credita et ementita Constantini donatione* (Weimar: Böhlau, 1976), 17–35, describing 25 known extant manuscripts; for Alberti, the introduction to Rocco Sinisgalli's edition of *On Painting* (Cambridge: Cambridge University Press, 2011), 4, which notes the existence of 20 manuscripts of the Latin version, and 195n1, which notes three of the (original) Italian.

72. The dates of 21 of those 22 range from 1416 to 1480, with one dated only "1400–1425" and the last dated 1505.

73. Griggio, "Copisti ed editori," 1039–47. Griggio establishes that the copy on which Gnesotto based his edition, Laur. 78, 24, was in fact derived from 78, 25, and not the reverse; and from the three other manuscripts provides numerous corrections to Gnesotto's text, which nonetheless, in the sum, do not materially change its meaning, not having "un peso rilevante nella comprensione di uno scritto in prosa dal contenuto molto chiaro e lineare" (1055).

(Michael de Salvaticis or Michael Germanicus), who was active in Venetian literary and chancery circles in this period; the second was written by Giovanni di Cenni d'Arezzo, another famous scribe (and professional notary), who was one of the first to adopt Poggio Bracciolini's reformed humanist script. The fourth manuscript belonged to the famed Venetian diarist Marino Sanuto the Younger (1466–1536), whose inscription notes it as "n° 1117" of his library.

Another early manuscript deserves mention: one transcribed in Guarino's house in 1428, which was likely the basis for the first (and most accurate) print edition (*editio princeps*) of the *De re uxoria*, not quite a century after its original composition.[74] The jurist André Tiraqueau (1488–1558), a friend of French author François Rabelais, commissioned the printing of the book, appropriately, on the occasion of his own marriage, as a gift for his father-in-law.[75] So the book that was born as a wedding gift in fifteenth-century Italy was reinvented, in the new medium of print, as a wedding gift in sixteenth-century France.

The print history of *De re uxoria*, like its manuscript history, is impressive.[76] It appeared in the original Latin in a total of five sixteenth- and seventeenth-century editions: after the *editio princeps* of Paris 1513 (reprinted 1514), also Hagenau 1533; Antwerp 1535; Strasbourg 1612; and Amsterdam 1639. Further, it was translated into four modern languages, the first being the translation into German by the theologian Erasmus Alber (Haguenau 1536; reprinted Erfurt 1561), who in the flush of the Reformation removed passages he found unnecessary and imported bits of Lutheran doctrine.[77] Second, following the 1536 publication of

---

74. Gnesotto, ed., *De re uxoria*, Introduction, 20; probably the same as Padua, Biblioteca del Seminario, cod. 449.

75. Gothein, *Francesco Barbaro*, 98–99. Ironically, Tiraqueau is known as well as the author of the notorious anti-female legal text, *De legibus connubialibus* (On the Laws of Marriage; 1524), regularly consulted by contemporaries. I am most grateful to Cheryl Lemmens for this information.

76. For the printed editions and translations named here, see the Bibliography, "*De re uxoria*: Editions and Translations."

77. Gothein's judgment of Alber's translation, contaminated by numerous Lutheran interpositions, in *Das Buch von der Ehe*, 87–88. Alber's work replaced an earlier German book on marriage compiled from Barbaro's *De re uxoria* along with other classical and humanist sources by the canon Albrecht von Eyb (Nürnberg 1472; reprinted ten times, the last in 1540): Albrecht von Eyb, *Das Ehebüchlein: Nach dem Inkunabeldruck der Offizin Anton Koberger, Nürnberg 1472*, ed. and trans. Hiram Kümper (Stuttgart: *ibidem*-Verlag, 2008), a bilingual edition in Middle High and modern German; print and manuscript exemplars at xxxviii–xli. Von Eyb (1420–1475) had studied intermittently at Bologna, Padua, and Pavia between 1444 and 1459, where he took a doctorate in canon and civil law, and became acquainted with the works of Barbaro, Guarino, Poggio, Lorenzo Valla, and Maffeo Vegio, among others. His *Ehebüchlein* has exceptional significance as one of the earliest works of German humanism. Manfred Lentzen underscores the differences between Barbaro's work and von Eyb's, but misses, in my view, the significant echoes: see "La concezione del matrimonio e della famiglia nel *De re uxoria* (1415) di Francesco Barbaro e nell'*Ehebüchlein* (1472) di Albrecht von Eyb: struttura e funzione del testo," in *Rapporti e scambi tra Umanesimo italiano ed Umanesimo europeo: l'Europa è uno*

Alber's work, the *De re uxoria* was translated into Italian by Alberto Lollio (Venice 1548) as *La elettion della moglie*, a work frequently reprinted, eventually in a revised edition as *La scelta della moglie* (Vercelli 1778), and at least twice again thereafter (Vicenza 1785, Naples 1806). Third, it was translated into French by Claude Joly, canon of the cathedral of Notre-Dame in Paris (Paris 1667), updating an earlier version, not printed, of 1548, another nuptial gift. It was translated, finally, into English (London 1677), by an anonymous author who believed he was translating from the Latin a work that had first been composed in Italian.

This long publication history in multiple linguistic guises testifies to the continued interest in Barbaro's discussion in quite different literary climates up to four centuries after his book's original composition. Given that many humanist texts began to lose readership as the Renaissance faded and the Enlightenment took hold—even the *Courtier* of Baldassare Castiglione lost its audience after the mid-seventeenth century, as Peter Burke meticulously documents[78]—Barbaro's *De re uxoria* must be judged a market success. Indeed, Claudio Griggio, editor of the canonical edition of Barbaro's voluminous correspondence, remarks in a somewhat puzzled tone that the success of the *De re uxoria* is a "most interesting aspect" of its story, for it achieved "extraordinary popularity" in an age characterized by a diversity and fluidity of interests, and circulated so widely—enjoying "a capillary diffusion" (*diffusione capillare*)—that it must be considered one of the "most read works" of the whole early modern period.[79]

The 1806 Neapolitan edition, however, marks a terminus lasting until the Italian and German philologists Attilio Gnesotto and Percy Gothein returned to the text in 1915 and 1933 respectively, seeking not a guide to living well, but an understanding of social and cultural values in a remote time. In 1952, Eugenio Garin, the leading Italian historian of Renaissance culture, included in his bilingual (Latin and Italian) collection of excerpts from humanist classics Barbaro's dedicatory letter to Lorenzo de' Medici.[80] Then in 1978, following a generation of the study of Renaissance humanism by American historians reconnecting with the European past, Benjamin G. Kohl and Ronald G. Witt included in their invaluable anthology of humanist works on government and society the dedicatory letter and the second book of Barbaro's treatise. Its publication coincided with the onset of the recovery of women's role in history driven by feminist scholars; accordingly, the work was much read in undergraduate classrooms by students fascinated by the repressive prescriptions that Barbaro imposed on wives, but who

---

stato d'animo, ed. Luisa Rotondi Secchi Tarugi (Milan: Nuovi orizzonti, 2001), 167–80. Sister Prudence Allen provides a useful overview of von Eyb and the *Ehebüchlein* in *The Concept of Woman*, 2:732–49.

78. In Peter Burke, *The Fortunes of the Courtier: The European Reception of Castiglione's Cortegiano* (University Park: Pennsylvania State University Press, 1996).

79. Griggio, "Copisti ed editori," 1036.

80. Eugenio Garin, *Prosatori latini del Quattrocento* (Milan: Ricciardi, 1952), 103–37.

were disinclined to register the import of his discussion of the wifely role in the social and cultural reproduction of an elite.[81] For their interests were other than those that animated Barbaro's contemporaries.

Despite the wide circulation of Barbaro's *De re uxoria*, however, it is Leon Battista Alberti's dialogue *Della famiglia* (On the Family)[82] that comes first to mind among modern scholars who wish to consider humanist views of marriage and family during the Renaissance. It takes the form of an extended conversation among several male members of the Alberti clan who have gathered at the death-bed of the patriarch, and as such, paints an intimate portrait of an elite Floren-tine family displaying both the mercantile and aristocratic values of that class.[83] Anglophone readers especially—in the footsteps of German sociologist Werner Sombart, who had found *Della famiglia* to be a treasure chest of bourgeois at-titudes and a harbinger of the modern age[84]—responded to the republican intona-tions of Alberti's work. In 1960, British scholar Cecil Grayson produced the first

---

81. For example, Frick's reading in "Francesco Barbaro's *De re uxoria*"; also Constance Jordan, *Renaissance Feminism: Literary Texts and Political Models* (Ithaca, NY: Cornell University Press, 1990), 40–47.

82. The following discussion draws on the version of the *Della famiglia* edited and translated by Renée Neu Watkins, *The Family in Renaissance Florence* (Columbia: University of South Carolina Press, 1969; reprint Lake Grove, IL: Waveland Press, 2004). A second full English version appeared two years later, edited and translated by Guido A. Guarino: *The Albertis of Florence: Leon Battista Alberti's Della fami-glia* (Lewisburg, PA: Bucknell University Press, 1971). Although Guarino's translation is more fluid than that of Watkins, it is the latter that has become the norm in Anglophone treatments of the work, and will be cited (in parentheses in the narrative) in the following pages. The original Italian text of *I libri della famiglia* appears in the first volume (1960) of Alberti's *Opere volgari* (bilingual Italian and Latin), edited by Cecil Grayson, 3 vols. (Bari: G. Laterza, 1960–1973); Grayson's text is reprinted in the edition of Ruggiero Romano and Alberto Tenenti, *I libri della famiglia* (Turin: G. Einaudi, 1969), thoroughly revised by Francesco Furlan in a second edition (Turin: G. Einaudi 1994), while retaining the earlier Romano and Tenenti introduction. For Alberti, see Anthony Grafton, *Leon Battista Alberti: Master Builder of the Italian Renaissance* (New York: Hill and Wang, 2000); Michel Paoli with Élise Leclerc and Sophie Dutheillet de Lamorthe, eds., *Les* Livres de la famille *d'Alberti: sources, sens et influence* (Paris: Classiques Garnier, 2013); Giovanni Ponte, *Leon Battista Alberti, umanista e scrittore* (Genoa: Tilgher, 1981); and the annotated bibliography by David Marsh, "Leon Battista Alberti," in *Oxford Bibliographies Online: Renaissance and Reformation*, http://www.oxfordbibliographies.com/view/document/obo-9780195399301/obo-9780195399301-0115.xml.

83. For that overlapping set of values, along with related Christian ones, see especially Gene A. Brucker, *Renaissance Florence* (New York: John Wiley, 1969; rpt. Berkeley: University of California Press, 1983), 101–9.

84. See Massimo Danzi, "Fra *oikos* e *polis*: il pensiero familiare di Leon Battista Alberti," in *La memoria e la città: scritture storiche tra Medioevo ed età moderna*, ed. Claudia Bastia and Maria Bolognani (Bologna: Il Nove, 1995), 47–62, at 58–59 and n37; Grafton, *Leon Battista Alberti*, 153; Paoli et al., *Les* Livres de la famille, 29, and in Paoli's essay in that volume, "La question de la richesse et de l'enrichissement dans les livres *De familia* d'Alberti," 121–53; Watkins, introduction to *The Family in Renaissance Florence*, 12, 14.

critical edition of Alberti's *Della famiglia*,[85] while but a decade later, in the space of two years, two different American scholars produced English translations.[86] Their enthusiasm, on reflection, seems odd, for Alberti does not so much celebrate the family as doubt its destiny.

Amid the sprawling discussions of *Della famiglia* there sounds a constant drumbeat: that of the fear of family extinction, which threatens because young men do not reproduce, not wishing to sacrifice their personal liberty to collective ends. That fear is underscored by the massive presence of Lorenzo, the dying patriarch of the family, whose imminent demise is the occasion for the gathering of the seven participants, all Alberti males of ages ranging from early adolescence to advanced old age.[87]

Lorenzo Alberti's double death—in this world, and in his son's book—prefigures the death of the family bank and the precarious future of its lineage. His actual death in Padua in May 1421, by which the author was orphaned, is reiterated in the fictive dialogue as its core and *raison d'être*. His deathbed speech articulates simultaneously the grave importance of a father for his children and his own failure to protect his sons[88]: "I leave you in exile, fatherless, outside your country and your house. It shall redound to your praise, my sons, if at your tender and weak years you set yourselves to overcome, if not wholly at least in part, the hard and bleak situation that confronts you."[89] He recommends education as an aid in the relentless struggle against misfortune, and beseeches his kinsmen to assume the task he leaves behind of promoting the interests of his sons.

Lorenzo's own self-diagnosed deficiency as a father is underscored by the celebration of paternal heroism by Lionardo, one of the younger Albertis:

---

85. Grayson, ed., *I libri della famiglia*.

86. Watkins, *The Family in Renaissance Florence*; Guarino, *The Albertis of Florence*.

87. Lorenzo, Adovardo, Giannozzo, and Piero, the elders; Lionardo, the most voluble interlocutor, aged twenty-nine in the fictive dialogue; and Battista (Leon Battista is thus written into his family story) and Carlo, both adolescent.

88. For the theme of paternal responsibility in Alberti's dialogue, see also Juliann Vitullo, "Fashioning Fatherhood: Leon Battista Alberti's Art of Parenting," in *Childhood in the Middle Ages and the Renaissance: The Results of a Paradigm Shift in the History of Mentality*, ed. Albrecht Classen (Berlin: Walter de Gruyter, 2005), 341–53. It is noteworthy that in Alberti's later work *De iciarchia* (On the Patriarch), the focus on the father and paternal responsibility is also relentless: see Alberti, *Opere volgari*, ed. Grayson, 2:187–286; in the same volume, see also Alberti's brief work *Uxoria* (On Marriage), 303–43, dedicated to Pietro de' Medici, portraying, much like the *Della famiglia*, a father advising his sons.

89. Watkins, *The Family in Renaissance Florence,* 40. Lorenzo speaks at length (33–45) at the beginning of the first of four books of the dialogue, and thereafter is silent except for a few sentences at 130–31. Subsequent references to this work will appear in parentheses in the text.

Even in old age, and all their lives before, fathers have worked in weariness and danger to earn a living which might maintain themselves and their families. Untiringly they have labored on in their last years, striving with every possible effort and care to leave their children better off after their death than they were themselves. Over and over again they have given themselves less reward in order to provide more abundantly for their children and make them happier. (Watkins, 103)

Despite this paternal diligence, the Alberti family is faltering; in Lionardo's words:

Thanks to the blows of fortune, it fell on adversity and stormy troubled days. I see and recognize this, that no family lacking the things we used to have in abundance, no family small in number of men, or poor, lowly, and friendless, let alone surrounded by enemies, no such family could ever be considered anything but wretched and unfortunate. So let us call that family fortunate which has a good supply of rich men, men who are highly esteemed and loved. Let us call the family unfortunate which has few men, and those obscure, poor, and disliked. (Watkins, 109)

The remedy is marriage and procreation—in a more desperate tone, a reprise of Barbaro's argument:

If a family is not to fall for these reasons into what we have described as the most unfortunate condition of decline, but is to grow, instead, in fame and in the prosperous multitude of its youth, we must persuade our young men to take wives. We must use every argument for this purpose, offer incentive, promise reward, employ all our wit, persistence, and cunning. (Watkins, 112)

But as Adovardo, a more senior Alberti, had argued earlier, it was Lionardo and his fellows who were failing to fulfill their responsibility to procreate. It grieved Adovardo "to see so many of you younger Albertis without an heir, not having done what you could to increase the family and make it numerous ...." (Watkins, 50)

[A]ccording to a count I took a few days ago, not less than twenty-two young Albertis no younger than sixteen or older than thirty-six are now living alone and without a female companion, since they have no wife. This grieves me. I see clearly the great harm it will do

our family if all the number of sons who might have been expected
from you young men continues not to appear. I think we should
gladly bear all the discomforts and unpleasant burdens in the world
rather than allow our family to stand desolate, with none to succeed
in the place and name of the fathers. (Watkins, 51)

To this rebuke, Lionardo responds mockingly that

... everyone who has nothing better to say to me, lacking conversation or an argument, begins to babble about providing me with
a wife. Here great streams of eloquence flow as they undertake to
prove to me the necessity and excellence of the conjugal state ....
(Watkins, 52)

But he will resist their patronizing lectures, for he would prefer to live free:

Often enough, with their overwhelming presumption, as they try
to kindle in me a wish no longer to remain free as I am, they spark
instead some righteous indignation .... The maidens who suit your
taste would not please me. Those who perhaps would not offend me,
never seem to suit the rest of you. So my spirit remains athirst, not so
much to avoid having my place and name in the family extinguished
and blank after my own passing, as just to escape the pestering of all
those friends and acquaintances who cavil, I know not through what
envy, at my liberty in being without a wife. (Watkins, 52–53)

Having uttered one of the most candid speeches in the whole humanist tradition (in the real voice, one suspects, of its author), Lionardo proceeds to other
matters that concern him little, beginning with the selection of a wetnurse, a task
he is unlikely ever to take upon himself. For he has identified precisely the problem with the argument for family continuity: its requirements impinge upon the
liberty of the young.

Under and about the predominant theme of the future of the lineage,
other themes are intertwined: household management, marriage, child rearing,
education, virtue, love, and friendship—as well as intimations of the author's
personal resentments and aspirations vis-à-vis the family to which he does not
quite belong. Notably, Giannozzo, an elder spokesman of the same generation as
the dying patriarch, discourses at length about the administration of farm and
business and household supplies, the latter requiring the minute instruction of
a young wife, the householder's agent in the sound management of the interior
spaces of his empire as he himself tends to the external ones. Some of the issues

that Barbaro raised also present themselves in Alberti's *Della famiglia*, especially in the second book entitled "De re uxoria": how a wife should be chosen—her robust health signaling her ability to bear children and the capacity of her kinsmen to pay even a modest dowry promptly are uppermost concerns—and her responsibility to care for young children.[90] But even as the importance of the wife is noted, her role is strictly subordinated to the patriarch's.[91] For men dominate Alberti's domestic universe, just as they dominate the dialogue that swirls around the dying sovereign whose moribund condition evokes the fragility and imminent failure of a clan that cannot attend to its own biological renewal.

Evidently, Alberti could in no way have escaped the deep pessimism that winds through the anxious pages of *Della famiglia*. He was, granted, a humanist of the first rank, as well as an artist and architect, whose works on painting and architecture, especially the groundbreaking treatise *On Painting*, frame the whole Renaissance understanding of the visual arts. But he was also—a fact of greater relevance here—an illegitimate son of the Alberti clan in an age when illegitimates were excluded from both inheritance and lineal role; and the Alberti family itself was, at the time of his writing, exiled from Florence.[92] Thus fallen from its former stature, it would fall further still in 1440, when, only three years after the completion of the final book of *Della famiglia*, the Alberti enterprises utterly collapsed.[93]

Before leaving Alberti, a juxtaposition will be useful between his *Della famiglia* and the *De re uxoria* of his Venetian counterpart.[94] For counterparts they were. Alberti was but fifteen years younger than Barbaro, and the first three books of *Della famiglia*, constituting its core, were written in 1434, when Alberti was thirty years old, nineteen years after the *De re uxoria*, written when Barbaro was

90. For Alberti's recommendations on the rearing of children, see also the essay of Remy Simonetti, "La conception et l'éducation de l'enfant: médecine et physiognomonie dans le *De familia* d'Alberti," 49–66, in Paoli et al., *Les* Livres de la famille.

91. Pioneer feminist Joan Kelly-Gadol, in a withering review not of Guarino's translation, which she prefers to Watkins's, but of Alberti himself, rapidly unmasks the latter's misogyny revealed in Giannozzo's speech—though it is not unusual for its time: *Italica* 53, no. 2 (1976): 263–65.

92. For the focus on males and the lineage in Alberti's work, the problem of the author's illegitimacy, and the "ambiguities" in which these cast the whole of the work, see the invaluable article by Thomas Kuehn, "Reading between the Patrilines: Leon Battista Alberti's *Della Famiglia* in Light of His Illegitimacy," in *I Tatti Studies: Essays in the Renaissance*, vol. 1, ed. Salvatore Camporeale, Caroline Elam, and F. W. Kent (Florence: Villa I Tatti, 1985), 161–87.

93. Watkins, *The Family in Renaissance Florence*, 5. A brief account of the decline and failure of the Alberti bank can be found in Philip J. Jacks and William Caferro, *The Spinelli of Florence: Fortunes of a Renaissance Merchant Family* (University Park: Pennsylvania State University Press, 2001), 34–39.

94. For Alberti's *Della famiglia* in relation to Barbaro's *De re uxoria*, see also Tenenti, "La *res uxoria* tra Francesco Barbaro e Leon Battista Alberti"; and for Alberti and Barbaro together with a third humanist writer on the family, see Manfred Lentzen, "Frühhumanistische Auffassungen über Ehe und Familie."

twenty-five. Both wrote in the early stage of Quattrocento humanism, when the work of Petrarch and his disciples had been absorbed, the most important Latin texts had been digested, and the Greek tradition had begun to be explored. Both had studied at Padua with Gasparino Barzizza, a master of Ciceronian rhetoric, and both had studied law: Alberti at Bologna, briefly; Barbaro at Padua, completing the doctorate.

Both authors, moreover, deal largely with the same roster of issues: the importance of family continuity, the selection of a wife, the proper rearing of the young. Yet there are profound differences between them, beginning with their different rhetorical approach: Barbaro writes in his own voice, systematically and authoritatively; Alberti distributes his arguments among different spokesmen, observes no system or limit in his presentation, and permits his material to sprawl to five times the length of Barbaro's *De re uxoria*. The differences in substance are also striking. While both authors discuss the selection of a wife, that matter is of central importance for Barbaro, while it is secondary for Alberti: the young man is depicted as choosing almost nonchalantly among the eligible women placed before him. Where Barbaro requires virtue as the first requirement in a wife, Alberti, who requires it as well, sets the bar very low: it is sufficient if the candidate is not "the sort who will bring scandal or shame to the house." (Watkins, 51) Barbaro, moreover, presents repeatedly an ideal of marriage as a conjunction of moral equals, who support and delight each other. Of this ideal, Alberti breathes not a word. While both authors are concerned with the rearing of the young, the accomplishment of that task is, for Barbaro, the mother's responsibility, and for Alberti's, the father's. For Barbaro, as well, a wife is assumed to be capable of management of household goods and servants, while for Alberti, she does so only as the subordinate of her husband, and an abject one at that. Both Barbaro and Alberti are concerned with the maintenance of the lineage; but toward this end, Barbaro's prescriptions are bold and confident—he has a plan—whereas Alberti is despondent and nearly desperate. For Barbaro, the realization of that goal depends on women; for Alberti, on men.

Curiously, although Barbaro's focus is on the role of the woman in the family—even though he does not entirely shed restrictive guidelines for female deportment and behavior inherited from both classical and Christian authors—it is Alberti's vision of the family, more exploratory and less prescriptive, that caught the imagination of twentieth-century scholars; and it is these who have forged our present understanding of humanism, and especially of "civic" humanism, humanism understood as reflecting the republican values of some members of the northern Italian elites. Barbaro's *De re uxoria*, in contrast, savoring of high aristocraticism, "has been to date investigated rather little,"[95] as Manfred Lentzen

---

95. Lentzen, "Frühhumanistische Auffassungen," 380: Barbaro's work "ist bisher relativ wenig untersucht worden."

delicately observes. And that is true, in modern times. But in its own day, it was far more widely known than Alberti's. Barbaro's work, as has been seen, circulated in more than 100 manuscript versions, five printed editions, and translations into four languages—the Italian version reprinted into the nineteenth century, when Napoleon had already descended upon Italy and rained the final blows on Renaissance civilization. Alberti's, in contrast, circulated in sixteen manuscript versions, and was not printed (except, in 1734, for a fragment, and that attributed to the wrong author) until its first modern edition in 1843.[96]

In his own time, then, Barbaro's *De re uxoria* enjoyed, in Griggio's words, "extraordinary popularity," and contributed to a great outpouring of humanist writing about marriage and family—so much so that Anthony d'Elia speaks, in his volume so entitled, of "the Renaissance of marriage in fifteenth-century Italy."[97] Humanists especially of a republican bent celebrated marriage as the mode of life characteristic of the citizen engaged in public life, as distinct from a clerical class that spurned marriage and embraced celibacy. That inclination was certainly embodied by Guarino Veronese, Barbaro's own teacher of Greek, who was the first to reinvent the genre of the ancient epithalamium as the humanist marriage oration.[98] The 336 marriage orations that d'Elia examines,[99] in their sum, present powerful pro-marriage arguments: first and primarily, as an institution that builds wealth while cementing social and political alliances; and second, an innovative message, as a partnership supplying emotional and sexual satisfactions. Feeding these positive themes were Barbaro's arguments in the *De re uxoria*, which circulated especially in the northern Italian ambit in which the most active nuptial

---

96. Francesco Furlan (in the revised 1994 Einaudi edition of *I libri della famiglia*) identifies the 16 useful manuscripts (plus a few other copies, fragments, and excerpts) at 431–36, and details the print history at 436–38. Echoing Girolamo Mancini, whose critical edition appeared in 1908, Watkins reports that Alberti's work was cited only eight times in the sixteenth and seventeenth centuries (Watkins, 3)—a meager reception in comparison to the multiple publications of *De re uxoria*. For readers of *Della famiglia*, see also Paoli et al., *Les* Livres de la famille, 26–29, and the essays by Paola Massalin, "Copistes et lecteurs du *De familia* dans l'entourage d'Alberti," 205–44, and Francesco Sberlati, "Un lecteur du *De familia* à la fin du XVIe siècle: Bernardino Baldi," 441–53.

97. Anthony F. d'Elia, *The Renaissance of Marriage in Fifteenth-Century Italy* (Cambridge, MA: Harvard University Press, 2004). Gothein (*Francesco Barbaro*, at 90) attributes that "immense mass" of marriage texts directly to Barbaro's treatise: "Das Werk Barbaros war für Italien der Auftakt zu einer unabsehbaren Menge von humanistischen Hochzeitsschriften, die alle auf ihm fussen." Claudia Corfiati also provides a briefer overview of humanist writing on marriage, with a useful review of the underlying classical and medieval misogynist traditions, repudiated by the humanists, in the first section of *Una disputa umanistica* de amore: *Guiniforte Barzizza e Giovanni Pontano da Bergamo* (Messina: Centro interdipartimentale di studi umanistici, 2008), 9–45.

98. Guarino proved himself in action: he married, and fathered 13 children (d'Elia, *Renaissance of Marriage*, 33, 195n153).

99. A finding list in d'Elia, *Renaissance of Marriage*, 139–79.

orators plied their trade.[100] Indeed, five of the authors very closely related to Barbaro—Guarino Veronese, Barbaro's teacher of Greek; Battista Guarini (1435–1513), Guarino's son; Ludovico Carbone (1430–1485), Guarino's student; and Guiniforte Barzizza (1406–1463), the son of Gasparino, Barbaro's teacher of Latin rhetoric—together account for nearly one-fifth (19%) of all the orations d'Elia surveys, and nearly one-third (31%) of those not written by that prolific author "Anonymous."

Other works opposing the inherited anti-marriage consensus are closely related to these orations. Giovannantonio Campano's *De dignitate matrimonii* (On the Dignity of Marriage, 1468) is, as d'Elia explains, an expansion of a marriage oration, and so repeats the expected themes.[101] Similar themes reappear in the dialogues of two Florentine chancellors, both prominent humanists: Poggio Bracciolini's *An seni sit uxor ducenda* (On Whether an Old Man Should Marry, 1437),[102] and Bartolomeo Scala's *Ducendane sit uxor sapienti* (On Whether a Wise Man Should Marry, 1457/1459).[103] Preceding these, in 1418 Guarino Veronese had written to Antonio Corbellini, an opponent of the notion, a brief epistolary defense of marriage, arguing that it was fully compatible with the life of a scholar.[104] Also related to Barbaro's circle, though once removed, was the discursive letter *De amore* (On Love, March 4, 1439) of Guiniforte Barzizza, advocating love between spouses, and repudiating the adulterous ideal of the courtly love tradition—which is defended in the epistolary reply of the Neapolitan humanist Giovanni Pontano (1426–1503).[105]

100. D'Elia notes that Barbaro is cited by "some authors" of epithalamia "as an authority on marriage": *Renaissance of Marriage*, 28 and 193n118.

101. Giovannantonio Campano, *Opera selecta*, ed. Friedrich Otto Mencke (Leipzig: Apud Iacobum Schusterum, 1734), 737–57. See d'Elia, *Renaissance of Marriage*, 118, 154 #149.

102. Poggio Bracciolini, *Opera omnia*, 2:673–705, for which see d'Elia, *Renaissance of Marriage*, 30–31, 120. For other works by Poggio in defense of marriage, see Corfiati, *Una disputa umanistica*, 41.

103. Bartolomeo Scala, *Humanistic and Political Writings*, ed. and trans. Alison Brown (Tempe, AZ: Medieval and Renaissance Texts and Studies, 1997), 262–73. See d'Elia, *Renaissance of Marriage*, 31–32, 126.

104. *Epistolario di Guarino Veronese*, 1:113–15; 3:88–89. See also Corfiati, *Una disputa umanistica*, 40; d'Elia, *Renaissance of Marriage*, 33–34.

105. Bilingual edition (Latin/Italian) in Corfiati, *Una disputa umanistica*, 110–33, with Pontano's response of 1439/1441 at 134–213. Barzizza's work reiterates major Barbaronian themes: the preeminent importance of virtue in a wife, along with the social standing of her family, and the lesser importance of beauty and dowry wealth. For Pontano's epithalamic poetry, of related interest, see d'Elia, *Renaissance of Marriage*, 103–4; also, for his erotic verse to his wife, Pierre Nespoulous, "Giovanni Pontano: poète de l'amour conjugale," *Proceedings of the Acta Conventus Neo-Latini Lovaniensis*, ed. Jozef IJsewijn and Eckhard Kessler (Leuven: Leuven University Press, 1973), 437–43; and Matteo Soranzo, "Poetry and Society in Aragonese Naples: Giovanni Pontano's Elegies of Married Love," in Jacqueline Murray, ed., *Marriage in Premodern Europe: Italy and Beyond* (Toronto: Centre for Reformation and Renaissance Studies, 2012). Nespoulous comments that Pontano is the first poet "à chanter en ver sa propre épouse" (442).

A fuller array of Barbaronian themes is found in the pro-marriage works of Desiderius Erasmus (1466–1536) and Juan Luis Vives (1493–1540), with whom, as with regard to many other topics, the thought of the Italian Renaissance humanists culminates.[106] Published a little more than a century after the composition of the *De re uxoria*, and a little more than a decade after the latter's first printing (Paris 1513), these works are, respectively, Erasmus's *Institutio christiani matrimonii* (Institution of Christian Matrimony, 1526),[107] and Vives's *De officio mariti* (On the Office of a Husband, 1529),[108] a companion piece to his earlier, better-known work *De institutione feminae christianae* (The Education of a Christian Woman, 1524),[109] to which discussion will return below.

As Anthony d'Elia notes, Erasmus wrote several works on marriage from the 1490s through the 1520s.[110] He discusses the *Encomium matrimonii* (In Praise of Marriage, 1498), a work on the scale of the marriage orations that his book explores. But attention will turn here, instead, to Erasmus's much larger *Institutio christiani matrimonii*—dedicated, ironically, to Catherine of Aragon, queen consort of English king Henry VIII, who would repudiate her. Here are found discursive treatments of the sacramental nature of marriage and canon law prescriptions that limit marital choices, as well as advice to both man and woman on the selection of a spouse. On the latter issue, while the need for the free (and carefully considered) consent of the spouses is recognized, consistent with church law, Erasmus also underscores the importance of parental participation and advice. But he is opposed to coerced matrimony, or marriages arranged primarily to acquire dowry wealth or family alliances. Above all, a point much reiterated, the

---

106. Martin Luther, as well, is a pro-marriage voice, as d'Elia discusses; but since his views are prompted by Reformation themes even more than humanist ones, this already long discussion will pass by, and leave his contribution to be assessed by others. The views of marriage offered by Thomas More in his *Utopia* are also omitted from this discussion.

107. Desiderius Erasmus, *The Institution of Christian Matrimony*, ed. and trans. Michael J. Heath, in vol. 4 of *Spiritualia and Pastoralia*, being vol. 69 of the *Collected Works of Erasmus* [CWE], ed. John W. O'Malley and Louis A. Perraud (Toronto: University of Toronto Press, 1999), 203–438.

108. Juan Luis Vives, *De officio mariti*, ed. and trans. Charles Fantazzi (Leiden: Brill, 2006), a bilingual edition in English and Latin.

109. Juan Luis Vives, *The Education of a Christian Woman: A Sixteenth-Century Manual*, ed. and trans. Charles Fantazzi (Chicago: University of Chicago Press, 2000). The edition of 2002—*The Instruction of a Christen Woman*, ed.Virginia Walcott Beauchamp, Elizabeth H. Hageman, and Margaret Mikesell, with Sheila ffolliott and Betty S. Travitsky (Urbana: University of Illinois Press)—is based not on the Latin original but on the sixteenth-century English translation, which circulated widely. In their comparative analysis of the *De officio mariti* with the *De institutione feminae christianae* (at lxi–lxvi), the editors find Vives more friendly to women in the former than the latter work, but in both they find his views of "women's nature and their place … distressingly constant" (lxiv)—missing, it might be suggested, the extent to which Vives advances the cause of women's education and dignity.

110. D'Elia, *Renaissance of Marriage*, 131; discussion of Erasmus on marriage, 131–34.

purpose of marriage is the procreation of legitimate children and their moral and intellectual rearing: for "their minds are empty, like a blank tablet on which you may write whatever you wish."[111]

Clearly, there are many issues in Erasmus's work that echo those treated by Barbaro in *De re uxoria*—the importance of spousal selection, the distrust of the dowry as a basis for marital choice, the insistence on procreation as the foundation of marriage, and the attention to the education of children. Erasmus could have identified all of these issues without consulting Barbaro, of course; and Barbaro does not concern himself at all, as Erasmus does, with the sacramental nature of marriage or the limitations imposed by canon law. On the other hand, Erasmus knew Barbaro's work—Barbaro is one of the Italian humanists Erasmus explicitly names in his *Ciceronianus*, alongside Leonardo Bruni and Poggio Bracciolini, among others[112]—and it is far more likely that he knew the treatise *De re uxoria* than the letters of that Venetian humanist. At several points in the *Institutio*, moreover, Erasmus so closely approaches statements made by Barbaro that his direct knowledge of the *De re uxoria* is implied, if not confirmed.

For instance, Erasmus names as experts on marriage the very Greek authors, and only those, on whom Barbaro principally relies: Aristotle, Xenophon, and Plutarch; and he speaks of natural principles fundamental to an understanding of marriage in much the same terms that Barbaro does.[113] Citing Pythagoras, like Barbaro, he praises the union of body and soul in marriage, making "two people one." (Erasmus, 219) His references to Juno, Venus, Mercury, and the Graces resemble Barbaro's discussons of those figures as protectors of marriage. (Erasmus, 224) He notes, as Barbaro frequently does, the importance of choosing a wife so that the children who will be born will be physically and morally fit. (Erasmus, 241, etc.) His discussion of the human appetite for procreation, instilled by God, is reminiscent of Barbaro's. (Erasmus, 244) A telling point: just as he is about to launch into his discussion of the duties of man and wife (Barbaro, of course, only speaking of the wife), Erasmus digresses, just as Barbaro does, to discuss the wedding ceremony. (Erasmus, 348)

Like Barbaro, too, recommending that infants be fed on mothers' milk, Erasmus echoes Barbaro's argument that the child is best fed on the substance that nourished it in the womb. (Erasmus, 356) Erasmus recommends, as Barbaro does, an equality between the spouses as supportive of marital harmony, and holds up the same speech of Andromache to Hector as an expression of spousal devotion.

---

111. Erasmus, *Institution of Christian Matrimony,* 435. An anticipation of John Locke!

112. Desiderius Erasmus, *Dialogus ciceronianus,* vol. 6 of *Literary and Educational Writings,* being vol. 28 of the *Collected Works of Erasmus* [CWE], ed. A. H. T. Levi (Toronto: University of Toronto Press, 1986), 414–15; cf. d'Elia, *Renaissance of Marriage,* 249n97.

113. *Institution of Christian Matrimony,* 216, 217. Citations of this work henceforth appear in parentheses in the text.

(Erasmus, 362, 375) Finally, Erasmus, like Barbaro, closes his treatise with an extended treatment of the rearing of children (Erasmus, 407–38), in the course of which he applies the metaphors of seeds and fields to describe the child's aptitude for learning, similar to Barbaro's employ of the same metaphors to discuss the aptitude of a wife for procreation. (Erasmus, 417) Enough said: Erasmus has many matters on his agenda that Barbaro does not address, but he gives ample indications of having read and learned from the Venetian on issues that concerned them both.

The *De officio mariti* of Juan Luis Vives, the younger contemporary of Erasmus, also offers an extensive discussion of marriage. Although the relationship between these two acquaintances and correspondents was sometimes strained, they shared a commitment to the classical tradition and to liberal studies, and both advocated the humane education of the young, the elevation (if not quite the equality) of women, and the responsibility of government to sustain (or at least not oppress) ordinary citizens. On marriage, they are in essential agreement.

For Vives, marriage is a lifelong commitment, whose main purpose is the birth and rearing of legitimate offspring. A man should select his wife because of her virtuous character, rather than her wealth or her beauty. Once married, a wife should tend dutifully to her responsibilities of domestic management, and should not waste thought or expense on lavish personal adornment. Love will bind man and wife into harmonious communion that will extend past childbearing into their later years, when habit and familiarity deepen their companionship. The husband, however, remains unquestionably the supreme head of the household, who is to direct its affairs and instruct his wife as needed.

These themes present in the *De officio mariti*, and others like them, resemble those in Barbaro's *De re uxoria*, although the connections between them may be indirect. At points, Vives more clearly echoes Barbaro. He defines, for instance, the double goal of marriage much as Barbaro does: "the production of children and a life of mutality."[114] And in the following discussion of the procreation of worthy children, he adopts Barbaro's metaphor of seed and soil in familiar tones: men of high fortune, especially, "must take [care] not to scatter such noble seed into unfruitful soil or otherwise taint such excellent seed with some of vitiated quality." (Vives, 47) In terms similar to Barbaro's, he affirms the chastity of the sexual act when performed within marriage; decries extravagant adornment in a wife, who "should deck herself out for no other eyes than his" (Vives, 187); discourages husbands from absenting themselves from the home; and urges diligence in household management.

The trilogy of works on marriage constituted by Barbaro's *De re uxoria*, Erasmus's *De institutione christiani matrimonii*, and Vives's *De officio mariti*

---

114. Vives, *De officio mariti*, 47. Subsequent references to this work are given in parentheses in the text.

establish a new platform of marital ideology on which discussion of marriage will build from the Renaissance into the modern era, when a new insistence on sexual freedom and female autonomy will require its revision. On the major issues the three authors concur: the goals of marriage as procreation and companionship; the diminished importance of dowry and the heightened expectation for the woman's moral and intellectual capacity as desiderata in the selection of a wife; and the appreciation of wifely competence in household management and derogation of extravagant adornment or behavior.

But Barbaro distinguishes himself from his successors—not only from Erasmus and Vives, but also from fifteenth-century humanist authors on marriage previously discussed—in his high-beam focus on the person of the wife. In the *De re uxoria*, the wife is critical for the procreation of worthy children in the successive processes of conception, gestation, parturition, lactation, and education. It is the moral and intellectual traits of wives that will be biologically transmitted to fetus and infant by the binary vehicle of blood and milk, and culturally transmitted to infant and child by means of the maternal spirit, the sublimation of those bodily substances. The importance given to the female role in Barbaro's vision is extraordinary, even though, in 1415, he fails to transcend the prejudices of the era—prejudices enduring until a few decades ago—that demanded the social subordination of women.

It is worth noting that in one other brief work, written in 1447, more than 30 years after the *De re uxoria*, Barbaro betrays a similar pro-feminine leaning. In a letter of consolation to his daughter Costanza, a nun, on the death of her cousin Luchina Miani, Barbaro pays tribute to both women.[115] He honors Costanza by addressing to her a work in sophisticated humanist Latin—few women of this era had the capacity to read such a composition, a capacity that must have been encouraged by her father. At the same time, he celebrates Luchina's impeccably Christian and equally stoical death, a most unusual subject for a male humanist in an era when the deaths of daughters (unlike those of sons) often passed by unnoted.[116] The work is all the more striking in that it departs in content

115. Barbaro, *Epistolario*, 2:549–55, letter 270 (December 6, 1447). Here Luchina is identified as a daughter of Barbaro's and wife of Pietro Miani at 549n; but she is more likely Barbaro's niece, the daughter of his brother Zaccaria, for which identification see Margaret L. King and Albert Rabil, Jr., ed. and trans., *Her Immaculate Hand: Selected Works by and about the Women Humanists of Quattrocento Italy* (Binghamton, NY: Medieval and Renaissance Texts and Studies, 1983; rev. ed. 1992), 106–11, and Allen, *The Concept of Woman*, 724–27. The English translation of Barbaro's letter appears in *Her Immaculate Hand*, 106–11.

116. There is the precedent, in ancient times, of Cicero's consolatory work on the death of his daughter in 45 BCE, a work that is lost, although we have a brief letter (*Epistolae familiares*, 4.6) in which he speaks of the loss. But Barbaro's work would in any case be quite different: it describes the courage of his daughter, rather than his own grief. There is, of course, a conspicuous tradition of consolatory works by humanists on the death of sons: see Margaret L. King, *The Death of the Child Valerio Marcello*

and style from Barbaro's other letters, the main literary product of his maturity, that mirror the kinds of political activity, at the highest level, in which he was regularly engaged.

Something of Barbaro's openness to female experience, along with his views on marriage, becomes visible in the vibrant Italian vernacular literary world of the sixteenth and seventeenth century.[117] The renowned early-sixteenth-century authors Ludovico Ariosto, Pietro Bembo, and Baldassare Castiglione all exemplify this outlook; and Ariosto acknowledges Barbaro, without naming him, by incorporating two of the Venetian's extended anecdotes as even lengthier passages of his epic *Orlando Furioso*.[118] While Ariosto might have taken one of these independently from Plutarch, its ultimate source, he could not have otherwise accessed the other, which was related directly to Barbaro by his first teacher, Giovanni Conversini da Ravenna.

In 1545 and 1548, additionally, with the publication of the *De re uxoria* in the Italian translation of Alberto Lollio, followed by the adaption of Vives's work on the education of women by the *poligrafo* Ludovico Dolce,[119] two of the most important pro-female works to emerge from the Latin humanist tradition became available to vernacular authors. Frequently reprinted, these works surely influenced the many letters, poems, and plays by women authors—and some by men—that flew from the Italian presses, with their claims for women's freedom of marital choice and desire for love and companionship in the married state.[120] Though unattributed, they likely left their impress on the two principal proto-feminist works published in the single year 1600 by women authors: Moderata

---

(Chicago: University of Chicago Press, 1994), and George W. McClure, *Sorrow and Consolation in Italian Humanism* (Princeton: Princeton University Press, 1991).

117. And into the eighteenth, when Gioseffa Cornoldi Caminer published excerpts from Barbaro's work in her *Giornale per donne* (Ladies' Journal, published in Venice, 1786–1788): Griggio, "Copisti ed editori," 1037 and n9.

118. The story of Brasilla in *The Wealth of Wives*, 114, appears (with names altered) in Ariosto's *Orlando Furioso*, canto 29:8–25; that of Camma (similarly altered), 48–49, in canto 37:46–76.

119. Lodovico Dolce, *Dialogo della institution delle donne* (Venice: Appresso Gabriel Giolito de Ferrari e Fratelli, 1545); frequently reprinted. Really a paraphrase of the *De institutione feminae christianae* (1524) (his *Education of a Christian Woman*) by Juan Luis Vives; see Paul F. Grendler, *Schooling in Renaissance Italy: Literacy and Learning, 1300–1600* (Baltimore: Johns Hopkins University Press, 1989), 87–88; see also Brian Richardson, who points to Dolce's consequential interventions in the text in his "'Amore maritale': Advice on Love and Marriage in the Second Half of the Cinquecento," in Letizia Panizza, ed., *Women in Italian Renaissance Culture and Society* (Oxford: Legenda, 2000), 194–208, at 196–97. For Dolce's role as a disseminator of ideas, see Ronnie H. Terpening, *Lodovico Dolce: Renaissance Man of Letters* (Toronto: University of Toronto Press, 1997).

120. For this discourse, see Richardson, "'Amore maritale'"; and, for the critique of marriage presented by contemporary comic drama, Laura Giannetti, *Lelia's Kiss: Imagining Gender, Sex, and Marriage in Italian Renaissance Comedy* (Toronto: University of Toronto Press, 2009), 193–232.

Fonte's *The Worth of Women, Wherein is Clearly Revealed their Nobility and their Superiority to Men*,[121] and Lucrezia Marinella's *The Nobility and Excellence of Women, and the Defects and Vices of Men*.[122]

A final point should be made about Barbaro's contribution to the discussion of the education of women. Although Barbaro does not explicitly mention women's education, at a time when the formal schooling of women virtually did not exist, his arguments invite it. His emphasis on woman as mother, both as a factor in the selection of the wife, and in the discussion of a wife's responsibilities, implicitly calls for the cultural development of the future wife, not only in the moral and spiritual dimension but, notably, in her intellectual capacity.

That call is answered by a steadily growing stream of voices advocating the education of women that arises soon after the composition of the *De re uxoria*. The Italians Leonardo Bruni and Lauro Quirini each wrote letters (in 1424 and 1443/1448, respectively) guiding noblewomen in their advanced studies of Latin texts, while Maffeo Vegio, in his *De educatione liberorum* (On the Education of Children, 1444), assumed that both parents, mothers as well as fathers, would supervise the schooling of their daughters as well as their sons.[123] Erasmus wrote often, though not systematically, in support of education for women, praising such learned women as Catherine of Aragon, the English queen consort, and Margaret Roper, daughter of the English chancellor and later martyr Thomas More.[124] In his *Institutio christiani matrimonii*, Erasmus recommends that husbands teach their wives,[125] in part by reading them sermons—a dreary prospect, perhaps, to our eyes, but more stimulating, possibly, during that era of vigorous religious debate. In the *De officio mariti*, similarly, Vives encourages the instruction of wives by husbands, but also recommends, quite remarkably, that women

---

121. Fonte, ed. and trans. Virginia Cox (Chicago: University of Chicago Press, 1997). Fonte is the pseudonym used by Modesta da Pozzo; the work was composed around 1592 and published posthumously.

122. Marinella, ed. and trans. Anne Dunhill, introduction by Letizia Panizza (Chicago: University of Chicago Press, 1999).

123. Bruni's in *The Humanism of Leonardo Bruni: Selected Texts*, ed. and trans. Gordon Griffiths, James Hankins, and David Thompson (Binghamton, NY: Medieval and Renaissance Texts and Studies, in conjunction with the Renaissance Society of America, 1987), 240–51; Quirini's in Isotta Nogarola, *Complete Writings: Letterbook, Dialogue on Adam and Eve, Orations*, ed. and trans. Margaret L. King and Diana M. Robin (Chicago: University of Chicago Press, 2004), 107–13; Maffeo Vegio, *De educatione liberorum et eorum claris moribus, libri sex*, ed. (books 1–3) Maria Walburg Fanning and (books 4–6) Anne Stanislaus Sullivan (Washington, DC: Catholic University of America, 1933, 1936); see also Vittorio Lugli, *I trattatisti della famiglia nel Quattrocento* (Bologna: A.F. Formíggini, 1909), 2:67–74.

124. J. K. Sowards, "Erasmus and the Education of Women," *Sixteenth Century Journal* 13, no. 4 (1982): 77–89.

125. *Institution of Christian Matrimony*, 373–74.

(whose literacy he now assumes) should read works about the education of children by the Greek author Plutarch and the humanists Pier Paolo Vergerio and Francesco Filelfo.[126]

But Vives made the most extraordinary contribution to the cause of women's education in his *De institutione feminae christianae* (1524),[127] as has been seen, the first major work ever to advocate the education of girls up to and including such advanced studies as philosophy and theology. Modern feminists assail Vives for the narrow educational regimen he prescribes, and especially for his conspicuous obsession with female chastity; but since the most obdurate objection to female learning was that it would lead to sexual dereliction, Vives's insistence that women's learning entailed no threat to chastity was essential to the success of his cause.

Building on the contributions of his humanist predecessors, Johann Amos Comenius, the Bohemian reformer and refugee polymath, advocated universal education for children of both sexes. Further, he singled out women as mothers as the critical teachers of early childhood in his diminutive work composed in Czech, published in German (in Lissa [Leszno] Poland, in 1633) as the *Informatorium der Mutterschule*, and translated into several languages, including English: *The School of Infancy*.[128] In it, he details how mothers are to provide physical care, moral guidance, religious training, and instruction in cognitive skills during the first six years of life before the child, at age seven, enters formal schooling. Comenius's recommendations were clearly taken to heart in England, where his works were much studied, and where it was commonly expected that mothers would exert enormous energy in the rearing of their children.[129]

In the eighteenth century, the Swiss-Italian pedagogical reformer Johann Heinrich Pestalozzi pursued Comenius's lead, detailing how a mother could lay the foundations of her children's education in his ponderous guide *Wie Gertrud ihre Kinder lehrt* (How Gertrude Teaches her Children, 1801).[130] The Comenian-Pestalozzian tradition culminates in the next century with the invention of the kindergarten by Friedrich Fröbel, an innovation that had notable success in the

---

126. *De officio mariti*, 134.

127. Dedicated, as Erasmus's *Institutio christiani matrimonii* had been, to the highly learned Catherine of Aragon, queen consort of England.

128. Johann Amos Comenius, *The School of Infancy*, ed. and trans. Ernest M. Eller (Chapel Hill: University of North Carolina Press, 1956). For Comenius, see especially Craig D. Atwood, *The Theology of the Czech Brethren from Hus to Comenius* (University Park: Pennsylvania State University Press, 2009), 366–97; King, "The Emergence of Mother as Teacher," 61–69, and sources there cited.

129. See Patricia Nardi, "Mothers at Home: Their Role in Childrearing and Instruction in Early Modern England" (Ph.D. diss., City University of New York, 2007).

130. Johann Heinrich Pestalozzi, *Wie Gertrud ihre Kinder lehrt, ein Versuch den Müttern Anleitung zu geben, ihre Kinder selbst zu unterrichten* (Bern: C. Gessner, 1801). For Pestalozzi, see King, "The Emergence of Mother as Teacher," 72–75, and sources there cited.

young United States.[131] Ironically, however, the kindergarten betrays the very ideals that had given it birth: for where Barbaro, Comenius, and Pestalozzi all envisioned a mother instructing her children amid her daily activities in her own home, Fröbel would remove them from that setting. At this moment, on the brink of modernity, the maternal role in early moral and intellectual training is transferred from women to men, and from the workshop of the family to an institution—for such it is, albeit disguised as a "garden."

The *De re uxoria*, a young man's first literary product, written some 600 years ago, matters, then, for this reason: not because we care, as he did, about the survival of the Venetian noble clans—for those are mostly gone, along with their palaces, sinking into the resurgent lagoon—but because of the spotlight he puts on the mother as the key agent of the enculturation of the young. Is she still? Some may believe that mothers been successfully replaced by fathers and daycare centers. Others may suspect that there is some truth to Barbaro's legend of blood and milk and soul force, the interconnected and indispensable fibrous web within which, before birth and after, a person is formed. Not long after his mother's death, and just weeks before his own, John Donne wrote of its ineluctable power:

> Wee have a winding sheete in our Mothers wombe, which grows with us from our conception, and we come into the world, wound up in that *winding sheet,* for wee come to *seeke a grave* ... when the *wombe* hath discharg'd us, yet we are bound to it by *cordes* of flesh, by such a *string,* as that we cannot goe thence, nor stay there.[132]

Note on This Translation

Barbaro's text is, as Claudio Griggio described it, "clear and linear"[133]—or, as Poggio Bracciolini commented in 1416, "so methodically ordered, that nothing could be more methodical."[134] Nonetheless, his sentences are long, allusive, and abstract. The difficulty has often been to concretize their meanings. In this, I have been guided and inspired by Percy Gothein, who crafted an ideal of the intellectual-as-statesman based on his studies of Renaissance Venice, and perished

---

131. See Irene M. Lilley, ed., *Friedrich Froebel: A Selection from his Writings* (Cambridge: Cambridge University Press, 1967). For Fröbel, see also King, "The Emergence of Mother as Teacher," 75–76, and sources there cited.

132. John Donne, *Sermons,* ed. George R. Potter and Evelyn M. Simpson, 10 vols. (Berkeley: University of California Press, 1953–1962), vol. 10, no. 11, at 233, delivered on February 25, 1631.

133. See above, note 73.

134. See above, 42.

under the Nazi regime.[135] With unfailing precision, he translates Barbaro's work into vivid, fluid German. My own translation seeks to achieve the same result in English. It is based on the critical edition of Attilio Gnesotto as corrected by Griggio.[136]

135. For Gothein, see Karlhans Kluncker, *Percy Gothein: Humanist und Erzieher, das Ärgernis im George-Kreis*, 2nd ed. (Amsterdam: Castrum Peregrini, 1986).

136. Gnesotto, ed., *De re uxoria*; Griggio, "Copisti ed editori," 1047–55.

DEDICATORY LETTER to Lorenzo di Giovanni di Bicci de' Medici

Our ancestors, my dear Lorenzo, out of kindness or necessity used to give gifts to those who were joined together in marriage, so that the token they gave of their love and support would be not only a pledge but also an ornament. As with so many other customs, this one has now lapsed since those days. For today, men with quite different ambitions burden themselves with debt so as to give rich gifts to those who are already rich. But in scattering their gifts about, as though sowing seed, they seem to me to resemble the Babylonian farmers about whom Herodotus, the father of history, writes, whose fields were so fertile that the good earth produced for each unit of sown grain a two-hundred-fold yield without fail, and often three.[1] But I would not characterize this extravagance as generosity or liberality: for these poor men who bestow gifts on the wealthy deprive themselves in their scarcity to supply others in their abundance. And so in hope of favor or in expectation of gain, they mortgage their possessions—and deserve therefore to be frustrated in their quest, it seems to me, having sought profit with a pretense of liberality and chased uselessly after a plethora of prizes.

This model I abhor, especially since my concern is with you, who possess such wealth, such riches, so many advantages on every front, who so far as I can see have no room in your abundance for any gifts of mine. For leaving aside those things which are the necessities of life, you possess precious furnishings, luxurious garments, and magnificent accoutrements of all kinds. Recalling, moreover, our many friendly conversations, I see that a gift would be more welcome and pleasing to you if it came not from Francesco's fortune, but from your friend Francesco. Therefore, I have undertaken to write and dedicate to you this brief commentary on the wealth of wives, which I judge will be of some use, since it suits this moment of your own nuptials. It avoids, moreover, the usual precepts,[2] which I could not, given the limits of my intellect, express better, nor explain more clearly than they already have been. Instead, I have for the most part followed those I learned

---

1. Herodotus, *History*, 1.193, describing the unique fertility of the Tigris/Euphrates valley, with the reference to yields of 200- and 300-fold at 1.193.3; alluding also to Virgil, *Georgics*, 2.458–460, utilizing the phrase *justissima tellus* (translated here as the "good earth") found at 2.460. In citing this passage from Herodotus, Barbaro suggests that the mindless gift-givers whom he profiles expect that their gifts will yield enormous benefits, in cash, power, or cultural advantage. In 1415, he seems to anticipate a culture of courtiers and sycophancy more commonly encountered in literary products of the sixteenth and seventeenth centuries.

2. Barbaro alludes, most likely, to contemporary discussions of marriage, mostly by clerical authors and rooted in patristic literature—which he himself cites when relevant.

from Zaccaria Trevisan[3]—that illustrious citizen of Venice, a man peerless in our age for his intellect, wisdom, justice, deep knowledge, and great deeds, and tightly bound to me by the law of friendship—in conversations about this matter we had from time to time. In these he gravely expounded to me nearly the whole of the elegant science of marriage as taught by the ancients.[4]

Nor did I undertake to write this commentary to instruct you in particular, but so that through you I might reach many of our generation; and when I communicate to them what is to be done, you will recognize in my instruction what you have already done, do now, and will do in the future. For who am I to instruct you, you who were crafted by nature to win honor, praise, and glory, and are further endowed with domestic paragons and the benefits of learning, which added to your native attributes open wide for you the road to glory?[5] For you imitate that excellent man, your father Giovanni, and your illustrious brother Cosimo, with the stores of whose authority, wisdom, and counsel you have been amply supplied. Around you also are other worthy and wise men from whose society you may profit. I saw when I was there with what diligence and regard you respected and esteemed above all the learned Roberto de' Rossi, from whose side, indeed, and quite rightly, you scarcely ever departed.[6] Joining us also were the most eloquent Leonardo Bruni, and the no less cultivated Niccolò Niccoli, to whom, I know, you listened closely and learned many things, among them many related to the present discussion.

Given all this, it will not perhaps be contrary to our friendship if you also attend to what I have to say about the things I have discovered. For it will please you all the more, it seems to me, if these thoughts of mine, written by my hand, come to you from me. When Xenocrates returned the fifty talents of gold that Alexander the Great had sent him, saying that he had no need of kingly gifts, Alexander replied: "Although Xenocrates does not require the munificence of Alexander, yet Alexander must be, and be seen to be, generous to Xenocrates."[7]

So, although you have been so reared that you will perhaps think my advice not at all necessary to you, yet the matter discussed here strikes me as one of

---

3. For Trevisan, see the Introduction, 2–3.

4. Barbaro writes that in these conversations, Trevisan conveyed to him *propemodum omnis elegans antiquorum ratio uxoria*; I have translated this as the "elegant science of marriage" so as not to lose the adjective "elegant," which Barbaro uses deliberately, and to approximate the sense of *ratio* here, which implicates not just a single principle but an entire field of learning. But as for *uxoria*: the literal meaning here is perhaps closer to "elegant science of wifeliness."

5. Cf. Pier Paolo Vergerio, *De ingenuis moribus*, ed. Kallendorf, 6/7, para. 4; here Vergerio speaks in similar tones of the natural endowments and possible future of Ubertino da Carrara.

6. For Rossi, Bruni, and Niccoli, see the Introduction, notes 49 and 50.

7. Cf. Plutarch, *Regum et imperatorum apophthegmata*, Alexander, 30; *De Alexandri Magni fortuna aut virtute*, 333b. Xenocrates of Chalcedon (c. 396/5–314/3 BCE) was a philosopher, mathematician, and leader of the Platonic Academy.

which young people in general, and those of our circle in particular, should be aware. For while all of philosophy is fruitful and beneficial, so that no part of it should be left unstudied and unknown, yet this part is most fertile and bounteous of all,[8] for it shows that marriage, which is the basis of the household and all its responsibilities, should be wisely, carefully, and honorably planned, instituted, and realized, with the highest seriousness and the most earnest devotion. What I have written will also be recognized immediately as the sign of our good will and firm friendship; and I shall have gained by writing a rare and extraordinary reward if my thoughts are pleasing and gratifying to you, to whom I owe so much. It will add to my happiness if the young commend my discourse, for whom I have written in my leisure so as to profit their activity, so that, if they are learned, they will delight in this confirmation of the judgment of learned men on the wealth of wives, or if without learning, they will become rightly informed. And if some part of what is written here is perhaps in your view less than satisfactory, yet you will readily approve the whole, as I hope and wish, just as at banquets, even if we hold back from certain particular foods, yet we normally applaud the dinner as a whole; nor surely do we let those things that the stomach refuses rob us of the pleasure with which we eat the others.

I begin, then, my discourse on the wealth of wives, and I will speak of those things—as briefly as so great a matter can be spoken about—which, as I have explained, I know would have pleased my friend Zaccaria,[9] that great man, and many other excellent men. Now what I have promised, I shall proceed to do! May you hear me with kind and attentive ears, and receive this work, such as it is, for the sake of our friendship, and in lieu of a glittering gift, on the occasion of your nuptials.

PROLOGUE: WHAT MARRIAGE IS

Before I discuss the choice of a wife and her responsibilities, I first wish to define here what marriage is, utilizing the views of learned men, so that we may understand from the start the subject of our future discourse.[10] Thus provided with a full overview, we shall more easily resolve the details, and arrive at sounder conclusions.

Marriage, then, is the perpetual conjunction of man and wife, lawfully instituted for the procreation of offspring or for the avoidance of fornication. About this subject there are many and diverse views; and to investigate and evaluate them all would be tedious. Instead, I shall turn to the most famous pagan and Christian thinkers, who by general consensus are considered authoritative.

8. Cf. Cicero, *De officiis*, 3.2.5.

9. Trevisan, that is, as above.

10. Cf. Cicero, *De officiis*, 1.2.7.

Now the Romans, so as to increase the number of legitimately born children, levied a tax on anyone who remained celibate into old age.[11] For they respected the pattern set by nature, which has instilled in every living species a desire for coition for the sake of procreation, and a belief that its success consists in having reproduced.[12] Indeed, the drive to generate in animals is powerful, as we see with birds, for example (so as not to discourse at too great length about other species), whose instinct to nest, which may be likened to marriage among humans, provides for both the birthing and the nourishment of their young.[13] In this way, just as the body is sustained by food, both animal and human species are perpetuated.

Lycurgus,[14] whose laws when observed made Sparta great, and when neglected caused her fall, targeted those for ignominy who were still unmarried at age thirty-seven. These men who had not yet married he barred from training in the palestra, so that its young men, seeking either to avoid that shame, or enflamed with zeal to win the crown of victory, would bestow upon the city greater honor and glory. Following this principle, a youth who while in the palestra had not yielded his place as courtesy required to the great general Dercylidas (who had never borne children while in Sparta, to which he had retired in old age) pointedly replied to his complaint: "Nor did you, not having borne children, yield to me."[15]

Time has shown that the children born of legitimate marriages are more inclined to honor, are more responsibly reared, and ultimately make better citizens; while the city composed of such citizens will be loved by its allies on account of its commitment to justice, and feared by its enemies on account of its courage. Experience, meanwhile, that great teacher, demonstrates amply that those who were conceived in lust and outside of wedlock are for the most part violent and dishonest and inclined to all that is base. But the splendor of their ancestors demands that those born honorably achieve excellence: they know that the glories of their forefathers will be more of a burden than a blessing unless by their own merit they match those forebears in dignity and eminence. For they realize that all eyes will be turned on them in expectation that they will in some way reiterate in their own lives the virtue they have inherited from their ancestors. So we may call

11. Valerius Maximus, *Factorum et dictorum memorabilium libri* (henceforth *Memorabilia*), 2.9.1.

12. Cicero, *De officiis*, 1.4.11.

13. Augustine, *De nuptiis et concupiscentia*, 1.5.

14. The legendary king of the ancient Greek city of Sparta, who supposedly established its distinctive laws, perhaps in the 8th century BCE.

15. Plutarch, *Lycurgus*, 15, and for this and following, Plutarch, *Apophthegmata laconica, Lycurgus,* 14; see also 16. The original text reads Dercylidas, substituted here for Callicles, a Sophist, the name that Barbaro used, relying on his manuscript version; see Gothein, *Das Buch von der Ehe*, 90n20. Free Spartan citizens, even more zealously than Greeks of other cities, exercised regularly in the palestra, or gymnasium, and were rewarded in competitions by a garland or crown.

those born thus honorably "the walls of the city."[16] When someone in his presence complained that Sparta lacked walls, Agesilaus said: "By God, the citizens themselves are the best and strongest walls of the city. For truly, we protect and defend our country, gods, household deities, altars, hearths, parents, wives, and children, not with wood or brick, but with virtue."[17]

And besides, what is more pleasant than to share our thoughts with our wives, and so resolve domestic cares? And to be wed to a prudent wife who in both good and bad is partner, companion, and friend? To whom you may confide your innermost thoughts about things that lie within her province, to whom you may entrust the little children that you bear together? To whom in sweet conversation you may unburden your cares and sorrows? Whom you so love, that your own hope of happiness depends in some measure on her well-being?

Cato the Censor held that wives were so worthy of care and reverence that to strike one's wife was a deed as vile as the desecration of the images of the gods, and should be prosecuted to the fullest; and he often said that in his view it was harder to be a good husband than a good senator.[18] By the bond of marriage, Adusius reconciled the feuding Carians, and by the same tie,[19] Cyrus settled the hostilities between the Chaldaeans and their neighbors.[20] Because of marriage, the Romans and the Sabines, on the very same day, turned from enemies to friends,[21] and marriage soothed the estranged hearts of Pompey and Caesar.[22] What is more incredible, by the tie of marriage, rather than any monumental bridge, Alexander made Asia and Europe one.[23] The list would be endless if I enumerated the philosophers, historians, poets, kings, and princes of cities, who jump forth from the pages of the monuments of letters[24] like the warriors who poured out of the belly

16. The notion that the citizens (collectively; not just those of the nobility) are the true "walls of the city" is ancient, appearing in, among others, Thucydides (*The History of the Peloponnesian War* II.78.3; VII.77.7) and Saint Augustine (*Sermo de urbis excidio* VI.6), as well as in Plutarch as follows.

17. Plutarch, *Apophthegata laconica, Agesilaus*, 29 and 30.

18. Plutarch, *Cato the Elder*, 20.

19. Xenophon, *Cyropaedia*, 7.4.1–7. Adusius is substituted here for the incorrect Cadusius in the Barbaro text.

20. Xenophon, *Cyropaedia*, 3.2.

21. According to legend, soon after the founding of Rome (c. 753 BCE), the first generation of Romans acquired wives by seizing them from the neighboring tribe of Sabines, an event referred to in literature as the "rape of the Sabine women."

22. The rival Roman generals Pompey and Caesar resolved their enmity, for a time, to join in the First Triumvirate (59 BCE), their reconciliation marked by Pompey's marriage to Julia, Caesar's daughter.

23. Plutarch, *De Alexandri Magni fortuna aut virtute*, 7.

24. Humanists frequently used the phrase *monumenta litterarum*, literally "monuments of letters," to describe the literary legacy of antiquity, suggesting that its many books had the weight and presence of monuments of stone and bronze; cf. for example Vergerio, *De ingenuis moribus*, ed. Kallendorf, 44, para. 36, among other *loci*.

of the Trojan horse, who celebrate this institution that binds two people in love and piety. But these things are well-known, so I shall omit them, especially since in so clear a case it is not necessary to produce witnesses.

Yet the Christian view of marriage must not be neglected, whose weight is so great that even without the aid of reasoned argument, its authority prevails. By its laws, marriages that are rooted in sacrament, faith, and offspring, are so assured that once they are instituted, as is apparent to all, they remain valid thereafter;[25] as Christ our Lord confirms in the Gospel, both when he prohibits the repudiation of a wife, and then when he attends a wedding as a guest.[26] From which it is evident that even if marriage is not sought for itself, yet, in my judgment, it is desired for the good that it yields. Wisdom, friendship, health we seek as goods in themselves; but we desire intellect, learning, and knowledge, as well as comity, intimacy, and sexual relations, and finally food, drink, and sleep, because they are necessary to secure those goods previously named.[27] Marriage, then, we believe to be good because it yields two benefits: first, our progeny, and secondly, friendship between the two sexes, which nature has wondrously bestowed upon us—otherwise the value of marriage would vanish for the elderly who did not have children, or those couples who no longer had any hope of begetting them, for whom marriage offers this great advantage that it removes from sexual relations all sin of incontinence. Accordingly, man and wife are joined by a law, a pact, a force so strong that no kind of separation can sever that union.[28]

Yet I am aware that some will oppose me fiercely from the outset, who will bring up the behavior of the cranky Xanthippe, and admire the wit of that Spartan, who when he took a wife who brought him not a penny, and was mocked for doing so, said to his critics, "It is an old and salutary proverb that advises us to choose the least of the evils before us."[29] Many other rejoinders to those skeptical of marriage can be adduced, including first of all this one of Socrates. When he brought Euthydemus home with him from the gymnasium, so he might enrich their friendship by a sacred act of hospitality, Xanthippe, in anger, overturned the table. Seeing that his guest was troubled, Socrates said, "Be of good cheer: we often endure fierce creatures in preference to tame ones, given that docile chickens hatch eggs much more fragile than the robust children birthed by our wives."[30] To these may be added the remark of Metellus Numidicus the censor, a most worthy

---

25. Augustine, *De bono conjugali*, 3.

26. For Jesus's teaching on divorce see Matthew 5:31, Matthew 19:3–9, and Mark 10:2–12; for his presence by invitation at the wedding at Cana, John 2:1–10.

27. Here I follow Gothein, *Das Buch von der Ehe*, 18 (explained in his note at 90n30) in grouping the three sets of subordinate goods in the service of the three stated "goods in themselves."

28. Augustine, *De bono conjugali*, 3.

29. Plutarch, *De fraterno amore*, 482A.

30. A loose retelling of Plutarch, *De cohibenda ira*, 461 D–E.

man, who in his discourse on marriage had this to say: "If we were able to live without wives, Senators, we would be spared many burdens; but since nature has contrived that we can neither live comfortably with them, nor in any way exist without them, we must choose long life over present ease."[31]

But enough has been said about marriage, about which learned men have written at length. But so as to clarify the essential points, I have reviewed them here. Now, once I have first defined how the proper wife is to be chosen, I shall briefly present a full analysis of the role of the wife, which to my knowledge was never undertaken by ancient authorities.[32] But first of all, it is necessary to warn that no marriage can be worthy that has not received a father's assent, as seen in the case of Cyrus, who when invited by Cyaxares, king of the Medes, to marry a most worthy woman with an enormous dowry, he said that he could not accept before he had secured his parents' approval.[33]

First Part: On the Choice of a Wife

CHAPTER 1: THE MORAL CHARACTER BEFITTING THE WOMAN CHOSEN AS A WIFE

The ancients, whose authority lives on because of their great learning and wide experience, thought that a prospective wife should be judged for her character, age, descent, beauty, and wealth, and that if any of these is neglected, we will certainly bring dishonor and sorrow to our families, and often grief to ourselves; but if we attend to them diligently, we win honor for our family, and for ourselves, reputation and enduring joy.

Virtue, then, is the preeminent requirement, whose power and worth is so great that, even if other qualities are lacking, yet the marriage should be considered a good one; and if it is present, then without doubt, the marriage will be successful. For the domestic matters committed to a wife's care will not be managed well unless the woman in charge guides, governs, and orders them with prudence, diligence, and industry. Citizens normally imitate the virtues of their rulers, soldiers of their generals, children of their parents, and maidservants their mistresses. Homer offers an apt example in chaste Andromache, whose hand-maidens were so trained that in chastity, diligence, and hard work they excelled

---

31. Aulus Gellius, *Noctes atticae*, 1.6.1–2. The speaker is Quintus Caecilius Metellus Numidicus (c. 160–91 BCE), the opponent of Gaius Marius, renowned for his integrity, and admired as an orator by Cicero.

32. Barbaro writes: *Nunc partis* [sic; i.e., *partes*] *uxorias, quas a majoribus nostris nusquam in ordinem digestas invenimus, quasi sub uno aspectu positas breviter exponemus …* .

33. Xenophon, *Cyropaedia*, 8.5.19–20.

and surpassed the servitors of Helen.[34] For the woman of whom we speak will easily rule her handmaidens, because she has ruled herself.

Nor can I approve of those who in choosing a wife seek some kind of rare excellence, and zealously require some quality that has not been seen for many centuries. From reading much, and hearing much, we have learned that even those of inferior rank will be found worthy who strive to excel by imitating the greatest examples. It is recorded that in the Olympic games, the boxer Philammon won the crown of victory, not because he was capable of defeating Glaucus, the famous athlete of times past, but because by his skill he vanquished the opponents of his own day.[35] So if perhaps the equals of Porcia, Cornelia, Pantheia,[36] glorious luminaries of womankind, have not been conferred upon our age, yet those who are diligent will find a wife who offers beauty, service, and delight. Finding such a wife is a task not too difficult to execute.

The consul and censor Marcus Cato, whose comments I mentioned earlier, took a young wife when he was already old, as described in this account taken from Greek sources, which I offer as a pleasant digression.[37] And so Marcus Cato, having often seen the daughter of his client Salonius, though he was much older than she, greatly delighted in her charm and manner. One day, as was his custom, the scribe Salonius accompanied Cato to the forum, when Cato said to him, "I have found a husband for your daughter, Salonius, who, unless his rather great age is a problem, will please you greatly." After these words, which are normally in such matters considered to be the first step, Cato confessed that he himself was the old man, and he most earnestly wished to have the other's daughter for his wife. Salonius in turn marveled that his daughter's qualities had made such an impression on Cato that, though she was humbly born, he would take her into his family, adorned as it was with consular and triumphal honors. What more is there to say? Cato married the girl.

This Cato had a son, also Marcus Cato, than whom no man was finer, if we are to believe his father, nor more observant of his parent. He was troubled by the announcement of the latter's marriage, and begged forgiveness if he had failed his father in any way, so as to cause his father to bring home a step-mother. Praising his son, the elder Cato replied that the qualities of this virgin enormously pleased him. "Nor should you think this was done so as to bring a

---

34. Based on *Iliad*, 10, and *Odyssey*, 4.

35. Demosthenes, *De corona*, 18.319. Glaucus of Carystus was an ancient Greek athlete.

36. Porcia the Elder, the sister of the Cato the Younger and wife of Ahenobarbus, was celebrated in a funeral oration by Cicero; Cornelia was the learned mother of the Gracchi, the heroic Roman brothers and reformers; Pantheia killed herself out of loyalty to her dead lover Abradatas, king of Susa, the story occupying much of the second half of Xenophon's *Cyropaedia*.

37. The following lengthy anecdote is based on Plutarch, *Cato the Elder*, 24. Barbaro knew the work well, as he had translated it from the Greek into Latin.

stepmother home to you, my dearest son, but rather so as to have many other sons just like you born to me, and to offer them as outstanding citizens to the republic." For the same reasons Peisistratus, who already had adult sons trained in the liberal arts, took a wife endowed, it was said, with exceptional modesty, since the great virtue of his sons increased in him daily the desire to procreate more of them. The sound judgment of Marcus Cato—than whose there was none greater—and of Peisistratus make clear to us how highly we must value good character in a wife.

Our own city is full of examples of this sort, of which it will be sufficient to name a few. Andrea Barbaro, an excellent man and father of our revered Marco,[38] an eminent citizen of honorable rank, took as his wife Lucia Viara, a woman of such remarkable and conspicuous probity that, having gained the necessary permission, he met and spoke with her in her home, and asked if she would consider marrying him, setting aside any consideration of wealth. And so, disdaining other much wealthier women, he took her as his wife for the sake of her virtue and goodness. This prudent man did not err in making this decision, since she cherished his children with such concern and piety that no greater harmony or peace could be desired than prevailed in their household.[39]

Many years later, this Barbaro, my ancestor, served as a pattern for the renowned and excellent citizen Giusto Contarini. For having ascertained the moderation, modesty, and exceptional beauty of Francesca, the daughter of Pantaleone Barbo, he first spoke to the father alone, declaring that he had grown more and more to love his daughter, and though she was poor, if Pantaleone were willing, he wished most earnestly to make her his wife. Pantaleone, a man of illustrious family and great learning, was delighted by this declaration. He requested time for deliberation, and summoned, as was customary, his friends and advisers. To these he laid the matter out fully, and they approved it wholeheartedly by unanimous consent. Giusto, who was advanced in age, was accepted by the most noble young woman, although she brought a very small dowry, as the family's circumstances dictated. I would call this a splendid marriage, which, having been established on a foundation of virtue, endured inviolate with the greatest faith and trust. Setting aside other examples, this one should be noted, that she treated the children of Giusto's former wife with such kindness and generosity that in their daily life, many of the stepchildren found that other than the name, she was in no way like a stepmother.[40]

38. Marco Barbaro was head of a collateral line of the Barbaro clan—an exceedingly wealthy family, according to the census of 1379; see Gothein, *Das Buch von der Ehe*, 91n39.

39. The children of a prior marriage, that is, those who would often be placed in the care of a new, young stepmother, a not always successful arrangement.

40. Barbaro here presents another case where a young stepmother takes over the care of children by a prior marriage.

Before all else, therefore, as I see you are also aware, my dear Lorenzo, the character of a wife must be pleasing, without which what hope domestic life may hold for us, I cannot imagine. Asked whether there would be Spartan victories in the future, Pausanias responded: "If a skilled general is in charge."[41] Which brings us back to the matter before us. What orders, guides, and illumines domestic life if not above all the diligence, frugality, and dignity of the wife? Not even the Doge of Venice can govern the city well, unless he is deeply learned in the civil law, ancestral customs, and the workings of the republic. Nor does a captain bring his ship out of a savage tempest and safely into port if he is ignorant of the art of navigation, nor will a charioteer who knows nothing of racing be victorious. So neither will the household be rightly managed, if the sterling competence of the housewife does not set the standard for everyone else. And just as in war soldiers who serve under a worthy general would be ashamed to desert the position assigned them, so neither manservants nor maidservants will fail in the household tasks with which they have been entrusted by a chaste and prudent matron.

Plato, that most profound philosopher, in his book on the *Republic* written with divine inspiration, prescribed that offices be assigned to the most worthy rather than the most ambitious citizens. For he saw that before long few would strive to achieve high office if these places were not given to the most worthy candidates but to the most aggressive. He proposed, accordingly, that magistrates be given a salary from the public purse, so that domestic anxieties would not distract them from performing their duties to the republic.[42] Likewise, we consider virtue in a wife of such great importance that, if our fortune permits, we should either pay no attention to the size of her dowry, or settle for a very small one, in order to obtain domestic honor and harmony. This quality by itself brings us greater glory than if we marry a wife laden with gold, but devoid of probity. To an Ionian woman who showed off her wealth by flaunting her treasures, Phocion's wife said, "Phocion is my wealth and my treasure, who for his service to the fatherland has now for twenty years been prince of the Athenians."[43] In the same way we may rightly glory in the worthiness of our wives, and pay no heed to those who, though enriched by the opulent riches of their wives, suffer endless troubles. These sorts of riches are transitory, while those named above are firm and stable and truly bind together the souls of man and wife. Philip, the father of Alexander, whose fortune and valor, according to Theophrastus, made him the foremost of kings, passionately loved a Thessalian woman, to such an extent that it was said he had

41. Plutarch, *Apophthegmata laconica, Pausanias,* 3. Barbaro, who mistakenly attributes this saying to the Spartan king Agesilaus instead of the general Pausanias, an attribution corrected here, means that the character of the wife is the primary consideration in marriage, as the skill of a general is in war.

42. Barbaro may have had direct access to Plato's *Republic,* 1.347a; but he certainly had Cicero, *De officiis,* 1.85–87.

43. Plutarch, *Phocion,* 19.

been enslaved by her love potions. Accordingly, his wife Olympias exerted herself mightily to get the Thessalian woman in her power; and when the queen found her rival was adorned with beauty, modesty, and virtue, she said, "Away with these calumnies! for you yourself perform love magic, with drugs compounded of the nectar of your probity."[44]

What else is there to say? Let us choose a wife of good character, whose frugality, joined to honor, comfort, and pleasure, we may cherish, treasure, and love.

CHAPTER 2: HOW OLD SHOULD A WIFE BE?

Since what is necessary has been said about a wife's character which, if she has been properly reared, is already formed or will soon be formed, now I shall briefly detail what my mentor Zaccaria and many other learned men have conveyed in writing, or learned from experience, about her age.

But first of all I would warn that a virgin should be chosen, not a widow; a girl, and no one of more advanced age: for she will more easily learn what is useful and necessary, and if any seeds of vice were once planted, they will be quickly uprooted. For we can easily imprint images in soft wax, while those impressed on surfaces that are hard and unyielding are difficult to erase. It is possible to shape tender minds with the lessons we wish to impart;[45] while for widows who have been accustomed to their own ways, or to those of strangers, if they are to be adapted to our way of life, an expenditure of great insight, extensive effort, and special care is required, and the goal is achieved only with great effort. For who will hope to straighten vines that are now old if they were allowed to grow wild at the start? And who will suppose that the stomach of a child nourished on the delicacies of Alexandria,[46] when his circumstances change, will live the life of an abstemious graybeard? Or who will expect that he will mature to be a man of fine character, who sees and hears petulance, lustfulness, audacity, and cruelty as a youth? So it is scarcely to be hoped that widows, who, having suffered, as it were, from some intolerable sickness from which they have just recovered, must now adjust to our mode of life. For this reason Timotheus, that noble flautist, wisely used to require twice the payment for instruction from those who had previously been taught that art by a different master, but only the standard payment from those who came to him completely untrained.[47] For these latter needed only to be taught, but the former first untaught before they could be instructed.

---

44. Plutarch, *Conjugalia praecepta*, no. 23.

45. Plutarch, *De liberis educandis*, 3 e–f (5.5). Strikingly, Barbaro adapts to the topic of virginal wives this passage in which Plutarch speaks of the plasticity of children's minds.

46. In late antiquity, the Egyptian city of Alexandria, founded by Alexander the Great, was a center of high culture and great luxury.

47. Cf. Quintilian, *Institutio oratoria*, 2.3.

From this follows the principle that experience also affirms, and is observed in nature: for those who explore the secret causes of things tell us that nature itself always intends what is best, so when it cannot beget a male, it conceives a female, who then is ennobled and perfected when joined to the male.[48] For this reason, we love women most of all who are joined to us by their first embrace. And why so? Because a virgin will more easily clothe herself with our character, discarding the garments of her own insufficiency, and so love us that much more passionately. For the Romans, on this account, even though they permitted divorce, still viewed widows who remarried as inconstant and wanton; and they awarded the crown of chastity to those who remained content with one husband while he still lived, while celebrating those who, even after his death, with sincere faith, piously and purely preserved the commitment of their soul to their husband.[49] But who would not condemn her as libidinous, whose embrace of many husbands could not satisfy her desires? Who will not joyously celebrate Dido, who was so chaste that she said of the death of her husband: "He who first took me to himself has stolen my love: let him keep it with him, and guard it in his grave."[50] Which should not surprise anyone, since crows and turtledoves, as nature has decreed, when their husbands have died, still preserve their chastity as widows.[51]

But I have wandered too far from the subject in condemning widows who remarry and accusing them of incontinence. Therefore let us return to our discussion. What most conduces to the peace of the household is that a similarity in character and interests joins husband and wife, or continues to keep them together. For this reason the ancients in their wisdom also placed Mercury, the Graces, and Persuasion in temples to Venus, thus signifying the great importance to a successful marriage of the harmony of wills, pleasantness, and affability.[52]

It must next be established at what age a woman is "ready for a husband," as Virgil puts it, and "old enough to be a bride."[53] Hesiod, the ancient poet, and Xenophon, that delightful philosopher, recommended an age of 15 for the woman,

---

48. Aristotle, *De animalium generatione*, 4.6 and 1.21.

49. Barbaro describes here the Roman ideal of the *matrona unavira*, a woman who had had, and remained devoted to, just one husband.

50. Virgil, *Aeneid*, 4.28–29, trans. A.S. Kline (2002), from the website *Poetry in Translation*, http://www.poetryintranslation.com/PITBR/Latin/VirgilAeneidIV.htm#_Toc342017.

51. For crows, see Plutarch, *Bruta animalia ratione uti*, 989a; for turtledoves, see Athenaeus, *Deipnosophistae*, 394h; Aelian, *Natura animalium*, 3.44; and Ambrose, *Hexameron*, 5.19. For these references, see Gothein, *Das Buch von der Ehe*, 91n47.

52. Plutarch, *Conjugalia praecepta*, 138 C–D. As Plutarch explains the presence of these figures in the entourage of Aphrodite (Venus), Hermes (Mercury) represents the need for rational communication between spouses, and Persuasion and the Graces the need for persuasion and collaboration instead of fighting and anger.

53. Virgil, *Aeneid*, 7.53, trans. A.S. Kline (2002), from the website *Poetry in Translation*, http://www.poetryintranslation.com/PITBR/Latin/VirgilAeneidVII.htm#_Toc3086149.

and 30 for the man.[54] Lycurgus, however, set the ages at 18 for the woman and 37 for the man, ages chosen as most conducive to the generation of children, in the procreation of whom thought had to be taken not so much for their number as their vigor.[55] On this point allow me, I pray you, my charming Lorenzo, to take a detour, which I know will not be unwelcome to you. For the same purpose, Lycurgus decreed that Spartan citizens should not spend the night in the same bedchambers with their wives, but rather have intercourse with them secretly during the day, so that freed from perpetual and, if I may put it this way, over-free coitus, they might better preserve their health in the long term, and produce more robust offspring.[56] For wisely, he saw that men are mortal, and inclined to give in to their lust for pleasure, from the lures of which he was determined to protect his citizens; so he arranged that they could not too assiduously indulge in such pursuits.

Lycurgus also established a plan for the education of women supportive of this end, which featured many games and contests, so that female honor would not suffer erosion due to idleness or inactivity. So he decreed for Spartan girls a program of running, discus throwing, and gymnastics, so that this regular exercise would encourage the birth of infants, both male and female, of innate hardiness. He also claimed that as a result of this law, Spartan women more readily bore the pains of labor in giving birth, during which, if complications arose, they fought courageously for the sake of their children.[57]

I approve also the recommendation that he[58] set forth for age at marriage, so that so far as possible the weakness of the female sex might be protected from the temptations of pleasure. These measures appear to have accomplished their end, because Spartan women excelled in every kind of worthy thing, yet especially for their chastity. To their excellence in this regard, powerful testimony is offered by the response of the noble Spartan Geradatas. Answering a foreigner[59] who had inquired what punishment an adulterer would suffer according to the laws of Lycurgus, he said that Lycurgus had said not a word about adultery, "since there are no adulterers in Sparta; nor should you marvel at that, stranger, since among us luxuries, fripperies, trifles, and other incitements of pleasure are everywhere condemned, while frugality, modesty, and chastity cannot be sufficiently praised."[60] Born and reared by laws such as these, Spartan women alone are known for giving

---

54. Hesiod, *Works and Days*, 695–705; also Plutarch, *Amatorius*, 753a.

55. Lycurgus did not propose ideal ages at marriage; for these, see Aristotle, *Politics*, 7.14.6.

56. Plutarch, *Apophthegmata laconica, Lycurgus*, 17.

57. Plutarch, *Apophthegmata laconica, Lycurgus*, 12.

58. Barbaro refers again to Lycurgus, although it is Aristotle's recommendation; see above, note 55.

59. Correcting Barbaro's *Xentus* for *xenos*; cf. Gnesotto, *De re uxoria*, 40 (18) n3; Gothein, *Das Buch von der Ehe*, 91n54.

60. Plutarch, *Apophthegmata laconica, Lycurgus*, 20.

birth not merely to males, but to men, as it is reported that Gorgo, the wife of king Leonidas, maintained; for when a guest of her husband criticized the women of Sparta, since they, more than women elsewhere, presumed to rule over their men, Gorgo responded: "And not without reason, since we alone give birth to men!"[61]

But all of this has gone on longer than is necessary. It is not really necessary, it seems to me, that we come to a final judgment as to which of these views of ideal marital age is better: each person will, naturally, judge that best which is most to his liking.[62] Nor indeed (as I hope) do you wish from me some set of binding unchangeable laws on marriage ready to present, as they say, to the Centuriate Assembly.[63] But I shall follow especially those precepts that are known from the books of scholars or tested by experience, among which these are many that are praiseworthy, but may be altered according to circumstances, time, and occasion. For we must exercise judgment and prudence, which the ancients considered to be daughters of experience and memory. Since we have spoken, then, concerning the age at which marriage should occur, the next topic to consider is the social position of the wife, a rather more serious matter.

CHAPTER 3: FROM WHAT LINEAGE SHOULD A WIFE COME?

I would prefer, my dear Lorenzo, to be able to discuss the whole matter of lineage, giving voice to the many things that occur to me on the subject: certainly I would argue forcefully that our ancestral heritage should be valued most highly, as I believe, rather than, as is the custom, of allowing it daily to decay. But only those few things that are most useful and important are touched on here, while the rest I shall perhaps treat more fully at another time.[64]

Let us start in this matter by looking to nature itself. A flourishing pasture, planted and sown, is a strong argument to us that for the sake of our offspring, we should marry women of noble birth. For seeds are better or worse according to their origins; and the best seed bears the finest fruits. And we know that many, and indeed the finest kinds of berries, nuts, and fruits, if they are not planted in proper and suitable soil, will not bear fruit;[65] and if they are transplanted to an ignoble field, they lose their noble spirit, and "forgetting the sap they once had, the fruits wither"[66]; while fine young shoots, if they are grafted to weak branches, yield inferior buds.

---

61. Plutarch, *Apophthegmata laconica, Lycurgus,* 13.

62. *Magno se judice quisque tuetur:* Lucan, *Pharsalia,* 1.127.

63. The body of Roman citizens gathered and ordered by "centuries," or hundreds, according to property owned; it had legislative, as well as elective and judicial powers.

64. As Gnesotto observes at *De re uxoria,* 41 (19) n1, it does not appear that he ever did so.

65. Cf. Matthew 13:1–23; Mark 4:1–20.

66. Virgil, *Georgics,* 2.59.

All this is true also of humans, who can anticipate worthier offspring from women of greater worth; whose importance is such that, in most children, it is the particularly the mother's image that we recognize in traits of body and mind. Nor is there any doubt of the great weight of the woman's role in the generation of children; for as many worthy physicians have held,[67] the procreation of girls is entirely from the woman.[68] This however is of enormous importance, that in civil law the condition of the child is determined by that of the mother. For indeed, as Roman law decreed, all those were considered freeborn who had their origin from freeborn mothers, even if their fathers were slaves;[69] which provision we note the legislators of Lycia[70] also upheld, among whom, if a freeborn woman married a slave or a commoner, yet the children born from her were deemed noble.[71] Further testimony to this principle comes from the poets, who ascribed divinity to those whose mothers were goddesses. The day is not long enough for me to name them all; but Achilles, Aeneas, and Orpheus were considered to possess divinity precisely on this basis.[72]

Maternal nobility greatly affects not only the birthing, but also the rearing of children. Who is so ignorant that he does not perceive the great influence that mothers exert on the children they bear? For though the finest seed is sown in a field, to return to the metaphor used earlier, unless that field is cultivated with skill and diligence, it struggles to produce the most despicable fruit. With nobly-born mothers, it is far more likely that the splendor of the parents will shine forth with even greater brightness in their offspring; while unless we diligently attend to these matters, our offspring will be notorious for their defects rather than ennobled by their lineage.[73]

Further, the achievements and reputation of ancestors often have the effect that their descendants both are, and are deemed to be, worthy of high honors. At the same time, they strive with their own particular virtue that accrues to them as though by the laws of nature. They know, too, that if this innate virtue is not realized in action, they will be judged harshly by all, and know that they have degenerated from the ancestral standard. Equally, like soldiers accustomed to

67. Whom Barbaro does not name, but he is most likely recalling the discussions among the physicians at the University of Padua, where he had studied, about the rival Aristotelian and Galenic understandings of conception and embryology; cf. Gothein, *Das Buch von der Ehe*, 91–92n58.

68. Or that of males, one would think; but so the text reads: *non nisi ex femina femellarum procreatio*. Or has Barbaro anticipated the interactions of *x* and *y* chromosomes?

69. Justinian, *Institutes*, 1.4; Barbaro had studied Roman law while at the University of Padua.

70. In antiquity, a small country of Asia Minor between Caria and Pamphylia.

71. Herodotus, *History*, 1.173.

72. But see also Cicero, *De deorum natura*, 3.18.45.

73. An alternate manuscript reading would suggest also the opposition of illegitimate and legitimate offspring: Gnesotto 42 (20) n2.

trophies who are prompted to boldness by the glowing memory of their glorious past, so the recollection of domestic example will forcefully spur them on, like runners in a race.

The person born to an honorable rank acquires new honors easily. Who doubts that they will be preferred by universal consent (unless there are others who surpass them in some other form of excellence) to those of more humble birth? Who does not understand that, even if they are unworthy of honor by their own merits, yet often much is granted them because of the worthiness of their ancestors? History tells us that many men chose to die for their country, both so that they might perform their duty, but also so that they might leave the memory of their name as a rich patrimony to their sons. The Athenians fed at public expense those who had died for the sake of their country.[74] In Rome, a pedestrian statue was erected in the forum to any who died while serving as ambassador, if that service caused his death, as a monument to his honorable sacrifice, and so his sons would be honored by it in perpetuity.[75] Among us, if anyone is known to have served the republic during difficult and perilous times by his exceptional determination, effort, and deeds, not only is he rewarded with goods, wealth, and honor, but so also his children: to some even honorary citizenship is given, and a distinguished title.

These things are said for this reason: to establish that forebears confer advantage and fame on their progeny. This is true not only of fathers, but also of mothers, whose virtue and merits have often conferred much honor on their descendants. Those not so fortunate have suffered greatly from their ignoble status, unable to break the barrier of nobility, nor in any way to emerge from the obscurity of their ancestors into the light; for new men have always been despised. As the old proverb put it, dogs will viciously bite and snap at strangers from back, front, and side, but are docile with those familiar to them. Let us esteem, therefore, the noble origin of both our parents, and communicate it to our children. While other things are uncertain, shifting, and transitory, this legacy of nobility is fixed with secure roots, can withstand any force, and will never be destroyed.

Not that I would, however, approve the judgment of those who, though humbly born, seek to marry noble wives. We can rightly compare them to those who, when they cannot mount the high hump of a camel, have the beast kneel down in the Syrian manner, so they can mount; for such men cannot elevate themselves, but rather debase their wives.[76]

Therefore we praise those marriages especially by which we acquire honor, and so make our children more powerful and resplendent. For this reason the

---

74. Diogenes Laertius, *Solon*, 55.

75. Cicero, *Philippics*, 9.2, "pedestrian" here signaling a dignified, erect pose.

76. Plutarch, *Conjugalia praecepta*, 8. But for Plutarch, the kneeling beasts were horses, for whom Barbaro substitutes camels—presumably because he had seen them in action in his travels.

ancient Roman custom began by which husbands were prohibited to take as wives women who were closely related to them, lest the warmth of feeling between the spouses would be constricted because of this close relationship, and their children would be deprived thereby of the many advantages which follow when man and wife share a mutuality of interests.[77] To this may be added the marriage among clans, which unions form a kind of web that strangle the city.[78] But that plague and pest of the Roman empire Claudius Nero extorted the decree from the senate that made marriage legal between uncles and the daughters of their brothers, so that he might, protected by public authority, pursue his unbound and impotent lust. Yet no one of any rank befouled himself by this crime except for one Roman knight, T. Alledius Severus, who did so, many worthy authors say, at the behest of Agrippina.[79]

Therefore let us take noble wives—just as you, Lorenzo, have most wisely done—so that our domestic life may be more pleasant, and having acquired sons ennobled both by nature and by nurture, and having prepared them for glory by the example of their forebears, we may abundantly bestow upon them honor and power. For they shall honor the memory of those from whom they have their origin, think about them always, incline their soul to them, so that the merit that they acquire not only from their father, but also from their mother, they may piously and righteously transmit, as though an inheritance, to their own descendants.

CHAPTER 4: SHOULD A WIFE BE CHOSEN FOR HER BEAUTY?

Now it is time for me to approach that issue with which the discussion of marriage usually begins, by those who would have omitted all that has been said above. In the following paragraphs I shall speak of beauty, which concerns, as many think, the most desirable bodily size, and the appearance of the hair, eyes, face, neck, and hands. Females of small stature, even if the rest of their bodies are properly composed, I find to be more apt for a whore than a wife; for their stature suits them more for pleasure than for the duty to procreate offspring. For this reason the Spartan Ephors laid a heavy fine on king Archidamus, when he took a wife of diminutive size, as though he wished to leave as progeny not kings, but kinglets.[80] And lest I go on for too long providing other examples, a woman's hair so greatly

---

77. Plutarch, *Quaestiones romanae*, #108.

78. In Barbaro's day, Venetian laws barring close relatives from voting in certain circumstances evidence this same anxiety about the potential of clan ties to distort the functioning of government.

79. Cf. Tacitus, *Annals*, 12.7. Barbaro writes Talledius, an error corrected here.

80. Plutarch, *De liberis educandis*, 1d (2.2). I have adopted "kinglet" from the apt rendering by translator Frank Cole Babbitt in vol. 1 (1927) of the Loeb Classical Library 16-volume bilingual edition of *Plutarch's Moralia* (Cambridge, MA: Harvard University Press; London: Heinemann, 1927–2004),

pleases men, that Homer often called his Helen beautiful on account of this one feature: her lovely hair.[81] And does not Virgil, when he describes a wise man, but also handsome, adduce in brief strokes this one component of beauty?: "like a god in shoulders and face: since his mother had herself imparted to her son beauty to his hair, a glow of youth, and a joyful charm to his eyes … ."[82] Believe me, Lorenzo, if Mars had seen Venus shorn of her hair, the ardor that possessed that bellicose god would have vanished posthaste, so that he never would have been entrapped by the arts of Vulcan.[83]

This beauty of which I speak, a citizen of your city of Florence, whom I do not name for the sake of honor,[84] considers to be either the sole or the most important requirement in a wife. Yet I would not concede to him that beauty—although I do not want to deprive it of all worth—is to be valued above all other things. Its power is indeed so great that it has vanquished, and may yet vanquish, the conquerors of nations. Jupiter himself, according to the poets the father of men and of gods, transformed himself into a rain-cloud or a swan or other various guises, so that he might enjoy that beauty by which he had been conquered.[85] I shall say no more about the others thought by the ancients to be gods over whom, according to Anacreon, Cupid triumphs.[86] Many were believed to be immortal, the ancients tell us, on account of their beauty alone. Indeed, Paris—he who disdained the lordship of Asia and victory in battle in order to pursue Helen, whom he found most beautiful—judged with the greatest diligence the contest in which those outstanding goddesses Juno, Minerva, and Venus competed to determine which was the most beautiful.[87]

Indeed it is a great and most beautiful thing that the appearance of loveliness in itself is viewed as divine and worthy of many honors. Who is so removed from the human condition that such beauty has not affected him? Nearly everyone loves those who are attractive, believes them deserving of authority, and willingly obeys them. As the wise poet Virgil aptly puts it: "… ability is more pleasing in a

---

available online at http://penelope.uchicago.edu/Thayer/E/Roman/Texts/Plutarch/Moralia/De_liberis_educandis*.html#copyright.

81. But as Gnesotto observes at *De re uxoria*, 45 (23) n2, he does not do so, and certainly not *saepissime*.

82. Virgil, *Aeneid*, 1.589–91, trans. A.S. Kline (2002), from the website *Poetry in Translation*, http://www.poetryintranslation.com/PITBR/Latin/VirgilAeneidI.htm#_Toc535054304.

83. Cf. Homer, *Odyssey*, 8:264–96.

84. It has not been possible to identify this Florentine figure.

85. Alluding to myths Barbaro may have read in Ovid's *Metamorphoses*, including those describing Zeus's conquests of Leda and Danae.

86. Cupid, the small blind son of Venus, who shoots the arrow of love creating victims of desire; Anacreon, a Greek lyric poet (582–485 BCE) who celebrated erotic love.

87. The myth of the judgment of Paris, retold by several authors, including Virgil, Apuleius, and Lucan.

beautiful body."[88] For even if virtue is better than beauty, yet I do not know that it is more appealing. The brave, the wise, the just—if they are ugly, the multitude respects rather than loves them. For this reason Plato used wittily to admonish Xenocrates, whose body was greatly deformed, that he should sacrifice often to the Graces;[89] for his wisdom, when conjoined with the baseness of his members, was repellent to most, and barely tolerable to many.

But to what end is all this discussion? Because we choose to live with beautiful wives—for whom many would even die. Nor is this love of beauty the same as lust, which a great and serious soul repels as rocks do the waves, but it does bear upon the procreation of offspring, and the joyful friendliness of a shared life. Virgil has Juno makes this point sensibly, who in persuading Aeolus names these benefits of marriage to a beautiful wife:

> I have fourteen Nymphs of outstanding beauty:
> of whom I'll name Deiopea, the loveliest in looks,
> joined in eternal marriage, and yours for ever, so that,
> for such service to me as yours, she'll spend all her years
> with you, and make you the father of lovely children.[90]

We must accordingly value beauty in wives, or any fool will know that I am telling a silly tale. I realize that in my zeal to acknowledge the force of beauty I have gone on at greater length than the matter requires; wherefore I come to a close, and move on to the next issue.

Although I have written here much about beauty, yet I want still to affirm, that if beauty be joined to noble character and other admirable qualities, I would value it highly; but apart from these, I would in no way praise it. For just as fire is easily ignited from kindling, and unless sturdier wood is added, then easily dissipates, so the love between man and woman, if excited by the loveliness of the body, unless a worthy mind, good character, and sanctity of life nourish it, is soon extinguished.[91] When it had been reported to Olympias that one of the king's courtiers had taken a wife who was beautiful to look at but, it was said, of dubious reputation, she said, "This young man, if he had had consulted prudent men older than he more often than he consulted with himself, would not have let his eyes

---

88. Virgil, *Aeneid*, 5.344, trans. A.S. Kline (2002), from the website *Poetry in Translation*, http://www.poetryintranslation.com/PITBR/Latin/VirgilAeneidV.htm#_Toc1537953. Gothein points out the echoes here of Plato's *Phaedrus*: Gothein, *Das Buch von der Ehe*, 92n71.

89. Based on Plutarch, *Conjugalia praecepta*, 28.

90. Virgil, *Aeneid*, 1.71–75, trans. A.S. Kline (2002), from the website *Poetry in Translation*, http://www.poetryintranslatiwon.com/PITBR/Latin/VirgilAeneidI.htm#_Toc535054291.

91. Plutarch, *Conjugalia praecepta*, 4.

choose a wife for him."[92] For this kind of loveliness, unless it is in itself a certain and explicit sign of probity, it is worthy of no praise or celebration. This point is made clearly by the great sage and poet Homer in his portrayal of Nireus, who was, after Achilles, the most handsome of all the Greeks; but who after he arrived in Aulus together with the others was never spoken about, nor in any way remembered.[93] For he performed no great deeds in Troy, whose proper reward is glory, making those who earned it demigods, memorialized by Homer, forever after.

Not only should wives not be cherished for their beauty alone, but not even whores should be; concerning which I bring to mind the man Philip of Padua.[94] Born to a rich father of noble origin, he was dying of love for a beautiful courtesan, from whose seductions his father's authority and kindness could not separate him. When his father heard that his son, with great peril to his reputation, was suffering with this disease, he resolved to cure it. He paid the mercenary harlot sworn to Venus to stay in his house with his son, where she slept with him and had intercourse with him, so that for a few days, overpowered by the titillation of his senses, the boy was lost, convinced she was his greatest and only good. But some time later, when passion had diminished with excess and he began to tire from overindulgence in pleasure, what he had especially loved in her he now despised, so that gradually the youth recovered, and, by his father's care, was liberated from a fierce and furious disease.

What kind of a wife will she be, if she who should be joined to us by dignity and friendliness is tied to us only by beauty?[95] But why do I extend this discussion further, as if I were discussing some weighty topic? Let us love beautiful women, if they possess the other qualities necessary to make marriage delightful for us, and honorable and advantageous for our progeny.

CHAPTER 5: SHOULD A WIFE BE CHOSEN FOR HER WEALTH?

Concerning character, age, birth, and beauty, I believe, I have spoken sufficiently. Now, as planned, I shall speak about wealth, the one remaining issue to be considered in choosing a wife, making a few points that are useful in this matter. Since therefore we value all that promotes the worthiness and honor of marriage, and our own ease, abundance, possessions, and riches, we must husband such wealth for its dignity and utility, whose fruits are gratitude, liberality, and magnificence, virtues which shine indeed with a supreme splendor. However much we may be

---

92. Adapted from Plutarch, *Conjugalia praecepta*, 24.

93. Homer, *Iliad*, 2.671–74.

94. Gnesotto speculates that Barbaro heard this story during student days in Padua: *De re uxoria*, xiii.

95. The London 1677 edition, at 36, based on Amsterdam 1639 and its alternate underlying text, here names a series of pairs of lovers omitted in the text before us: Menelaus and Helen, Vulcan and Venus, Minos and Pasiphae, Theseus and Phaedra, and the emperor Claudius and Messalina.

by nature grateful, beneficent, and munificent, yet in our roles as generals, ambassadors, or physicians, we shall not merit high praise unless we have declared those virtues in our actions.

So wealth is most useful for many purposes. For it permits us to reward others fittingly, and allows us to confer much on our closest friends and connections; and in turn, we shall benefit our own children with the wealth, riches, and benevolence of those to whom we have been generous—for parents are loved and respected in their children. No duty can be viewed as more pressing than that of repaying a benefit, such that whoever has willingly failed to do so, he has surely sinned against God Almighty, his country, his parents, his family, his friends, and his patrons. He betrays all those, in sum, by whose beneficence he has been bound but whom he has not benefited in turn, nor repaid.[96] By the excellent laws of the Persians, accordingly, ingrates were severely punished; for as Herodotus reports, the worst vice among them was to lie, but the next, to be in debt. And why not? Arguably, he who is not ashamed to be in debt to another, will both in many ways often fail or fall short in performing the office of a good man, and will also frequently lie.[97]

We value wealth most highly for this reason, therefore, which even if we ourselves do not require it, yet, as is abundantly evident, it is honorably employed for the benefit of friends and the whole human race. Alexander sent to Phocion, that excellent man, a great weight of gold as a gift, but that austere and upright man refused it, since money was of no use to him. Alexander then asked whether he had any persons bound to him because of their honorably shared studies or style of life; it would be right to exercise liberality and bestow a benefit on them. "For whatever you choose to do, Phocion, as such you will be seen." The incredible wealth of Darius, in fact, was scarcely sufficient for Alexander, since he most liberally assisted the fortunes of those whose health and well-being were dear to him.[98] Such liberality will be also a great aid to our children, so that, as is most commendable, freeborn youth may be reared and instructed in excellent studies and arts. Endowed with these benefits, these offspring may be worthy of those honorable men, their fathers, and render their ancestors still more illustrious.

This being the case, a diligent accounting must be made of wealth, lest we are judged to have begrudged our family members and advanced instead our own ease and comfort. As for that, however, if wine is mixed with water, even if there is a greater portion of water than of wine, yet we call it wine, so wealth and possessions we consider to belong to the man and not his wife, even if the woman contributed the greater and more weighty part; since what matters, I would judge,

96. The above several sentences on the duty to repay benefits are based on Cicero, *De officiis*, 1.42–50.

97. Herodotus, *History*, 1.138.1.

98. Based on Plutarch, *Regum et imperatorum apophthegmata, Alexander Magnus*, 27.30. Barbaro substitutes Phocion for Xenocrates, the fortunate recipient in the original.

is not who has brought the most, but who has best improved the household's fortunes. Wherefore, just as the physicians hold that our health requires that moisture be dispersed through all parts of the body, so in the same way we suggest that those who are joined in marriage should fuse into one whole not only their wealth (about which we now speak), but also their loving and conjoined souls. For this reason it was rightly established by Roman law that neither husband nor wife should hold any wealth for himself, so that they would understand that nothing was owned privately, but all things were held by both in common, by which principle the household would be managed with greater care, diligence, and good faith.[99] What Dion said to Dionysius is true: everyone is more diligent in caring for his own affairs than those of another.[100] For which reason princes should be taught that the cities of their realm are like their own homes, the citizens their children, and themselves the householders, so that they will manage with care, counsel, industry, and vigilance those over whom they have authority, considering their health and fortune, and furthering their prosperity. But more about this later.

I wish that we lived in that age long ago when young people could be taught, and not misled as they are now, that they should not too greatly esteem wealth and possessions in marriage: truly that would have better served the interests of the human community. But most young men have been from their childhood so infused and imbued with the love of gain that they will perform any labor and expend any effort to acquire and achieve it, not neglecting any path by which they think they may satisfy their avarice. I prefer, however, not to incite or inflame our youth to acquire wealth through marriage, but rather I urge them, if they can afford to do so, to consider the other factors I have written about here in choosing a wife. I fear I shall be criticized for saying this; yet I must say what I believe. I cannot accuse those enough, who however wealthy they may be themselves, still zealously seek wives who possess in no way the qualities necessary in a wife.

For just as mirrors adorned with gold and pearls are of no use to us if they do not accurately reflect the image before them, so I count wealth in a wife utterly useless unless she reflects the image of her husband's character in the cordiality of her manner.[101] Alexander is praised because, as many attest, he took as his wife Barsines, a daughter of the royal line of Artabazes, by whom he fathered his son Hercules; she was a modest girl learned in Greek literature, but poor, while he with his great soul disdained marriage to a daughter of Darius and a measureless mountain of gold.[102] There can be found many, both princes and private citizens, who as in other things so also in their contempt for wealth in a wife were and

---

99. For the above passage, see Plutarch, *Conjugalia praecepta*, 20, 34; Xenophon, *Oeconomicus*, 7.13.

100. Ps.-Aristotle, *Economics*, 1.6=1344b.

101. Plutarch, *Conjugalia praecepta*, 14.

102. Plutarch, *Alexander*, 21.

are considered great, with whose praise, like a galaxy of stars, history sparkles. But there is a greater number of those whose appetite cannot be satisfied with any quantity of estates, of villas, or of luxurious furnishings; and since they are impoverished in the midst of great wealth, so they desire not more worthy, but more lucrative marriages. And just as those untrained in the equestrian art make much of horses with splendid equipage; and those ignorant of the military art vaunt their golden helmets; and those without learning display their worthless books—useless, dull, and full of lies, though bound with gilded covers; so most men seek out wives whose coffers are full—not coffers, in truth, but glittering coffins, as my learned and beloved mentor Guarino used to say.[103] For inside these, while their ornamented surface is encrusted with a variety of adornments, there is within nothing worthy, but rather the greatest filth, fetor, even defilement,[104] and many other such horrors that only the dead can bear. The excellent Phyrgian writer Aesop, whose fables convey serious messages in a humorous tone, wishing to advise us concerning this matter, told this charming tale: a fox having taken on the job of musician took up a lyre, whose rounded lower part was crafted in the form of a human head, designed marvellously with skill, art, industry, and fitted out with gold and gems, which he closely observed, and said: "This head is magnificent, certainly, but it has no brain inside."[105] We might say the same of wealthy women, unless they are able to fulfill the office of wife.

The rash Paris took wealthy Helen for his wife; but the prudent Ulysses took chaste Penelope, than whom no other in her time was more pure or modest. This latter marriage the ancients admire, love, and endlessly praise; the marriage of the former, in contrast, was recorded for posterity as wholly ignominious, inasmuch as it brought to Asia fire, plague, devastation, and ruin. These tragedies, clearly, happened because, to serve his passions, Paris went in search of wealth.[106] For this reason Lycurgus prudently decreed that wives should be married without dowries, so that Spartan girls would neither remain unmarried on account of their poverty, nor marry on account of their wealth. For he understood that Spartan men would naturally seek for virtue in their wives, not wealth, and Spartan women would strive more earnestly to acquire virtue.[107] So that this goal might be more easily accomplished, those ancient demigods, as though perched in a watchtower so

103. Barbaro recalls his teacher Guarino Veronese, for whom see the Introduction, 3, 4–6.

104. Reading *inquilinus* as *inquinatus*.

105. Aesop's fable of "The Fox and the Mask," no. 27 in Perry's Index to the *Aesopica*, http://mythfolk-lore.net/aesopica/perry/27.htm, and found in, among others editions, *The Fables of Aesop*, ed. Joseph Jacobs, illustrated Richard Heighway (London: Macmillan, 1922), available at http://en.wikisource.org/wiki/The_Fables_of_%C3%86sop_%28Jacobs%29/The_Fox_and_the_Mask. I am most grateful to Cheryl Lemmens for locating this fable, not available in earlier standard editions.

106. Plutarch, *Conjugalia praecepta*, 21.

107. Plutarch, *Apophthegmata laconica, Lycurgus,* 15.

that they could see long into the future so as to benefit their posterity, decreed that wives not bring a dowry to men—as we do in our age—but that men should bring a marriage-gift to their wives, so that husbands would not depend on the fortunes of women, but would rather exert themselves to care for their wives, to whom their own welfare, and that of their children and all their household, would be committed.[108] This wise ordinance should be reinstated, I believe—if only bad customs had not altered our minds, and luxuries over time corrupted us—and not left to die. For if we pay farmers and laborers to cultivate our fields, so that we may spend the profit in turn on things that are useful to us, why should we not also do so for a wife, from whom we expect such necessary, and such sweet fruit?

But unless we first free ourselves from pleasure, that seductive tyrant, and cast away the precious garments and fripperies befitting a lecher, and the other supposed necessities we do not really need, and quell that desire that is content with no limit, we shall never be able to think rationally and freely about marriage. But since this subject has been explored at length, there is not much more to be said at this time. So let our young men collect themselves, and consider marriage with more care and less greed—here they might follow your example—lest for the sake of money, or in the hope of gain, they make themselves slaves to a dowry, and so kindle a domestic fire that cannot easily be put out. If they wish to do what is best for them and their families, as I recommend, they will select wives endowed with virtue, youth, nobility, beauty, and wealth. If any one of these should be lacking, I shall soon explain which should be preferred; but first, as is both excellent and necessary, I must respond to my critics.

CHAPTER 6: FOR WHAT CAUSES IT MAY BE NECESSARY TO ALTER THESE PRECEPTS

Perhaps someone will ask, "What are you doing? You have assigned to yourself the task of offering advice on the selection of a wife, but then you ignore those who are poor and humble, and only instruct the very wealthy." The response to this is obvious. I would greatly prefer that these jottings of mine could be equally useful for all. But if there is someone who cannot follow my advice, either because of lowliness of birth or lack of funds, let him rage at his misfortune, not my precepts.[109] So let us return to the matter before us.

I also suspect that others will agree that all the points I have argued above should be duly observed, but contend that they are to be wished for, but not easily attained. Their objection forces me now to introduce this comparison: indeed,

---

108. Codex Justinianus, 5.3.20. *Pace* Gnesotto, *De re uxoria*, 52 (30) n4, Barbaro is not here speaking of Spartan, but later Roman law.

109. The whole of this paragraph is drawn from Plutarch, *De liberis educandis*, 8e (11).

they cannot all be Lorenzos,[110] to whom, superbly endowed in soul, body, and fortune, wives of every sort and every rank are available. So to these I believe it is sufficient to give the same response which I gave above, since that argument is also valid here.

Yet there frequently occur many circumstances, whether of time, or necessity, or chance, in which it is permissible, as learned men agree, to alter our rules. For as Pericles sagely advised Tolmides,[111] we must consider the decision of time, the wisest of judges.[112] And just as the suitors of Penelope, when they despaired of obtaining her, eagerly and willingly pursued her handmaidens,[113] so if we cannot win as wives the most excellent of women, let us, to the extent that our dignity allows, take those whom we can. Nor should we act like those ridiculous suitors—like children, who to the amusement of all observers put on their parents' shoes—who, though low-born and poor, strive to marry women whose sublime and consummate merit is in every way apparent. I do not hesitate to warn them, lest to the derision of all, they be seen to resemble the Aesopian camels who, in the council of the beasts, expressed a desire for horns like the deer; in response, their own ears were nearly all ripped off, as a lesson to others that they should remain content within their own limits.[114] Young men should pursue wives, then, in accord with their capacity; the failures of others will amply warn them, so let them take care, so as not themselves to become an object of scorn. Regarding which that old saying comes to mind, useful in many circumstances, and particularly apt in this one: equals are best suited to equals. For what could be more pleasant, what more comfortable, what more easy, than to take as a wife a woman equal to oneself?[115] Thus I strongly disagree with those for whom nothing appears more equal than inequality itself.

After this the issue of character must be considered, to which in this matter of marriage I always accord first place. For if her character inclines to things other than virtue, or at least an aptitude for good behavior, I shall not find there grounds for great praise. The great orator Demosthenes, when asked what was the first requirement of eloquence, responded, "pronunciation." To this same requirement he accorded the second and also the third rank of importance, so that clearly he awarded it the victor's crown as a prerequisite for oratory. To this may be added the weighty testimony of Hortensius, who although in other regards he

---

110. An allusion to Cicero, *Cato the Elder (de senectute)*, 5.13: "not everyone can be a Scipio or a Maximus … ."

111. The Athenian general, active in the 450s and 440s BCE.

112. Plutarch, *Pericles*, 18.

113. Plutarch, *De liberis educandis*, 7d (10).

114. Not Aesop but Flavius Avianus, "De camelo," in *The Fables of Avianus,* ed. Robinson Ellis (Oxford: Clarendon Press, 1887), 10–11, no. 8.

115. Plutarch, *De liberis educandis*, 13f (19).

was inferior to many, in this skill he was believed to surpass nearly all others.[116] The preeminence Demosthenes gave to pronunciation in the matter of oratory, we may assign, in that of marriage, to virtue. Wherefore let us esteem character, to be placed in the forefront ahead of all other qualities, since without this a marriage cannot properly be approved; for a sound marriage is characterized before all else by obedience, ease, and comity, and leaves no room for insults or rebuffs or any of the issues brought before the goddess Viriplaca.[117] A certain Roman repudiated his wife, who was noble, rich, and beautiful, which aroused a great deal of astonishment and criticism; to which he replied, wanting to defend his decision, with foot outstretched, "This sandal, as you can see, is both new and beautiful; but that it hurts me, I alone know."[118]

Not dowry, therefore, nor family origin, nor beauty, as I see it, but rather virtue and moral goodness should determine the choice of a wife who is to cherish nothing more than the will of her husband.[119] If the girl has been reared nobly to be of sound character, the component of beauty is secondary. Socrates urged young men to regard themselves in their mirrors: if they find they are ugly, their virtue may make them handsome and desirable; but if they are comely, they should beware lest their sins steal from them this gift of nature.[120] So is it too with wives: though they were not born beautiful, if they have youth, chastity, and noble birth, they are incontrovertibly beautiful enough, to agree with Gorgias, who argued that the excellence of a wife should be measured by her reputation, not her beauty;[121] but if they happen to be beautiful, we shall love them all the more. If they excel in other ways, marriages to women humbly-born or poor, as the great king Agamemnon shows by his example, should not be disapproved. For he valued the captive Chryseides more than Clytemnestra, the daughter of Jove,[122] since he judged her to be superior in body, face, prudence, and many skills beside.[123]

He who is eager to accumulate wealth should change course, and realize that it is better for him to acquire a good rather than a wealthy wife. Themistocles testified to this when he responded, having been asked by some father whether he should give his one daughter in marriage to a man who was good but poor, or one less worthy, but rich: "I would greatly prefer that you have for a son-in-law

116. Quintilian, *Institutio oratoria*, 11.3.6 and 8.

117. For the Romans, the goddess Viriplaca was one of Juno's manifestations, charged with reconciliations especially of couples, and to whom was devoted a temple on the Palatine hill.

118. Plutarch, *Conjugalia praecepta*, 22; *Aemilius Paullus*, 5.2–3.

119. Plutarch, *Conjugalia praecepta*, 22.

120. Cf. Plutarch, *Conjugalia praecepta*, 25.

121. Plutarch, *De mulierum virtutibus*, 242f.

122. That is, Zeus.

123. Homer, *Iliad*, 1.113–15.

a man who lacks wealth, than wealth which lacks a man."[124] What that prince among the Greeks holds for husbands, I hold true for wives. For it is right that we choose wives for ourselves, not wives for their riches. Accordingly the Ephors justly punished those Spartans who promised to take the daughters of Lysander as wives while he was alive, but declined to do so once he was dead; for though they had courted these young women when wealthy, they scarcely hid their contempt for them when they had become poor, despite their fine breeding.[125]

What more is there to say? To sum up, we must take care that we marry those women who in all regards are honorable, loving, and pleasant. If there is any uncertainty, we must diligently inquire about each detail. And just as it pleased Automedon and others who served as master of the horses,[126] we consider those horses sound and worthy in whom more features can be approved than censured, so we shall count those women worthy of the honor of matrimony in whom we recognize either many of the qualities we have defined, or the most important ones. Nor do I wish to burden the men of our generation with so many prerequisites for a wife—for all that I wish and desire is difficult and nearly infinite, yet I require all of it; but let them demand virtue, and with it, they may be confident that all else will follow. Concerning these matters, it seems to me, there is no point in saying more. All the rest is common knowledge, and those striving judiciously and wisely will easily succeed.

CHAPTER 7: CELEBRATING THE WEDDING

It remains for me to speak of wifely duties, about which there is such fullness of joy, sweetness, loveliness, and all that is in every way so beautiful to behold, that, overwhelmed by the force of ideas, I almost neglected one thing that must first be presented here. For surely, before I come to the second part of this work, I must say a few words about the wedding ceremony itself, which, though they are now forgotten and nearly obliterated, I shall recover from the records of antiquity. For it will illumine this matter which is now before us if we apply our minds to what the wise men of antiquity believed concerning the pomp and splendor of weddings, whose customs indeed we have to a great extent imitated. Concerning this matter there exist many profound precepts, while many more still can be adduced, which should not be neglected, since they pertain to so great a matter. So if I am expected in this commentary to describe how a man should take his chosen wife in matrimony, I shall supply a few brief notes taken from records of the distant past.

124. Based on Plutarch, *Regum et imperatorum apophthegmata, Themistocles*, 11.

125. Plutarch, *Apophthegmata laconica, Lysander*, 15.

126. Automedon was equerry to Achilles; he is used here as a stand-in for all expert horse handlers.

Marriage has its origin in God,[127] who from the time of creation conferred reason on the learned, exigency on the barbarous, law on the nations, and caused nature herself to come into being. From the first, the ancients ordered these sacred things with such great care that God himself was the most visible and important witness to the sacred union of man and woman. At this event, the eternal God, as he is known to us, would be invoked—or Hymen by the Athenians, or Talassius by the Romans—to make the marriage good, fruitful, joyous, and fortunate.[128] Now this Talassius was an agreeable youth, beloved, commended, and praised by all, and among the comrades dearest to Romulus conspicuous for martial glory. Amidst the rape of the Sabines, a certain exceptional young woman sought refuge with him, who, while he protected her honor, was seized by some of his unknowing companions. But with his gracious and popular appeal, Talassius liberated her from imminent danger. Their joyful marriage followed, introducing the custom of invoking his name in connection with weddings.[129]

So great is the strength, so strong the connection of this matrimonial contract (to return to the matter from which we have strayed), that the love of children for parents, although it glows brightly, is exceeded by the splendor of its binding force. For in his love for his wife, the husband is permitted, by the authority of both ancestral example and our own religion, to fix the eyes of his soul on her to such an extent that, putting all else aside, he may revere, delight in, and serve her alone.[130] Homer's powerful witness may be noted here, whose Hector, while he bravely faces the deaths of his parents, brothers, and even his country, cannot bear to think about the terrible destiny awaiting his cherished wife Andromache. In this moment, that valiant pagan hero is so weak, so soft, that he seems to have become someone else altogether. Exalted by the glory of his great deeds, he was unconcerned about his own fate, but deeply anxious about hers, lamenting with groans and sighs.[131] Lest I go on too long, then, we shall be content with this one example: for there is a huge crowd of them, and many more than I would wish, from every race and nation, which are often conflated with each other, and their authors charged with impiety.[132]

---

127. Cf. Virgil, *Eclogue* 3.60.

128. Hymen, the Greek god of marriage ceremonies and other festival occasions; Talassius, a legendary figure invoked at weddings, for whom see following note.

129. Plutarch, *Romulus*, 15; but also Plutarch, *Quaestiones romanae*, 31; Livy, *Histories*, 1.9.12.

130. As, for instance, in Genesis 2:24: "That is why [referring to Eve's creation from Adam's rib] a man leaves his father and mother and is united to his wife, and they become one flesh."

131. Homer, *Iliad*, 6: 450–65.

132. Barbaro refers to two issues that Giovanni Boccaccio addressed in his encyclopedic *Genealogia deorum antiquorum* (Genealogy of the ancient gods): the complex duplications and conflations of classical tales and myths, and the discrediting of their pagan authors for unbelief.

For now I omit the wreaths, with which both the bride and the doorposts are customarily decorated. And I pass by for the moment the carpets and other elaborate accoutrements, of which I do not at all disapprove, but judge rather to be suited to the magnificence of the event. The custom endures of placing a ring on the bride's finger, specifically the one next to the shortest finger of the left hand, which is called the ring-finger, it is believed, for this reason: that so placed, the ring presents to her eyes a perpetual monument of her great love for her husband; and from this finger, according to some authors, a nerve extends directly to the heart.[133] Then, as was the custom, water and fire were placed before the bride, so that she could touch both, so as to demonstrate her responsibility for the procreation of children. For just as heat and moisture, which qualities these elements possess, are the cause of generation, so the marriage of male and female exists above all for the generation of offspring.[134]

It is customary, too, that brides avoid touching the threshold of their husband's house, but they are carried over it, so as to declare, for the sake of modesty, that they do not enter willingly but are in some way coerced.[135] Similarly, among those ancients it was sacred law that virgins be married only on certain days, and particularly on the First Days of the months, which were dedicated to Janus, so that if it seemed that they had been taken by force, the sin would be expiated. Yet no religious stricture prevented widows from marrying at this time—since, as Verrius Flaccus writes, it was permitted to drain tilled fields on the sacred days, but not to plow new ones.[136] A pagan custom also required that if anyone approached the gateway to the temple of Janus who seemed dishevelled and rude, he was not permitted to touch the threshold, but was to be carried over it. On festal days as well, such as those of the Lupercalia, Megalensia, or Circenses,[137] or any other spectacle attended by a large gathering of the people, virgins were not permitted to be married, while widows were allowed to do so. Some think that these rules were established for the excellent reason that on these days virgins recalled what they could never forget, that the Sabine women were raped on a festival day—which event was not only shameful in itself, but triggered a terrible and devastating war. But marriage was not prohibited on this day to widows, or to those who had been repudiated by their husbands; for it was seen to be no

133. Macrobius, *Saturnalia*, 7.13.7.

134. Plutarch, *Quaestiones romanae*, 1.

135. Plutarch, *Quaestiones romanae*, 29.

136. Macrobius, *Saturnalia*, 1.15.21, reports this pronouncement of Marcus Verrius Flaccus, a Roman grammarian and philologist of the first century CE, based on ancient calendrical prohibitions.

137. Major Roman festivals: the Lupercalia, celebrated February 13 to 15, assured the purification of the city and restoration of health and fertility; the Megalensia were celebrated April 4 to 10 in honor of the goddess Cybele, the Magna Mater (Great Mother); the Circenses were games celebrated on August 28 at the Circus Maximus for the Sun and Moon.

great cause for shame if those who had prior husbands either dead or still living celebrated their weddings while the people at large were off and otherwise occupied at the theater.[138]

If our resources permit, weddings may be celebrated with magnifience, lest we be denied this kind of honor. For many famous men have praised banquets and gladiatorial games and the provision of public entertainments; with these Theophrastus so busied himself, that he considered this kind of expenditure, which purchased the good will of the multitude, to be the fruit of wealth.[139] Or I might name here the aediles Quintus Mucius, Gaius Appius, Hortensius, Silanus, Publius Lentulus, Scaurus, Pompey, the Crassi, and the Luculli, who, as was their duty, zealously performed the function of providing public entertainment.[140] Still, this sort of expense has been and is condemned by many sage men;[141] though I find no one who forbids splendor in weddings, and many who would praise it. The learned Aristotle, who is often called the lord and prince of philosophers, in the books he left on "ethics,"[142] also approved of this kind of magnificent show for high-ranking men.[143] The respected and renowned philosopher Manuel Chrysoloras chose a wife for his nephew John,[144] a learned and upstanding man of the equestrian order, whose wedding was celebrated with a most splendid show; and when one of his companions charged that the display diminished the dignity of that grave philosopher, he replied, "God preserve us! It is permitted us on joyous occasions to have magnificent celebrations; and for the honor of our family, so long as we do no injury to our neighbors, this kind of splendor is never prohibited."

What more is there to say? The thing speaks for itself, as it always can exceedingly well, and does not require a longer exposition. Besides lavish banquets, which may be condemned in other settings but are suitable for weddings, we may, in the Sabine fashion, also introduce witty conversation so that no opportunity may be lacking for refreshing both body and soul.[145] For the same purpose, actors

---

138. Plutarch, *Quaestiones romanae*, 105; Macrobius, *Saturnalia*, 1.15.21.

139. Cicero, *De officiis,* 2.16.56.

140. Cicero, *De officiis*, 2.16.57, where Cicero names some but not all of the figures Barbaro introduces: Quintus Mucius and Lucius Crassus, colleagues as aediles; and the aediles Gaius Claudius Appius, Hortensius, Silanus, the Luculli, Scaurus, Publius Lentulus, and Pompey. He does not name the Crassi.

141. Cicero, *De officiis*, 2.16.56.

142. Barbaro was familiar with the *Nicomachean Ethics,* which he presently cites.

143. Aristotle, *Nicomachean Ethics,* 1122b, 1123a.

144. John Chrysoloras, nephew and disciple of Manuel (1355–1415), famed statesman and initiator of Greek studies in Italy and revered teacher of Barbaro's teacher Guarino, who was the likely source of this anecdote.

145. Pliny, *Natural History*, 31.41, at end, attributes to salt the capacity to promote relaxation, delight, and hilarity, and further discusses the Sabine commerce in salt; drawing on this passage, Barbaro

may be employed, whose reputation in Rome was so great that, when all the great practitioners of that art had died, players were summoned from your Etruria, the most flourishing province of Italy. Of these the most senior and expert was named Histrus,[146] as Cluvius Rufus reports,[147] as a result of which the others afterwards were all termed *histriones*—just as the Epicureans, Pythagoreans, and Gnathones[148] acquired the names of their founders.

In former times as in our own age, all those invited to the wedding—close family and kin of all sorts—will delight in attending, so that all to whom either the honor or the pleasure of the ceremony pertains may join with the others in rejoicing. Solon, one of the seven sages, required the new bride to eat a Cydonian apple, so as to signify that her voice and speech should be pleasing and sweet to her husband.[149] When she enters the bridal chamber to perform her marital duty, the virgin's face is veiled, and in the dark;[150] with Venus as handmaid, her husband embraces her as his spouse; then, "nestled in her bosom, languor spreads through all his limbs."[151] Thus do we imagine it happens, unless her virgin bashfulness, as is right, pertinaciously resists the lawful embrace. And so that nothing sorrowful might interrupt this joyous celebration, it was the custom to scatter nuts, so that over the clamor of children collecting them, the sounds the newlywed emits due either to pain or lost innocence might not be heard by the crowd gathered outside.[152]

There are many reasons why I should say no more. First, if I continue to speak about this matter, I shall offend your ears, which, now that you have devoted your soul, concern, and passion to these divine humanities,[153] should be greeted by nothing but pure speech and a grave and learned message. Further, because I think enough has been said to gently urge our friends[154]—to the extent that the sanctity of our religion allows—to love and admire our ancestors, whose

---

associates with the Sabines the addition of witty or "salty" conversation to the banquet experience.

146. Plutarch, *Quaestiones romanae*, 107.

147. Correcting Claudius Rufus in original; cf. Tacitus, *Histories*, 1.8.

148. For the Gnathones (Parasites), see Plutarch, *Quaestiones convivales*, 707e. The Epicureans and Pythagoreans were philosophical schools founded by Epicurus and Pythagoras respectively.

149. Plutarch, *Conjugalia praecepta*, 1. The Cydonian apple can be identified as the quince, a fruit thought to freshen the breath and cure sore throat.

150. Plutarch, *Quaestiones romanae*, 65.

151. Virgil, *Aeneid*, 8.405–6. My translation.

152. Cf. Servius, *Commentary* on Virgil, *Eclogue* 8.29, 30.

153. Barbaro writes *haec divina studia humanitatis*, conflating the concept of the *studia humanitatis*, those disciplines favored by the humanists, with what is "divine" and "sacred"—i.e., Christian. He will do so again below; see note 298.

154. Barbaro writes *ut nostros humaniter admoneam*, "nostros" here suggesting others of the young set to which both he and Lorenzo belonged.

virtues are recorded in letters, and to imitate them in other things, but in this one most especially. But so as best to engage that audience, I have not poured forth all things, but so to offer a pleasing variety, I have gathered from many places these few notes pertaining to this issue. Nor do I cease to exhort them to be deeply grateful to those ancient authors, from whom in long nights of study, if they do not fail in the task, they will not only improve themselves, but also win wives of sharper wit,[155] and celebrate more splendid nuptials. Concerning this enough. We come to greater things.

Second Part: On the Duties of a Wife

CHAPTER 1: ON OBEDIENCE

The next task, as was established from the start, is to discuss the duties of a wife, to which matter this discourse now turns. It is the second part of this work, as the discussion of the selection of a wife has preceded this inquiry into her duties. And it is its final and culminating part, presenting recommendations of such a kind that if wives comply with them—either by their own choice or guided by their husbands—no critic will ever be so unjust as to say that I have not so defined the duties of a wife that young men throughout the whole course of their lives may secure the joy of peace and tranquility.

Three things, then, are required of a wife to make a marriage praiseworthy and admirable: that she love her husband; that she live virtuously; and that she manage domestic affairs soberly and diligently. I shall explore the first of these, once a little has been said about a wife's capacity for obedience—than which nothing is more pleasing, nothing more desirable—for it is the master and guide of her capacity for love. That this is so did not escape the ancient sages, who established that when an offering was made to Juno, the goddess of marriage (who was also called Gamelia on that account), the gall bladder was excised from the sacrificial beast, signifying by this wise regulation that the marital state should be free of all rancor and bile.[156] In the same way, many learned men approved the response of a Spartan woman who, outraged by the curses hurled against her husband by some crazed old woman, said, "Get away from me! When I was a girl I learned to obey my parents, and now I must obey my husband, if I am to be what I ought to be."[157]

155. Barbaro writes *instructiores uxores*; but it is unlikely at this date that he means women who have been instructed in the humanities—especially when he is urging his own male contemporaries to take on that pursuit.

156. Plutarch, *Conjugalia praecepta*, 27. In ancient Athens, *gamelia* referred to the rite or law of marriage.

157. Plutarch, *Lacaenarum incertarum apophthegmata*, 23.

For the husband rules: the wife must yield to his will. Thus Gorgo can rightly be condemned, who when asked whether she would go to her husband, she replied, "By no means; but let my husband come to me."[158] That great man and general Cyrus instructed his soldiers that when the enemy burst upon them all in a tumult, their assault should be greeted with silence; but if they came silently, instead their approach should be met with clamor and fury. So it should be with wives. If her husband, roused with anger, bellows so that her ears can hardly bear the sound, the wife should endure the noise with silence; but if he is wordless and laden with sorrow, she should with sweet and sensible speech address, comfort, encourage, soothe, and console him.[159]

Those who handle elephants do not wear white, while those who handle wild bulls avoid red: for these colors greatly excite and enrage those beasts. Similarly, as many authors report, tigers are excited by drums, which agitate them greatly. Wives should be instructed accordingly. If they have a garment their husbands dislike, let them put it aside, lest they quarrel with those with whom they must live in peace and harmony.[160] Headgear designed to protect the ears are of greater use, I suggest, to wives than to boxers. For the latter need only protection from blows, while the former are vulnerable to writs of divorce, and the consequent burden of shame.[161] Accordingly, wives must take great care lest any cause for suspicion, jealousy, or anger is aroused because of what they hear.

It would be helpful in this matter to imitate the prudence of king Alexander. For whenever someone came to him with a complaint about another, he used always to cover one of his ears, reserving it so that he might then hear the person who desired to defend himself.[162] Indeed, Hermione seems to have spoken the truth when she spoke and testified in a ringing voice that she had been ruined by wicked women whom she thought were her friends. Wives, therefore, if they encounter such talk, should not admit such female calumnies, but block up their ears and drive away the slanders, lest fire, as the proverb says, be added to fire. Let them learn and imitate the response of the great king Philip: when his courtiers once urged him to rage against the Greeks, who although he had bestowed many benefits upon them yet accused and cursed him, he said: "What would they do if we actually inflicted an injury on them?" In the same way, when malicious women say, "Your husband doesn't appreciate you, though you are obedient and loving,"

---

158. Plutarch, *Lacaenarum incertarum apophthegmata*, 25; *Conjugalia praecepta*, 18. See Gothein, *Das Buch von der Ehe*, 95n4 for Barbaro's misconstrual of this passage.

159. Plutarch, *Conjugalia praecepta*, 37.

160. Plutarch, *Conjugalia praecepta*, 45.

161. Plutarch, *De recta ratione audiendi*, 2. Barbaro follows Plutarch too faithfully here; divorce was a risk wives faced in antiquity, but not in Christian Europe prior to the Reformation, when some communities accepted divorce.

162. Plutarch, *Alexander*, 42.2.

the wife should respond, "What would happen then if knowingly and willingly, though chaste, I had abandoned my chastity, and though loving, had ceased to love him?"[163]

A householder whose slave had run away found the fugitive laboring in a mill, having in effect already atoned for his error; to whom the master said, "In what better place could I have found you than here?" In the same way, a wife whose jealousy plagues her husband, who on that account ponders and plans divorce, should hold back, I would suggest, and say to herself: "Will not that whore, for whom I would lose my home, be even more joyful and fortunate if she sees me shipwrecked, while she in the meantime, sailing with following winds, finds secure harbor in my marriage bed?"[164] Euripides used to criticize those who had the lyre played as they dined: for the music was more likely to arouse anger and sorrow than to calm those who were intent on pleasure.[165] In the same way I would accuse those wives, who when peace and comity prevail, sleep with their husbands, but if anger intrudes, they go off to sleep separately, and deny Venus, by whose playful arts they might easily have been reconciled. So, too, thought Homer's Juno, "in whose care are the marriage ties."[166] For when she spoke of Thetis and Oceanus, if I remember correctly,[167] she sought to resolve their quarrels, and reunite them by means of love and lovemaking.[168] And in Rome, when tension arose between man and wife, the couple went to the temple of the goddess Viriplaca, where they could speak freely together without witnesses; and with harmony restored, they returned home together.[169] Surely domestic peace and well-being are advanced if the wife nurtures her husband's good will with special diligence.

When Gorgias of Leontini gave his oration at the Olympic games held in honor of the great all-powerful Jove on the need to settle the peace of all of Greece, Melanthus said: "This orator of ours attempts to persuade all of us that we should settle a peace, though he himself has not made peace with his wife and his housemaid—just three persons whom he cannot persuade to reach an agreement"; for his wife was beset with jealousy, while Gorgias was enamored of the servant.[170] When Philip, likewise, who had long been enraged with both Olympias and Alexander, questioned Demaratus of Corinth (who had just returned from

163. Plutarch, *Conjugalia praecepta*, 40.

164. Plutarch, *Conjugalia praecepta*, 41.

165. Plutarch, *Conjugalia praecepta*, 38. Cf. Euripides, *Medea*, 192–200.

166. Virgil, *Aeneid*, 4.59; trans. A.S. Kline (2002), from the website *Poetry in Translation*, http://www.poetryintranslation.com/PITBR/Latin/VirgilAeneidIV.htm#_Toc342017.

167. He does not; Juno speaks of Tethys and Oceanus: see Homer, *Iliad*, 14:20–209.

168. Plutarch, *Conjugalia praecepta*, 38.

169. Valerius Maximus, *Memorabilia*, 2.1.6.

170. Plutarch, *Conjugalia praecepta*, 43. Melanthus is most likely the artist Melanthios: see Gothein, *Das Buch von der Ehe*, 96n15.

Greece) closely and carefully about the concord of the Greeks, the latter replied: "I think it's shameful, Philip, for you take such pains over the peace of all of Greece now under discussion, when you have not yet made peace with your own wife and son."[171]

A wife who wishes, therefore, to settle differences among her children and servants, first let her settle those with her husband, lest she be criticized for doing that for which she faults others. If she is to perform her duty of maintaining and securing peace and quiet in her marriage, then nothing should more occupy her mind than the need in all matters to assent to her husband. But of these things, enough said.

CHAPTER 2: ON LOVE

Now we come to conjugal love, whose extraordinary force and unmatched dignity (as we learn from illustrious authors) seem to constitute a model of perfect friendship. So as first to address the principal issue concerning this topic, I shall set aside many other matters which ought properly to be explored. I would wish, then, that a wife love her husband with such earnestness, faithfulness, and delight that nothing is lacking in concern, attentiveness, or good will. Let her be so bound to her husband that, without him, she could find nothing at all to be good or pleasant. Such love must be genuine, as I see it; for as in all things, there is no better, no quicker path, to seeming to be something, than actually to be it.[172]

How much labor, how much effort must a lazy farmer perform if he wishes to be viewed as diligent? How much skill, how much knowledge are required for an inexpert doctor, or horse-trainer, or lyre-player, if in those activities in which they are inept, they wish to appear to others to be proficient? Many and various circumstances will intervene, causing the false honor accorded these would-be practitioners of agriculture, medicine, horsemanship, and music to evaporate. These fellows, if they will follow my advice, will more easily, swiftly, and surely attain a secure and solid reputation if they silence those who trumpet their inflated and spurious achievements. And since in every situation truth conquers imitation, let the farmer diligently cultivate his field with energy and skill; let the doctor heal the bodies of men; let the horse-trainer coax, goad, and compel unruly horses to his will; and let the musician sing his song so that nothing could be more pleasing or sweet to the ears. And wives, likewise, if they wish to seem to love their husbands wholeheartedly, let them love them from the heart.

Wives should constantly observe their husbands closely to detect their varying moods, responding now with solicitude, now with gaiety. For when things are going well, celebration is in order, but consolation is needed when they go badly.

171. Plutarch, *Regum et imperatorum apophthegmata, Philippus*, 30.

172. Cicero, *De officiis*, 2.12.43; Xenophon, *Memorabilia*, 1.7, and 2.6, at end.

In the same way, wives should share with their husbands whatever cares may afflict them, so long as these are matters fit to convey to the ears of a decent man, feigning nothing, dissembling nothing, hiding nothing. Often the anguish and trouble of the soul may be lightened by words and counsel that a husband sweetly conveys, for in attending to and sharing all the pain and burden of her cares, he may make them vanish, or at least diminish them. And if these troubles are very serious and distressing, she would do best to set them aside until she is ready to whisper them in confidence to her husband. So I would wish wives, in sum, to live with their husbands as though their souls were somehow intermingled—so that, as Pythagoras describes friendship, the two become one.[173]

In order easily to achieve this end, the citizens of Crete (who for many centuries now have been part of our empire[174]) only permit their daughters to marry those with whom they had exchanged, as virgins, mutual signs of love. For they believe that those husbands will be dearer to their wives who were dear to them even before the marital knot was tied. As nature has established, they note, and custom has affirmed, all actions (except for a very few) unfold in the course of time—for we are not instantly burned when we put our hands in the fire, nor is wood immediately set ablaze when thrown in the midst of the flames. Accordingly, they think it necessary that, just as in choosing friends, so also when it comes to husbands, young girls should select with careful deliberation those who most resemble them in mind and soul: for a husband can neither be wisely chosen in an instant, nor genuinely loved. They themselves will discover how successful this custom may be; but certainly it will not be denied that it accords with the fullness and constancy of love. I cannot pass by in silence those who—behaving quite differently—extort their husbands' love by potions and magic spells. I would compare these women to fishermen who use drugged bait—as they often do in parts of Etruria[175]—and so render the fish tasteless and almost useless. They also resemble travelers who prefer to be led by the blind than to follow those who see.[176]

Love that is mutual, therefore, and voluntary, should be zealously sought, increased, and preserved. Its power is exemplified by the life and the deeds of famous women, and those who imitate them will prove their capacity for virtue, love, and constancy. Pantheia wondrously cherished and loved her husband

---

173. Cicero, *De officiis*, 1.17.56.

174. The island of Crete had been since the thirteenth century a colony of Venice. Zaccaria Trevisan, Barbaro's mentor, had served as Captain of Candia in Crete in 1404, and is presumably the source of Barbaro's anecdotes about contemporary Cretan customs.

175. Etruria was the ancient Latin word for the Italian region once dominated by the Etruscans, called Tuscany (*Toscana*) by Barbaro's contemporaries, of which the capital was Florence, the home of his dedicatee Lorenzo de' Medici.

176. Plutarch, *Conjugalia praecepta*, 5 and 6.

Abradatas, king of Susa;[177] as a captive, she kept faith with him and acquired for him the friendship of Cyrus the Great; and so as to outfit him in due splendor, she did not squander, but rightly employed all her great wealth and treasure. While fighting valiantly against the Egyptians, the allies of Croesus, Abradatas died honorably, both so as to please Cyrus and be worthy of his wife Pantheia, his duty as a powerful general and brave soldier accomplished. Pantheia searched for his body and, so as to sanctify his death, nobly slew herself upon it. The dying Cassandane, as well, so loved her husband that it was harder for her to part from Cyrus than to part from life. On her death, no ungrateful husband, Cyrus grieved for her at length, and commanded all his many subjects to wear mourning in her honor.[178]

The wife of Themistocles, in the same way, was so absorbed by her love and passion for her husband that it seemed she thought of nothing else. Indeed, this most illustrious Greek prince yielded to her in all things, so that she was considered to be the most powerful person in Greece. For whatever she wanted, so, too, did Themistocles; and whatever Themistocles wanted, so, too, did the Athenians; and what the Athenians wanted, so, too, did all of Greece.[179] Likewise Thesta, the sister of Dionysius the elder, was given in marriage to Polyxenus, who, mistreated by the tyrant, fled Sicily in fear of him.[180] Dionysius called for his sister, accusing her that though she was aware of her husband's flight, she had told him nothing about it. Constant as always, and freed by the unique license of virtue, Thesta responded: "Do I seem to you, Dionysius, to be such a vile and wretched woman that, if I had been aware of my husband's flight, I would refuse to be the companion and partner of his fortunes? I would have much preferred to be known as the wife of the Polyxenus, even in exile, than as the sister of Dionysius the tyrant." Admiring her greatness of spirit, when they had expelled the tyrants, the Syracusans conferred royal honors upon her during her lifetime; and on her death, those of every rank and every class—indeed, all of Syracuse—attended her funeral.

Armenia, the wife of Tigranes, is another example of such female nobility. For in that expedition that Cyrus led against the Assyrians, unable to bear his absence, Armenia followed Tigranes everywhere, in the face of every kind of danger, an undefeated companion of undaunted spirit.[181] And again, Homer's

---

177. Susa (in Asia Minor) was the capital city of the Persian empire during the period of high Greek civilization. Abradatas was its (possibly fictional) king during the reign of Cyrus the Great (600/576–530 BCE). The following anecdote is a summary of books 4–7 of Xenophon's *Cyropaedia*.

178. Herodotus, *History*, 2.1.

179. Plutarch, *De liberis educandis*, 1c–d (2). Themistocles (524–459 BCE) was an Athenian statesman and general.

180. The following anecdote is from Plutarch, *Dion* 21. Dionysius the elder (432–367 BCE) was tyrant of Syracuse.

181. Xenophon, *Cyropaedia*, 3.1.41–43. Tigranes I, king of Armenia (r. 560–535 BCE), was a close companion of Cyrus the Great.

Andromache declares in these words how much she loved her husband Hector, who embodied for her every possible form of love: "... you are father to me, and my honoured mother, you are my brother, and it is you who are my young husband."[182] Crazed by word of his death, she rushed across the city to mount the walls of Troy, which she paced in her distress.[183]

At this point the virtue of that excellent woman Camma should be recounted, whose remarkable tale I shall now narrate in detail; for though her story may be lengthy, yet its merit, novelty, and variety will be pleasant both to you, and to those others who pick up this work.[184] The two kinsmen Sinatus and Sinorix incontestably outshone the other princes of Galatia[185] in strength, fame, and glory. Of these, Sinatus took Camma as his wife, who was without peer not merely for the loveliness of her body, but also for her remarkable virtue. Endowed with chastity, integrity, prudence, and greatness of soul, she captured the hearts of all with an extraordinary kind of love. She won still more fame when, for her own merits and those of her ancestors, she was promoted to be priestess of Diana, a goddess especially revered by the Galatians. All eyes turned on her when, arrayed always in her magnificent priestly robes, she performed the sacrifices.

Sinorix first fell in love with this woman, and then decided to kill her husband, his kinsman, since while the latter still lived, he would be unable to satisfy his lust. So blinded by love, the ruthless Sinorix surprised the unsuspecting Sinatus and slew him with his sword. Soon after he asked Camma to marry him, while she, bearing courageously the death of her husband, zealously desired and patiently awaited the time and occasion to exact vengeance for the crime of Sinorix. Sinorix pressed for the fulfillment of these funereal nuptials, dismissing his deed as having been caused by honest error—as though we could think honest a deed contaminated with dire evil. At first Camma rejected his suit; but soon her family, to gain a perpetual connection to a powerful prince, pressed her strongly to accept his offer. Then, as though persuaded, she promised that she would, and cordially received the young man who came into her presence, and with him entered the temple of Diana so that, with the goddess as witness, they might seal their faith and covenant.

Thereupon, taking in her hands a celebratory cup, Camma drank from it first, then gave the rest to Sinorix. But the mead in the cup was mixed with poison; and when she saw that Sinorix had drunk it, her eyes and all her visage shone with

---

182. Homer, *Iliad*, 6.429–30, in the translation of Richmond Lattimore (Chicago: University of Chicago Press, 1951); also quoted in sources known to Barbaro: Plutarch, *Conjugalia praecepta*, 48, and Plutarch, *Brutus*, 23.

183. Allusion to Homer, *Iliad*, 22.460–63.

184. Plutarch, *Mulierum virtutes*, 20.

185. Sinatus and Sinorix were tetrarchs not of Gaul, as Barbaro writes, but of Galatia, a Roman province in Asia Minor.

joy. Turning to the statue of Diana, she spoke thus: "You, divine parent, are my witness: I did not wish to outlive my Sinatus, I swear, for the sake of my own life (which were I to live still would afflict me with pain, but leaving it behind may liberate me from all my troubles), but I was determined to live to realize the events of this day; for I would have taken no pleasure in living after the funeral of my husband, sorrowful to me and bitter to his country, had I not been inspired by a certain fierce hope of one day avenging him. Vengeance won, I now descend to my dearest Sinatus, the best of husbands. You, cruel Sinorix, are destined not for a wedding and the bridal chamber, but for a tomb." A moment later, the poison having spread through all their members, first Sinorix died, then Camma.

Stratonica, a final example, so loved her husband Deiotarus, that her one purpose was to fulfill his will.[186] She was saddened, therefore, and distressed, when she saw that Deiotarus realized that she could not give birth, and that there would be no heir to the kingdom. Whereupon, on her own accord, she chose a woman of worthy appearance and character, Electra by name, with whom she persuaded, urged, and exhorted her husband (who much admired the kindness and loyalty of his wife) to have intercourse. Calmly, thereafter, and with the greatest love and loyalty, she took as her own the children to whom Electra gave birth, and nourished, educated, and honorably reared them.

I would go on too long if I were to tell the tales of the passionate fondness of Tertia Aemilia for her husband Publius Cornelius Scipio;[187] or the great affection of Julia, Porcia, Artemisia, and Hypsicratea for theirs;[188] or of the other exemplars of marital love, whose stories are readily available to all of those who have any familiarity with history. Many precepts about marital love have also been recorded, which I shall now deliberately pass by, for I fully trust that other authors will for their part thoroughly and accurately explore how wives should revere and love their husbands. What they present will be of the same nature, I hope, as is what I have said in these pages.

CHAPTER 3: ON MODERATION

The next topic concerns moderation, in which enduring love between husband and wife is often rooted, and therafter protected and preserved. This quality not only pleases husbands, but also impresses all those who observe it. It is evident principally in a wife's expression, gestures, speech, dress, eating, and lovemaking. I shall discuss briefly what I have learned of these from native intelligence, study,

186. Plutarch, *Mulierum virtutes*, 21. Deiotarus (105–42/40 BCE) was a Galatian king and ally of Rome.
187. As described by Valerius Maximus, *Memorabilia*, 6.7.1. Scipio, surnamed Africanus, was victor of the Second Punic War.
188. For these figures, see Valerius Maximus, *Memorabilia*, 4.6.4 and 5, 4.6.ext 1 and 2.

or experience; of these the first two, which are of the same sort, I shall discuss together.

Above all else, the surest image of the mind, the face, found in no living creature except man, should display the signs of an upright, reverent, and temperate soul.[189] For in it, the sentiments that nature otherwise deeply hides are easily discovered; indeed, better than words can, it reveals and declares many things, for it is from the expression of the face, and manner of walking, that the condition of our souls is announced. Even in dumb animals we observe anger, joy, and similar affections of the soul, both in the movements of the body and in the eyes, which testify and plainly declare with what kind of passions the soul may be affected. Many find that the pattern of lines especially about the mouth conveys much about the nature of any creature.[190] But I am digressing.

At every time in all places, therefore, wives should appear modest. In this they will excel if in their eyes, their gait, and every motion of their whole body, they preserve balance and constancy. For the wandering of the eyes, a hasty walk, too much movement of the hands or other parts of the body are always indecorous, and betray an underlying levity or vanity. Therefore wives must take care that their brow, face, and gesture, by which we penetrate with a critical eye to the most intimate feelings, all contribute to maintaining decorum. Diligence in this matter will bring them joy and honor, while negligence will result in anguish and censure. Yet a wife's face should not be ungracious, with a stern expression, but rather pleasant; nor should her bodily motions seem awkward, but suitably grave. I strongly urge that she not laugh excessively, which is vulgar in everyone, but is especially vulgar in women; but if she happens to be present for a free exchange of jests, she will not be faulted if she smiles modestly, relaxing a little her usually serious posture. Demosthenes used to rehearse his movements before a mirror, so that he could see with his own eyes what he should do and what to avoid when he came to deliver his oration.[191] The same approach is recommended for wives.

I recommend that wives consider and reflect daily on what dignity and gravity require, lest they be deficient in any point of decorum. Spartan wives, we know, used to walk out in public with covered face, while virgins were unveiled. Asked about this practice, the Spartan Charillus responded: "Our ancestors permitted this freedom to girls so that they may find husbands; but they prohibited

---

189. The next two paragraphs are drawn from Cicero, *De legibus*, 1.26–27, and *De officiis*, 1.34–36.125–32; 1.29.103.

190. Barbaro appears to be familiar at least by report with Aristotle's *Physiognomonica*, of which the English translation by T. Loveday and E.S. Forster, 52–77, in the *Opuscula* (Oxford: Clarendon Press, 1913), vol. 6 of *The Works of Aristotle*, ed. W.D. Ross, is available online at https://archive.org/stream/worksaristotle00arisuoft#page/n3/mode/2up; and cf. also Pier Paolo Vergerio, *De ingenuis moribus*, ed. Kallendorf, 12/13, para. 9.

191. Plutarch, *Demosthenes*, 11.2.

it to married women, so that they might understand that their duty was not to find husbands, but to guard and cherish those that they had."[192] The custom observed by our citizens of Crete is similar, for they allow unmarried girls to stand out of doors, and to sing and in all sorts of ways joke and play games with their suitors. But those wedded to husbands remain at home and very rarely leave, like Vestals pledged to sacred offices, as though it were a kind of sacrilege for them to look at men not related to them. Surely they learned this custom from Xenophon, whose belief that women should not show their faces abroad is plainly seen in this story he tells. For when Tigranes with his parents and beloved wife Armenia came home from Cyrus, with everyone praising his good looks, his character, the strength and elegance of his body, Tigranes asked Armenia whether she thought Cyrus handsome. But calling on the immortal gods as witnesses, Armenia said "I never took my eyes off you; therefore I am completely ignorant of Cyrus's form or face."[193] Gorgias would have approved, for he advised that wives remain enclosed at home, so that nothing about them, except their good reputation, would be known abroad. For Thucydides, however, not even this was sufficient: for him, that wife was best concerning whom there circulated not even a whisper of either praise or censure.[194]

But we, who follow the rule of moderation, have allowed women greater freedom. For we do not require wives to be bound in chains, as it were, but permit them to walk out openly in public, this indulgence shown them serving as a testimony to their virtue and probity. Yet the relationship between wives and their husbands should be quite unlike that of the moon and the sun. For when the moon is close to the sun, it is invisible; but when it is far away, it shines brightly, visible to all. In the same way, I suggest that wives should be seen when they are with their husbands, but when these are away, they should stay quietly at home.[195] Moreover, with their eyes—for sight, as with paintings, often called silent poetry, is the sharpest sense—as well as in the movements of their head and whole body, they should always display decorum and propriety.[196] I have spoken of the face and gestures; now I shall speak of words.

CHAPTER 4: ON SPEECH AND SILENCE

Isocrates advised men to speak both of those things of which they had certain knowledge, and of those about which they could not honorably keep silent.[197] We

---

192. Plutarch, *Apophthegmata laconica, Charillus*, 2.

193. Xenophon, *Cyropaedia*, 3.1.41.

194. Plutarch, *Mulierum virtutes*, introduction.

195. Plutarch, *Conjugalia praecepta*, 9.

196. Plutarch, *Quomodo adulator ab amico internoscatur*, 15.

197. Isocrates, *Ad Demonicum*, 41.

urge women to concede the first of these as proper to men, but to adopt the second as proper for themselves. In women, loquacity cannot be sufficiently censured, as wise and learned men have advised, but silence cannot be sufficiently applauded. On this account, the ancient laws of the Romans barred women from defending cases at law, either private or public. And when, according to the annals of the Romans, Amaesia, Afrania, and Hortensia defied this injunction, their action was censured, reproved, and rebuked.[198] Likewise, when Marcus Cato the Elder saw Roman women who, defying the limits set them by nature and disregarding the norms of matronly restraint, often walked in the forum, petitioned for support, and spoke with strangers, he railed against them, reproached them, and restrained them, as the dignity of a great citizen and the majesty of that empire required.[199]

We are told that newcomers to the Pythagorean sect were commanded to be silent for at least two years, so they would not basely succumb to falsehood, deceit, or error, or stubbornly defend notions they had not yet sufficiently investigated.[200] Wives, however, we require to be silent—since the opportunity for levity, vulgarity, and shamefulness is always present—for an unlimited expanse of time. Let them respond modestly when called by those close to them, report on their health, and when the place and occasion permits, speak briefly, so that they seem to have been provoked to speech, rather than to provoke it. Women should also strive to be praised for the dignified brevity of their conversation rather than its splendid prolixity. When the Greek woman Theano reached out her hand from her mantle, a certain youth turned to his companions, saying "How lovely is that arm!"; to whom she responded, "It is not a public one." So like her arms, so also a woman's words should not be public; for the voice of a woman who speaks out in public should be feared as greatly as the nakedness of her limbs. It follows that women must avoid conversation with strangers, by which their affections and character may easily be made known.[201]

Silence is also often praised in great men. The Pythagorean Spintharus of Taranto lauded Epaminondas, that excellent Greek prince, who, though he knew much, spoke little. For in this matter, as in most others, he observed the wise dictates of nature, life's schoolmistress, who clearly conveys her view of silence: for in her great wisdom, she gave to us two ears, but only one tongue, and that doubly guarded in a palisade of lips and teeth.[202] For through this portal of the ears, as Theophrastus and many other learned men assert, virtue is planted in us, bearing excellent and delightful fruit, while the other senses, which nature bestows on us

198. Valerius Maximus, *Memorabilia*, 8.3.1–3.

199. Livy, *Histories*, 34.2; also Valerius Maximus, *Memorabilia*, 8.3.

200. Aulus Gellius, *Noctes atticae*, 1.9.3–4.

201. Plutarch, *Conjugalia praecepta*, 31.

202. Plutarch, *De recta ratione audiendi*, 3. Correcting Pindar, as Barbaro writes, to Spintharus.

as agents and messengers, may occasionally supply knowledge, but more often ignorance.[203]

Yet one of our fellow citizens,[204] whom it is unnecessary to name to you here, praises silence only in those whose intellect cannot garner praise; or whose wisdom, eminence; or whose eloquence, fame; to whom I generally respond, that in every matter my judgment takes into account the person and the place, as well as the time. For though, as he wishes, I would grant men a chance to speak when they wish, yet I believe such speechifying is entirely alien to the modesty, reserve, and constancy of a matron. Hence the author Sophocles—who in my view is not lesser than this fellow citizen I have mentioned; rather, most men would say greater—called silence in a woman her single finest ornament.[205] Thus women should consider they have attained the glory of eloquence, if they have adorned themselves with the splendid ornament of silence. For what is desired in them is not the honor won in a declamatory contest, nor the applause and adulation of the crowd, but an eloquent, well-mannered, and reticent silence. But what am I doing? I must take care, since I preach about silence, that I not seem to you to talk rather too much.

CHAPTER 5: ON DRESS AND OTHER ADORNMENT

It is now time to speak about dress and other bodily attire; for neglecting the best precepts in this matter threatens not only matrimonial wealth, but often the patrimony as well,[206] as all who have studied this matter can attest. But if wives truly embrace moderation, a virtue never sufficiently praised, and give proof of their modesty, they will both preserve the wealth of the household and that of the whole city besides. This salutary precept should be followed: they should adjust the splendor of their apparel more to avoid ignominy than to gain applause. Now those wives born to a high rank, if their fortunes permit, should not be clothed in plain or undistinguished garments; these matters must be judged according to circumstances of place, person, and time. Who can look without laughing at a priest attired in a soldier's rough cloak, or one who attends a learned convocation dressed like a senator, or who sports a toga to a horse race? So I would not approve a wife clothed either frivolously or carelessly, but the one dressed so as to preserve

---

203. Plutarch, *De recta ratione audiendi*, 2.

204. Barbaro writes "civis tamen quidam noster"; more likely a Florentine, as before, than a Venetian.

205. Sophocles, *Ajax*, 293.

206. Barbaro is playing with the terms *matrimonium* (meaning matrimony, the state of marriage, and all that pertains to marriage, including matrimonial property, consisting principally of the dowry) and *patrimonium* (meaning explicitly the wealth that is accumulated by the patriarchal family and passed down through the male line). His wordplay cannot be entirely rendered in English.

decorum. For too much indulgence in fine dress is the pathway to vanity,[207] and could cause wives to abandon their husbands for their lovers, as rumor and experience inform us.

The example of king Cyrus may serve to warn our wives that they should not pursue lavish adornment too zealously, for he seemed indeed, on account of his outstanding wisdom and remarkable moderation, to live up to his name: in Persian, "Cyrus" means "Sun." When legates of the king of India came to his uncle Cyaxares to negotiate peace with the Assyrians, Cyaxeres, in order to showcase the most select regiment of his army, ordered Cyrus, their commander, to come immediately with all his troops to the courtyard of the royal palace and the open marketplace. Cyrus obeyed his order speedily, impressive in discipline and dignity, but plainly dressed, although Cyaxares had sent him a purple robe and precious chain and other Persian adornments, so that the nephew of the king and commander of his army might appear duly splendid and magnificent. But all these things the great-souled Cyrus despised, and both he and others thought he was sufficiently adorned when, as a valiant warrior with an army ready for battle, almost before the royal messenger had returned to the king, he presented himself to Cyaxares.[208] For wives, as well, such parsimony in dress will be the finest ornament.

Dionysius the tyrant of Syracuse sent as a gift to Lysander two precious robes for the splendid adornment of his daughters; but Lysander refused them and ordered them returned to Dionysius, saying that his daughters would be more splendidly adorned without them.[209] Julia, the daughter of Caesar Augustus, realizing that her excessive costume was an annoyance to her father, found cause the next day, dressed plainly, to see and salute him. But while Caesar was delighted, Julia admitted that she had sought to please her father's eyes with her present attire, but with that she had worn the previous day, those of her husband Agrippa.[210]

Others may believe what they wish; but I am convinced that heaps of curls and all those pretty ornaments are designed for other men, so that wives expend all this care and effort to please their admirers rather than their own husbands. For at home these fineries are set aside, while abroad these destroyers of our wealth—our wives—cannot be sufficiently decked out or adorned.[211] For surely a plethora of precious clothing is of little use to husbands, but rather often painful, while it always provides pleasure to lovers, for whose sake such fripperies are created. In my mind, the men who permit their wives this apparel—and are rightly called uxorious—are like those who so prize the splendid exterior of their house, that in order to delight neighbors and visitors with an elegant gilded façade, they

207. Cf. Vergerio, *De ingenuis moribus*, ed. Kallendorf, 88/89, para. 73.

208. Xenophon, *Cyropaedia*, 2.4.1–6.

209. Plutarch, *Conjugalia praecepta*, 26.

210. Macrobius, *Saturnalia*, 2.5.5.

211. Terence, *Eunuchus*, 1.1.79.

neglect necessary expense inside the walls. They also resemble unskilled but wealthy barbers, to whom no one goes, except for youngsters who need their hair cut. Nor are their elaborately-wrought ivory mirrors of use to them, but rather the cause of sorrow, when with heavy hearts they espy noble adolescents frequenting neighboring barbershops, despising theirs. As well, this showy splendor, this most magnificent bazaar, this luxurious display make it pleasant to loiter in courtyards, in entryways,[212] in arcades, and constantly to roam the whole of the city. For this reason Egyptian women were wisely forbidden to wear fancy shoes, which might encourage them to wander abroad. Indeed, if we took away their showy attire, most women would willingly and diligently stay at home.[213]

Yet this one custom should be retained, I believe—however much our morals have declined: which is that, if finances permit, women be adorned with gold, gems, and pearls. For these are the signs of a wealthy, rather than a luxurious woman, and declare the amplitude of her husband rather than amuse the eyes of lovers. I should add that these are a more durable form of wealth, and require little care. They can also readily serve often as a great aid in both private and public affairs. Who does not know what great benefit, on one occasion, this kind of magnificence brought to the Romans, by which, at a time of great peril during the Punic War, the city raised money—called by the ancients the "sinews of war"—as authorized by the Oppian law?[214] Yet in this kind of display I would afford wives less liberty than the laws themselves concede; rather, I would wish that they abstain from licentious dress and other adornments, so that observers conclude not that they could not dress more luxuriously, but that, for the sake of honor, they refused what they could have had.[215] With this we are done with dress and adornment.

CHAPTER 6: ON FOOD AND DRINK

Now we shall consider food, of whose great importance in every regard all will agree with me who have given the matter some thought. Who doubts that those delicacies that the multitude believes affords us the good life instead tear at and shatter the sinews of virtue? Who is so abstemious that he is not swiftly corrupted by them? Who has been so lost to these pleasures, that sobriety, vigilance, caution, cannot recall him to the joy and honor of a moderate existence?

212. Cf. Aulus Gellius, *Noctes atticae,* 16.5.

213. Plutarch, *Conjugalia praecepta,* 30, which Barbaro somewhat misconstrues: see Gothein, *Das Buch von der Ehe,* 97n58.

214. Correcting "Appian law," as Barbaro writes; see Livy, *Histories,* 34.1.3, and Valerius Maximus, *Memorabilia,* 9.1.3; and cf. Gothein, *Das Buch von der Ehe,* 97n60. The Oppian Law required matrons to surrender their gold and jewels to the public treasury.

215. Augustine, *De bono conjugali,* 3.

If wives, then, are not to fall short in any aspect of modesty, I would wish that, first of all, they diligently abstain from these things that arouse, implant, and increase the craving for pleasure. Great and wise men instructed nuns to observe fasting vigils and practice temperance in food and drink so that fleshly appetite would not sully their pure thoughts and weaken their devotion. The ancient Romans forbade the use of wine by women, as now also do the Turks and Persians.[216] In order to enforce this rule more easily, family members in Rome customarily kissed, so that by the odor itself the guilt of an intemperate woman would be declared. Those who transgressed the law were not only disgraced, but as Cato attests, they were also heavily fined; for intemperance of this kind often tempts and induces to impermissible pleasures.[217] For this reason, some ancients wisely placed together in the same temple the images of the goddess of love and the god of drunkenness and revelry, so that those who came seeking the image of Venus would first encouter the statue of Bacchus.[218] For indeed the minds and souls of those who have succumbed to intemperance are rendered so impotent that they can think nothing difficult, remember nothing honorable, understand nothing godly, but deprived of reason and judgment, take for their highest good some swamp of titillation, which beasts, if they could speak, as Cicero writes, would call pleasure.[219] Cyrus parried the attack of Spargapises, the son of Tomyris, who led a splendid army, but was unmanned by the consumption of wine, which extinguished his ardor and sapped his courage, while Cyrus, strong and energetic, yearned for battle, fought, and triumphed.[220] Did not the softness of Capua diminish the strength of Hannibal more than the slaughter of Cannae dispirit the Romans?[221] What need is there of examples? Unless moderation is strictly observed in the consumption of food and drink, the mind is driven beyond the barriers of honor to shipwreck and devastation.

There is scarcely any, of all the many kinds and forms of living creatures, who if coddled and overprotected as children, could ever achieve in adulthood a semblance of moderation or of good morals. Those who follow nature as guide

---

216. Barbaro writes of the "Syris et Persicis," but intends the Muslims of the contemporary Levant and Middle East; see Gothein, *Das Buch von der Ehe*, 97n63.

217. Valerius Maximus, *Memorabilia*, 2.1.5; Aulus Gellius, *Noctes atticae*, 10.23.1–3; Plutarch, *Quaestiones romanae*, 6.

218. Pausanias, *Descriptio graeciae*, 2.23.8, mentions such a temple. In this passage, Barbaro conflates the Roman god of wine and drunkenness, Liber, with the Greek Bacchus/Dionysius, and names Liber as the father of Aphrodite/Venus, who was, according to poetic tradition, like Bacchus, the child of Zeus/Jupiter.

219. Cicero, *De finibus*, 2.6.18.

220. Herodotus, *History*, 1.211.

221. Valerius Maximus, *Memorabilia*, 9.1; Livy, *Histories*, 23.18.14–16. Cannae (216 BCE) and Capua (211 BCE) were two sites of the Roman struggle against Hannibal in the Second Punic War; Hannibal won the first, but lost the second.

require little, but those who seek pleasure to some kind of voluptuous excess will always crave what is immense and infinite. I commend the frugality of that Spartan, who having caught a small quantity of fish, gave them to the innkeeper to be cooked—who, as cooks do, requested also cheese, oil, vinegar, and more, so that he could season them properly. To whom the Spartan said: "If I had all of those things, I would hardly need the fish."[222] Shameful lusts and excessive lovemaking do not merely follow upon Alexandrian delicacies and Syracusan feasts, but rush after them. It was the excellent custom of the Spartans, so as to portray the deformity of intemperance in drink to their wives and children, to admit drunken helot slaves to their banquets; and when these made fools of themselves by the many stupidities they exhibited, were viewed as not only pitiful, but also miserable and wretched. Nor do I believe that the illustrious men gathered there delighted in the torments of the helots, but recognized that what was base in those slaves, was certainly to be judged despicable in free men.[223] In the same way, wives should closely observe their drunken maids, so they will be aware of what they must carefully guard against in themselves. For although as Homer says, "In a tired man, wine will bring back his strength to its bigness,"[224] yet excessively consumed, it stupefies the mind and weakens the senses to a condition of senectitude; for the quality of its fervor is such that the natural heat of our bodies, when overcome by its fiercer heat, increases extraordinarily.[225] Evidently, as well, that dangerous and volatile vapor is a great impediment to understanding, for those affected cannot form thoughts, nor construct an argument, nor refute an objection, nor discourse on any subject. What more is there to say? The poets tell us that too much drink caused many men to turn into pigs, donkeys, and lions. It is especially necessary that women avoid drink, since as Aristotle informs us,[226] they who are of slower intellect and remote from important matters are more inclined to this kind of vice. Children, accordingly, whose welfare is the point of all that is said in this commentary,[227] will greatly benefit from the moderate character and habits of their mothers. Thus Diogenes quite aptly said, when he observed a drunken child, "The parents who conceived you were drunkards."[228]

How much being reared by a temperate mother can benefit the children to whom she gives birth, we shall discuss a little later. For now we must advise

---

222. Plutarch, *De esu carnium*, 1.5.

223. Plutarch, *Demetrius*, 1.4; cf. also Vergerio, *De ingenuis moribus*, ed. Kallendorf, 22/23, para. 18.

224. Homer, *Iliad*, 6.261, trans. Richmond Lattimore (Chicago: University of Chicago Press, 1951).

225. Aristotle, *Problemata*, section 30, 1:953b.

226. Aristotle *Politics*, 1.13.6 and 8:1260a; ps.-Aristotle, *Economics*, 1.3.4. See also Gothein, *Das Buch von der Ehe*, 97n72; also 91n45a.

227. *Liberis etiam, ad quos haec omnia maxima ex parte referuntur* ... . Barbaro is vague but his meaning can't be missed; and it is here that he identifies the thesis of his work.

228. Plutarch, *De liberis educandis*, 2a (3).

and exhort our wives that they should follow the path of nature, and disdain and dismiss pleasures—in whose domain, virtue can in no way exist. And they should approve and imitate the frugal repasts of Lucretia, rather than the sumptuous delights of the Tarquinian daughters and of Cleopatra.[229] So doing, they will protect their own honor and that of their children, for whom they must do all things. Now we proceed to a brief discussion of the regulation of sexual behavior.

CHAPTER 7: ON MARITAL RELATIONS

This is the main point: the same principles valid for food and drink hold also largely for sexual relations; for sexual intercourse, too, must follow the path of right living, as a tender chick follows after its mother. And while this may be confirmed by many explanations and examples, yet it is more useful, and the wisest possible course, to begin this discussion with nature itself, about which I shall briefly comment.

First and foremost, since, as was discussed above,[230] the conjunction of man and wife was created principally for the sake of offspring, and should be valued for that end; intercourse must be undertaken in the hope that it will result in the conception of a child. The behavior of most animals plainly displays and conveys to us what nature has decreed. She has assigned to them certain laws of sexual relations according to this principle: that living creatures, though mortal, may in a sense be rendered immortal through the perpetual succession of descendants.[231] So in this matter beasts may serve as an example to us humans, whose desires are freer and nobler, that we are to have sexual relations not for the sake of pleasure, but in order to procreate offspring. When the ship is full, therefore, we are admonished, to use the words of Julia, the daughter of Augustus, no passenger may enter[232]—nor are beasts to be thought bestial on this account, since they never engage in sexual intercourse when already pregnant, but always for the sake of procreation. But if there are women who wish to defy this prohibition, I would insist that they restrain themselves, so that in that aspect of moderation from which chastity takes its name,[233] they may indeed be, and may be considered, chaste.

---

229. See Gothein, *Das Buch von der Ehe*, 97n74: either women of Tarquinia (Etruria) or daughters of Roman king Tarquinius; and in either case, women of wealth and privilege.

230. In the prologue, "What Marriage Is," above, 67–71; cf. Augustine, *De bono conjugali*, 3.

231. A Darwinian anticipation!

232. Macrobius, *Saturnalia*, 2.5.9–10. When a woman is pregnant, that is, the "ship is full," and she should not engage in sexual intercourse whose purpose of conception has already been achieved.

233. *Pudicitia*, translated as "chastity," relates to a number of Latin terms, including those meaning "shameful" and, indeed, the "shameful" parts of the (usually female) body, the pudenda. Thus the "aspect of moderation" Barbaro defines as chastity takes its name from the sexual organs which are thereby regulated.

This matter, I imagine, is best managed if husbands guide their wives from the start to be servants of necessity rather than lust.[234] At the same time, wives should bear themselves with such modesty and marital decorum that in the sexual act itself they will be at once loving and lovable, but neither shameless nor impudent, which would detract from their decency and even make them less desirable to their husbands—though the latter say nothing about it.

Herodotus has written that women dispense with their modesty along with their undergarments—which would be true if we were concerned with fornicators; if wives are with their husbands, however, they should listen to our advice and always observe decency.[235] When a woman raging with lust was forcefully dragged away from Philip, she said "Release me—when you dim the lamp, any woman at all is the same as all the others." This can rightly be said of adulteresses; but wives, even if the lamp is taken away, should be quite unlike such whores.[236] Did not Hesiod forbid them to be entirely unclothed at night? For, as he says, even the nights belong to the immortal gods.[237]

For it is never right to neglect duty: so a wife should not be seen unclothed, but chastity must be preserved in all places, so that even in darkness a wife behaves modestly before her husband. Thus Phocion, when his wife tried to persuade him to explore unusual and improper pleasures with her, pointedly responded that he would gladly accede to other women in these matters, but that a wife was intended, surely, for honor, not for pleasure.[238] For the same reason Cato the Censor ejected Manilius from the senate when, with his daughter present, he ardently kissed his wife.[239] But if it is improper to kiss one's wife, or amorously to embrace her, in the presence of one's family, it is surely most proper that wives present nothing wanton, nothing shameful to the eyes of their husbands, whom they are required above all to please. Hieron heavily fined Epicharmus, the comedian, who exposed his wife to an indecency.[240] For the honorable condition of marriage is so venerable, that no aspect of it should be made public to the eyes and ears of strangers. The Athenians nicely demonstrated their decency in this matter, when they restored inviolate to Philip the letters to his wife Olympias that they had

234. Augustine, *De nuptiis et concupiscentia*, 1.8.

235. Plutarch, *Conjugalia praecepta*, 10, citing Herodotus, *History*, 1.8.

236. Plutarch, *Conjugalia praecepta*, 46.

237. Hesiod, *Works and Days*, 727–30.

238. Cf. Plutarch, *Conjugalia praecepta*, 29, at end. Instead of the Athenian statesman Phocion of whom Plutarch writes, Barbaro here mistakenly names the Roman emperor Commodus, who was both insane and a lecher: see Gnesotto, *De re uxoria*, 84 (62) n5; Gothein, *Das Buch von der Ehe*, 98n81.

239. Plutarch, *Cato the Elder*, 17, and *Conjugalia praecepta*, 13.

240. Plutarch, *Regum et imperatorum apophthegmata*, *Hiero*, 5.

intercepted. For clearly they deemed it unsuitable that foreigners, and indeed, enemies should share the secrets of a spouse.[241]

Wives must always, therefore, give this matter care and thought: here they may find honor, here triumphs, here a golden crown; for nothing is so pleasant or delectable, that it should divert them from the duty of a chaste mind. While there are many worthy women whom they might imitate, I think that Brasilla may be first among them, whose outstanding deed our age should not neglect to celebrate. Born in Durazzo to noble parents, as certain authors tell, she was captured in an enemy raid and faced the prospect of rape; but although in the greatest danger, given her great beauty, she preserved her chastity pure and uncorrupt, exerting her intellect, virtue, and greatness of soul. For she placated the fury and tamed the ferocity of her captor Cericus[242] with a flow of words: she promised that if she might keep her chastity, she would provide in compensation a certain magic unguent that would prevent his being killed by the weapons of his enemies. The words of this innocent and chaste woman, and his own devotion to magic, persuaded him to believe her. While the noble virgin, surrounded by his guards, gathered some roots, he eagerly awaited the outcome. Then bravely she called him over, promising to prove her success not with words, but with herbs.[243] Thereupon, anointing her neck with ointment, she bared her throat to him. Cericus, then, suspecting nothing, struck off her head with his sword—and was left astonished at her demonstration of determined chastity.[244] What more is there to say? Examples and exhortations are not lacking, if wives wish to be what they should be. And so that I no longer postpone the other things I promised I would discuss, I shall make an end here to this discourse of marital relations.

CHAPTER 8: ON HOUSEHOLD MANAGEMENT AND ON SERVANTS AND OTHER STAFF

It is now both time and place for me to discuss household management. I hope you do not expect an extended treatment concerning this matter, since we largely know by experience the most useful precepts. In the small space available here, therefore, I shall treat only glancingly what learned men have written,[245] since not

---

241. Plutarch, *Demetrius*, 22.1, and *Praecepta gerendae reipublicae*, 3.

242. Cericus is a latinization of the Bosnian name Čerič.

243. Barbaro juxtaposes the Latin words *verbis* (words) and *herbis* (herbs), an exact rhyme for which here the assonants "words" and "herbs" are substituted.

244. See Gnesotto, *De re uxoria*, 86 (64) n1, for many possible sources for this story—all of which vary from the one Barbaro knows, however, as he had heard it from one of his teachers, Giovanni Conversini da Ravenna: see Kohl and Witt, *The Earthly Republic*, 214n76.

245. The learned men Barbaro principally relies on are Aristotle (the ps.-Aristotelian *Economics*) and Xenophon (*Oeconomicus*).

everything they have to say pertains to this discussion and time, and anyone can themselves obtain from their books whatever information they require. It will be sufficient, in this little commentary of mine, to note what is essential and can be briefly and easily stated. It seems, then, that household management is concerned principally with three things: with possessions; with servants and other staff;[246] and with the rearing of children. This last topic will be treated in due course, when discussion of the first two has been completed.

Great diligence is required in the care of our possessions, and the management of servants and staff; for both possessions and servants are necessary, as without them the well-being and order of the whole household cannot be sustained. In these, then, the regulation of domestic affairs largely consists; and unless they have been ordered by the precepts and guidance of the wife, they lack all foundation, and are prone to collapse and fail. For just as nature gives men vigor of body and soul so that, as well as for other reasons, they may enrich their households by their industry, labor, and many bold ventures, so also (or so it seems to me) nature makes women weak, so that they may more carefully supervise all that is in the home: for fear generates worry, and worries elicit vigilance. To what end is wealth brought into the home, unless once within its walls, a wife guards, preserves, and distributes it? Why else do we have the fable of the daughters of Danaus, who were consumed by the perpetual and useless labor of refilling a leaky jug?[247] In this I am of the opinion—that you, Lorenzo, I am confident, would also approve—that no small advantage is achieved by this wifely custodianship. For it was aptly said by the wise Augustus Caesar that Alexander would have garnered more honor and praise if he had been able to guard and conserve what he had won, rather than to have achieved greatness as a gift of fortune.[248]

It follows that wives should not be denied due praise if, as is their duty, they manage all the things that constitute the home. They should endeavor, therefore, just as Pericles as ruler of Athens did every day, to think about their governance of their household. And they should constantly examine themselves as to whether they have in any way fallen short in care, concern, and diligence. It greatly conduces to their success in this matter if they remain at home—a requirement especially important for them—and dutifully supervise all things.[249] Here there comes to mind this response of the prudent stableman, who when asked what it was

---

246. Barbaro has in mind different subsets of servants: manservants and female servants, hired servants and slaves, and children and adults, as appears in different contexts.

247. Ps.-Aristotle, *Economics*, 1.3.4 and 6: 1344a; Xenophon, *Oeconomicus*, 7.21–25, and 40. Labor is wasted, that is, if household implements are not in proper repair, under the supervision of the housewife.

248. Plutarch, *Regum et imperatorum Apophthegmata, Caesar Augustus*, 8.

249. Xenophon, *Oeconomicus*, 7.35.

that made a horse fat, he replied: "The eye of his master."[250] To commend wifely duty to posterity, there were affixed[251] to the bronze statue of Gaia Caecilia, the daughter of Tarquinius, a plain shoe, a distaff, and a spindle, as emblems of domestic industry worthy of imitation.[252] What lazy farmer can hope to have diligent farmworkers? What sleepy general will rouse his soldiers to be vigilant on behalf of the republic? If a housewife wants her handmaids to serve the household, she will not only instruct them in words, but also identify, explain, and show how to do that which must be done.

Nothing is indeed more desirable in household management than that each thing be assigned to and kept in its place. For order—than which there is nothing more beautiful or useful—is always of first importance. A chorus or an army that is not arrayed in its proper ranks, we know, cannot properly be called an army, or a chorus.[253] Wives, I suggest, should imitate the queen bees, who know, receive, and conserve all that is brought into the hive, to be stored until they are needed; and they remain within the honeycombs, while the honey slowly matures and reaches perfection. Wives may send their maids and manservants abroad, if they recognize some need to do so; but if it is useful for them to remain at home, so they should declare, require, and command.[254] They will consider it their duty to see that in the pantry and wine- and oil-cellars, nothing occurs that is disadvantageous to their husbands. For in the same way that generals regularly count the numbers of their soldiers, so wives should frequently and carefully register the provisions stored in their homes, lest they discover to their shame that what should be sufficient for a year proves to be scarcely enough for a month.[255]

This behavior of Pericles greatly confuses the ignorant, and can threaten the household stores: for he would sell all the harvest that he gathered from his fields, then later purchase each day from the market whatever was needed at home;[256] but this daily purchase of grain, wine, and wood might seem more suited to a vagrant or itinerant soldier, than to a citizen and householder, and unworthy of his liberality, his rank, and his fortune. This behavior should be attributed rather to the steward's incompetence, or, very likely, to the negligence of the wife or her staff, than to the judgment of one of the wisest of men. Yet I believe that this Ro-

250. Plutarch, *De liberis educandis*, 9d (13); Ps.-Aristotle, *Economics*, 1.6.3: 1345a; Xenophon, *Oeconomicus*, 12.20. That is to say, the wife's careful management will cause the household to prosper.

251. Accepting Gnesotto's emendation of *refixerunt*: Gnesotto, *De re uxoria*, 88 (66) n2.

252. Plutarch, *Quaestiones romanae*, 30. Gothein notes that Gaia Caecilia is the wife, not daughter, of Tarquinius Priscus: *Das Buch von der Ehe*, 98n93. The distaff and spindle, tools used for managing raw wool and winding spun thread, was associated specifically with female labor.

253. Xenophon, *Oeconomicus*, 7.2–4.

254. Xenophon, *Oeconomicus*, 7.32–36.

255. Xenophon, *Oeconomicus*, 7.36.

256. Plutarch, *Pericles*, 16.

man custom is worthy of imitation, so that women of high station not be assigned the meanest tasks: for by the treaty struck with the Sabines, noble women were exempted from the grinding of grain, kitchen work, and other servile labors.[257] But naturally, if a husband's health required it, or to show hospitality to guests, they might resume those duties; for where a husband's health is concerned, not only should no effort be spared, but to begrudge such labor would be detestable. I am especially delighted to see that, as the learned poet and philosopher Homer reports, Andromache so loved and cared for her Hector, that she undertook even to fodder his horses, who were her husband's pride and joy, both dutifully and capably.[258] If a wife, therefore, is sensible of her duty and reputation, she will know that she owes everything to her husband, and will act accordingly; and if he is a hospitable man who invites guests to his home, she will not refuse to perform her service in the kitchen, just as those tasks were not shunned by those brave and noble men Achilles and Patroclus. For when Ulysses and Ajax came to them seeking a reconciliation, Achilles put his lyre aside, received them courteously, and earnestly performed tasks which, had they not been deemed proper as acts of friendship or hospitality, would have seemed scarcely worthy of ordinary servants.[259] But enough of these things, since my intention was to speak briefly and not belabor details, especially since the writings of learned men have more thoroughly and amply treated this subject than could any presentation of mine. So I move on to the other topics before us.

As promised, it is now time to speak of servants, who, so long as they are not left unsupervised, will provide no small adornment, utility, and delight. This outcome will be achieved if wives carefully instruct them, nor become angry with them unless they err in something about which they had been clearly directed. As in other cases, in this matter I would like wives to imitate queen bees, who allow none of their company to be lazy or negligent.[260] Marcus Cato the Elder so diligently followed this precept of household management that he, though a censor, has been censured for failing to act well in this case: for he sold his slaves when they reached old age, unwilling to tolerate their staying useless at home.[261] Wives should consider it their pressing duty to teach skills to ignorant handmaidens, and to promote any who has proved dependably faithful and diligent to the custody of the cellar. Frugal wives should assiduously seek out a reliable steward, speak to him in a kindly fashion and treat him well, so that by these wifely efforts the household will each day become better managed.[262] They should provide ser-

257. Plutarch, *Quaestiones romanae*, 85.

258. Homer, *Iliad*, 8:186–89.

259. Homer, *Iliad*, 9.182–224.

260. Xenophon, *Oeconomicus*, 7.32–33.

261. Plutarch, *Cato the Elder*, 4.

262. Xenophon, *Oeconomicus*, 7.41 and 9.11–12.

vants the food they need so that they can thrive and perform the constant labor required of them, and adequate clothing befitting the climate, the setting, and the season.[263] Wives must be aware of those servants, as Hesiod counsels,[264] who cannot be separated from their own children and kinfolk; for it will be necessary for these to nourish these dependents, even if furtively, along with themselves. They should also be understanding if any of the servants becomes sick, and see that they are properly cared for. For this compassion and generosity will make servants loyal and well-disposed to the welfare of the household.

But to return to an earlier example, we see how clearly among bees, the workers never desert their queen on account of her care and kindness toward them, and with the greatest willingness always provide whatever she requires.[265] This should not strike anyone as unusual, since other animals also display a special kind of gratitude, which is seen in many cases, as in this next example. In order to save themselves during the Persian war, the Athenians decided to evacuate their city and entrust themselves to the sea. As they were hastily leaving the shore, they saw the dog of Xanthippus the Elder frantically running, wagging his tail, whimpering and barking, because he could not reach his master. Then while the dog swam through the waves toward the ship, Xanthippus halted in his flight, and took the desperate dog aboard. When the dog later died, so as to preserve the memory of his devotion, Xanthippus buried him in a noble sepulcher placed high on a hill, which for many years to come was called the Cynotaphium,[266] or Dog's Tomb: a perpetual monument left to posterity commemorating the mutual love that united master and servant.

In dealing with servants, it will be very useful if they be assigned specific tasks—just like legates, tribunes, and centurions in military affairs, and praetors, censors, treasurers, and other kinds of magistrates in the governance of cities—so that being responsible for a few specified things they may perform their responsibilities well. Likewise, if wives wish to manage well the business of their household, they will distinguish between the different functions of overseers and workers, so that whatever should be done by each person, and what is expected of them, is perfectly clear. For unless a place is designated to each person in a ship, even though no storm arises, still all things will be in tumult.[267] Heaven itself, the domicile that we await, we know to be composed of a series of parts each joined

263. Ps.-Aristotle, *Economics*, 1.5.

264. Cf. Hesiod, *Works and Days*, 373.

265. Xenophon, *Oeconomicus*, 7.37–38.

266. Plutarch, *Cato the Elder*, 5. On Barbaro's reading of this story, see Gothein, *Das Buch von der Ehe*, 99n107. Modern scholars refer to the promontory as Cynossema, which also means "Dog's Tomb." I am most grateful to Cheryl Lemmens for this information.

267. Cf. Xenophon, *Oeconomicus*, 8 and 9.

to the other, and all smoothly interconnected.[268] In playing the harp, diverse tones struck at the same time come together in harmony, than which there is nothing sweeter or lovelier to be heard. Likewise, if servants and provisions are all given a due place and purpose, they will work together for the splendor and utility and delight of the household. Therefore, as I have said before, wives should receive, protect, and distribute all that is in the house with care, prudence, and grace. And whatever they have ordered with zeal and diligence and labored to improve, they then carefully perfect, so that the common welfare of the household may be strengthened and increased. But of this matter, enough said.

CHAPTER 9: ON THE EDUCATION OF CHILDREN

It remains to speak about the education of children, that most important and rewarding of a wife's responsibilities. For diligence in the accumulation of household wealth avails nothing, in truth, as that excellent guide Socrates used to say, unless extraordinary determination and energy have been devoted to the moral and intellectual training of the children who will inherit that wealth.[269] Because of this early care, children are enormously attached to their parents, to whom they are indebted for everything, and rightly so: for if their parents did not provide them with nourishment and instruction, they would be utterly abandoned and forlorn. If indeed we owe all things to the authors of our life—a desire for which nature instills in all mortals, and which we protect as best we can—how much more will we owe them if they also provide a liberal education and the precepts of moral living?

Concerning this, if you reflect deeply with all your mind and soul, you will conclude that if mothers are not bereft of natural instinct, the duty of educating their children is so incumbent upon them, that they cannot refuse it without imperiling their ability to function at all: for in every way nature signifies that the love for offspring is innate, and can in no way be denied.[270] But so that this may be more plainly shown, I shall now speak about the procreation of children before they are born—even though time does not permit me to treat the matter fully, and nature has so positioned those parts of the body in such secret places that they cannot be observed without shame, and hardly spoken of with honor.[271] But what cannot be left unsaid, I shall set forth.

---

268. Cf. Cicero, *Tusculan Disputations*, 1.11.24; *On the Nature of the Gods*, 1.4.9. Barbaro alludes to the interconnected spheres and operations of the Ptolemaic model of the universe, common to the ancients and Christian Europe.

269. Plutarch, *De liberis educandis*, 4e (7). Correcting Crates, an error in the manuscript Barbaro utilized, for Socrates.

270. All of the preceding based on Plutarch, *De amore prolis*, 3, at end.

271. Plutarch, *De amore prolis*, 3.

The blood that women otherwise expel in their monthly effusions is retained at nature's command precisely at that time when it is needed to surround and nourish the fetus while it grows for the appointed time until birth.[272] Later, in all animals that give birth, once the fetus is born, nature supplies milk as nourishment, and fills the breasts from which, as from welling fountains, the infant drinks, so that gradually his members grow and he thrives. Two breasts, moreover, are supplied, which are beneficial if the mother has given birth to twins, so both may suck and feed at the same time.[273] While these things are arranged in this manner by divine providence, it would have been done in vain, if nature had not also instilled in the mother an exceptional love and warmth towards those she has brought into the world.[274] The particular care and diligence of nature can be observed also in this, that while in other species she has placed the nipples under the belly, she has instead affixed them to the breasts of the human mother, who may thereby at the same time nourish the babe with milk and enfold it in a warm embrace, easily and conveniently kiss it, and, as it is said, receive it wholly to her bosom.[275]

So nature has assigned to mothers the office of birthing and educating their children not only as a necessary burden, but as an expression of exceptional love and kindness. A fine example of maternal duty, if we care to attend to it, can be observed in that stern and savage beast, the bear. The bear is wholly devoted to the rearing her young: for as soon as the unformed fetus is born, she grooms the newborn with her tongue as if it were a kind of tool, and so shapes it, that she properly could be called not only the mother of her cub, but indeed its sculptor.[276] Why do we linger over these small matters? For they illustrate how nature itself has instilled in mothers such love for their offspring, that once having given birth, animals that were timid become fierce, the lazy become industrious, and the gluttonous starve themselves. For did not Homer tell of a bird who suffers hunger so that she could bring food to her chicks, and so that all might be well with them, deprives herself?[277]

Mothers will be deserving of great blame, therefore, if they neglect the care of their children and live only for themselves. Rather, they should spare no exertion in this task, so that in their old age they may have their children about them as their friends, aides, and caretakers. If mothers wish to live worthy lives, therefore, they must not reject those to whom they have given birth, but rather, they should provide for their children in body and in soul. Let them feed them,

272. Plutarch, *De amore prolis*, 3.

273. Plutarch, *De liberis educandis*, 3d (5).

274. Plutarch, *De amore prolis*, 3.

275. Plutarch, *De amore prolis*, 3.

276. Plutarch, *De amore prolis*, 2; cf. also Pliny, *Natural History*, 8.54.

277. Plutarch, *De amore prolis*, 2.

offering their breasts, so that those whom they nourished with their own blood when they were yet unknown, now that they have come forth into the light, now that they are human, now that they are known, now that they are loved, let them rear those who now cry out for them, performing in every way they can the role not merely of nurse, but the office of mother.[278]

The wife of Marcus Cato the Censor suckled her infant with her own milk,[279] which custom remains alive today among Roman women. And since, indeed, the bond formed between those who eat together encourages a kind of camaraderie and love,[280] so as to make the children of her servants more friendly to her own infant, such a mother sometimes offers them her breasts.[281] We ask and urge all noble women to imitate Cato's wife, because it is of the greatest possible consequence that the infant should also be fed by her in whose womb, and from whose blood, it was conceived.[282] For there exists no more suitable or salutary nourishment to be offered to the infant as a familiar and trusted food than that very blood, aglow with natural warmth and vigor. The potency of maternal milk is nearly as great as that of semen in forming the qualities of mind and soul, as is clearly evident in many things. The hair of goats suckled on sheep's milk gradually becomes softer, for instance, while the pelts of lambs who are suckled by goats are visibly coarsened. In trees, similarly, as is well-known, the sap and soul have greater potency than the seed: when strong and vital plants are transplanted to an alien soil, their sap deteriorates and they grow inferior shoots.[283]

Noble women, therefore, should try to suckle their children, lest they fail to thrive when fed on lesser and alien milk. If, as often happens, mothers are truly unable, for valid reasons, to suckle their own offspring, nurses should be sought who may substitute for them in that office—not servants, nor foreigners, nor drunks or whores, but well-born and well-bred women commanding proper speech. Otherwise the tender infant can be corrupted by vulgar words and behavior, and by drinking in error, impurity, and disease along with the very milk, be infected by a pernicious contagion, and degenerate in both body and soul.[284] For in the same way that the limbs of the infant can easily be guided and formed, so also from infancy, its character may be aptly and harmoniously composed. Great care must be taken, therefore, in choosing nurses, as the mind

278. Aulus Gellius, *Noctes atticae*, 12.1.11–17. Cf. also Xenophon, *Oeconomicus*, 7.19.

279. Plutarch, *Cato the Elder*, 20.

280. Plutarch, *De liberis educandis*, 3d (5).

281. Plutarch, *Cato the Elder*, 20.

282. For this extended discussion of the power of maternal milk, see Aulus Gellius, *Noctes atticae*, 12.1.11–17.

283. Barbaro returns here to points made in the first part of the treatise, Chapter 3: see 78–81.

284. Plutarch, *De liberis educandis*, 3c–d (5).

at this age is so pliable that the affections and defects of the nurse, like a seal in soft wax, can leave their impress on the fabric of the child.[285] The wise poet Virgil demonstrates how powerful is the character and nature of the nurse when his Dido calls Aeneas not only fierce as a beast but also hard as iron, as though "Hircanian tigers nursed you."[286] In the same way, the lighthearted poet Theocritus reviled Cupid as savage, not because Venus was his mother, but because he had sucked from the breasts of a lion.[287] Mothers, accordingly, should think it worthwhile, honorable, and most commendable to suckle their children, whom they will thereby nourish also with great love, trust, and care—or they should commit this part of their responsibility to well-trained nurses who will act not from false or mercenary motives, but will genuinely cherish and value their charges.

Once their children have grown past infancy, mothers will need to commit much thought, care, and energy to guide them to excel in qualities of mind and body. They should teach their children to revere Almighty God, first above all, and then their country and their parents, so that from their earliest years they develop the habit of piety, the foundation of the other virtues. Only those children who fear God, obey the laws, honor their parents, respect their elders, love their peers, and cherish those younger than they, will give grounds for hope. Let these children greet everyone with an open countenance and friendly words, especially seeking to know the best of them. Let them learn to be temperate in food and drink, thereby laying, as it were, the foundations for the lifelong practice of moderation. Let them be warned to flee those pleasures that are accompanied by any dishonor, and apply their mind and soul to those studies that will be to them in later years honorable, useful, and pleasurable. If mothers have been able to instruct their children in these things, as youths they will more easily and solidly acquire the benefits of learning. We see often that the orders and commands of princes are gratefully received, while the same instructions issued by ordinary figures are unwelcome. Who does not know how, in the same way, even the bland and ordinary words of a parent have great authority with children? For this reason the wise Cato the Elder, so as not to fall short in his duty as a father to his children, diligently taught them their letters, among other things.[288] The Illyrian woman Eurydice, as well, should be given her due praise: for as an adult, she taught herself to read, opening that great storehouse of virtue and knowledge, so that it might be

---

285. Plutarch, *De liberis educandis*, 3e–f (5).

286. Virgil, *Aeneid*, 4.367; trans. A.S. Kline (2002), from the website *Poetry in Translation*, http://www.poetryintranslation.com/PITBR/Latin/VirgilAeneidIV.htm#_Toc342017. Quoted by Aulus Gellius, *Noctes atticae*, 12.1. 20. Hircania was a region on the southern coast of the Caspian Sea that had been under Persian and Macedonian rule.

287. Theocritus, *Idylls*, 3.15–16.

288. Plutarch, *Cato the Elder*, 20.

said she not only gave her children life, but also showed them, as best she could, through the bounty of education, how to live rightly and well.[289]

Mothers should correct children who laugh too much, or who speak brashly: for the former is a sign of foolishness, the latter of fury. They should warn them that it is improper even to speak about anything that is improper to do. Mothers should forbid filthy or disrespectful language, and any unseemly or obscene speech should be greeted not with a smile or a kiss, but a whip. They should teach their children, further, never to mock others for their poverty, or their humble ancestry, or other such calamities, by which behavior they arouse enmities that do not go away, and acquire, besides, the habit of arrogance. They should have their children engage in sports, in which they willingly exert themselves so that, if the need occur, they will be able to tolerate more stressful challenges.

In the presence of their children, I would have mothers avoid anger, avarice, and lust, for these sins deplete virtue. In this way, from their infancy their children will despise, reject, and hate these despotic vices, and, shuddering at blasphemy, revere and honor greatly all that is sacred. For what adults will not scorn those who, at such an age, despise what is holy? So it is of the greatest importance that children be taught from a very tender age to abstain from swearing; for we cannot really expect much of those who swear freely over some trifling matter, while those who swear often may find that they have unknowingly damned themselves. They should be taught plainly to speak the truth! The Persians did not permit the institution of the marketplace, for they believed it was a place of lying, trickery, and false witness.[290] As elsewhere, so also at banquets, children should be taught to say little unless asked, lest they talk too much or disrespectfully—behavior which is intolerable at this age. And it will be an impediment to learning, if they impudently wish to expound what they have not thoroughly understood.[291] Cato replied cleverly when, as a young man, others rebuked him for his silence: "It will not trouble me in the future," he said, "when I shall have learned those things that need to be said."[292] If children learn these principles from their mothers at the earliest possible age, they will more easily and successfully achieve the gravity and rectitude of their parents.

Many other things could be said which, because they pertain rather to fathers, I shall pass by for now—and all the more so, because I suspect there are some who say that this disquisition of mine on marriage is so immense and infinite that the patriarchs of our age could not hope to meet its standard. To them I can only respond in this way: I did not set out to describe what was being done,

289. Plutarch, *De liberis educandis*, 20.

290. Herodotus, *History*, 1.138.1; see also Aulus Gellius, *Noctes atticae*, 11.11.1–2.

291. Cf. Xenophon, *Cyropaedia*, 1.2.3; cf. also Vergerio, *De ingenuis moribus*, ed. Kallendorf, 16/17, para. 13.

292. Plutarch, *Cato the Younger*, 4.

but to show what ought to be done. Who is so unjust a critic that he will not approve of marriage made for the best reasons, just as you have done, who in choosing a wife for her character, age, birth, beauty, and wealth have taken the best of women, who is loving to her husband, who is modest, and who is skilled in household management? Who, I say, has so dark a view of things, that he will not himself hope for all these great benefits, and think that wives of this sort will not excel in all of these ways?

Your peers, therefore, my Lorenzo, should be inspired to imitate you and eagerly follow your path, who have chosen as your wife Ginevra, who in virtue, beauty, nobility of birth, and wealth, is the most splendid young woman anywhere to be found. What more luminous, what more worthy example could I put forward than yours?[293] Since you, a citizen of Florence, Italy's most glorious city, and made illustrious by those admirable men, your father, your grandfather, and your ancestors, have taken for yourself a wife whose wealth all men, and whose modesty, loyalty, and prudence, the best of them so celebrate and admire, that they think her most blessed and fortunate to have you for a husband, and you equally so to have her for a wife? And who all pray to God Almighty, now that you have completed the most excellent and estimable rites of marriage, that you may give birth to splendid children for yourselves, and worthy citizens for the republic?

These matters that I have discussed would perhaps be seen as trifling if they had not been made conspicuous by your nuptials. For young men will indeed profit more greatly if they follow your example, than if they merely had my writings to guide them. For just as laws are of greatest benefit to a city when it is known that an excellent prince obeys them, so also, since your own deep understanding of matrimony[294] bears out my precepts, we need not despair that they will be of use to the young.

But let my discourse end where it began, with you, Lorenzo: you now have, instead of a present, my treatise on the wealth of wives. Whatever I have said in it—not so as to admonish you (as I said at the outset[295]) but so as to declare the love we share—will be, I trust, acceptable to many; but to you, I know, in whose name I undertook this endeavor, it will most certainly be. But as you read these jottings of mine, if anything strikes you as weighty or learned, you may give the credit to Zaccaria Trevisan,[296] a man worthy of the highest praise—whose memory I celebrate—and to Greek books,[297] from which I have extracted whatever pertains to

293. Cf. Vergerio, *De ingenuis moribus*, ed. Kallendorf, 12/13, para. 10.

294. Barbaro writes *ratio uxoria*: the same phrase used in the dedicatory letter, which I translated as the "science of marriage"; see above, note 4.

295. See above, 65–67.

296. Zaccaria Trevisan, Barbaro's mentor; see above, Introduction, 2–3.

297. Gnesotto comments that he should really have said "Greek and Latin books," for he uses both: *De re uxoria*, 99 (77) n4; but it is the extensive use of Greek sources that is exceptional.

the matter before us and presented it here. Having been immersed in these Greek studies for only a few months, yet I have managed already to extract from them rich and delightful fruit. In this task I have been empowered by the mind and soul of the eminent and erudite Guarino Veronese, my teacher and most devoted of friends. Ever since I, together with some other of my peers, took up and entered upon the study of the humanities, he has been my guide, and such a guide, that by his efforts these sacred studies,[298] to which I had been devoted since child-hood, have become more fruitful and satisfying. So be pleased now to take this wifely necklace,[299] then, if I may so call it, on the occasion of your nuptials. You will treasure it, I know, either because it is the kind of gift that cannot, like other necklaces, be broken and worn by use, or because it comes to you in all sincerity from a soul that is entirely yours.

༄

298. Barbaro writes *divina studia*, which in this period usually means theological studies; but here clearly he intends the *studia humanitatis*, or "studies of humanity," a byword for the humanist disciplines of history, moral philosophy, grammar, rhetoric, and poetry, which by insinuation are likewise "divine." This is the second instance of Barbaro conflating the *studia humanitatis* with the "divine" or "sacred." For the first, see above, note 153.

299. As Barbaro writes: *monile uxorium.*

Bibliography

De re uxoria: *Editions and Translations*[1]

Editions:

Paris 1513/1514, editio princeps
Fr. Barbari patricii Veneti oratorisque clarissimi de re uxoria libelli duo. [Paris]: Josse Bade [Jodocus Badius Ascensius], 1513; [Paris]: Vaenundantur in aedibus Ascensianis, 1514.[2]

Haguenau 1533
Francisci Barbari ... de re uxoria libri duo. Haganoae: Secer, 1533.

Antwerp 1535
Francisci Barbari Patricii Veneti oratorisq clarissimi De re vxoria libri duo. Antverpiae: Apud Martinum Caesarem [Merten de Keyser], 1535.

Strasbourg 1612
De re uxoria: libri duo. Praemissa sunt duorum Poggii Florentini & Pauli Vergerii de hisce libris iudicia / alt: *Francisci Barbari, ... de Re uxoria libri duo ante annos septuaginta octo in imperiali Haganoa editi, nunc in lucem reproducti a Joachimo Cluten* ... Argentorati: Typis J. Caroli, 1612.

Amsterdam 1639
De re uxoria: libri duo ut venustate sermonis praeclari, ita & praeceptis optimis & exemplis uberrimis ex omni Graeca Latinaque historia collectis redundantes. Amstelodami: [Typi]s Ioannis Ianssonii, 1639.

Padua 1915/1916
De re uxoria, in partes duas. Ed. Attilio Gnesotto. *Atti e Memorie della R. Accademia di Scienze, Lettere ed Arti in Padova,* n.s. 32 (1915–1916), 6–105.[3]

---

1. The *De re uxoria* circulated in more than 100 manuscript versions (Griggio, "Copisti ed editori"), mostly of Italian origin, the great majority written prior to the first printing of Paris, 1513.

2. Manuscript located and printed at the instigation of jurist and scholar André Tiraqueau, a gift for his father-in-law on the occasion of his marriage: Gothein, *Francesco Barbaro,* 98–99.

3. Minor emendations to this critical edition based on further manuscript investigation in Griggio, "Copisti ed editori," 1047–55.

Translations:

Haguenau 1536	Alber, Erasmus, trans.	*Eyn güt büch von der Ehe was die Ehe sei, was sie güts mit sich bringe, Wie eyn weib geschickt sein soll, die eyner zu ð Ehe nehmen will, etc.* ... Getruckt zü Hagnaw: Durch Valentinum Kobian, 1536.
Venice 1548	Lollio, Alberto, trans.	*Prudentissimi et graui documenti circa la elettion della moglie.* In Vinegia: Appresso Gabriel Giolito de Ferrari, 1548.
Erfurt 1561	Alber, Erasmus, trans.	*Vom H. Ehestand. Sechs Gottlicher Lehr, des inhalt im folgenden blat zu sehen.* Zu Erffurd: truckts Georgius Bawman ..., 1561.
Paris 1667	Joly, Claude, trans.	*Les deux livres de l'estat du mariage ... Traduction nouuelle. Avec quelques traités chrestiens & moraux touchant les offices domestiques.* Paris: G. de Luyne, 1667.[4]
London 1677	Anonymous trans.	*Directions for Love and Marriage: In Two Books.* London: Printed for John Leigh at the Bell, and Tho. Burrell at the Golden Ball, under St. Dunstan's Church, in Fleet Street, 1677.[5]
Vercelli 1778	Lollio, Alberto, trans.	*La scelta della moglie.* Vercelli: Dalla Stamperia Patria, 1778.[6]
Vicenza 1785	Lollio, Alberto, trans.	*La scelta della moglie.* Vicenza: Nella Stamperia Turra, 1785.

4. Revises an earlier translation, not printed, of 1548, also intended for the celebration of a marriage: Gothein, *Francesco Barbaro*, 99.

5. Translated from the Amsterdam 1639 edition, in the belief that it had been translated from an Italian original, as the publisher writes in a prefatory letter to the reader: "This treatise was first written in Italian, and so well liked of that it was translated into Latine (sic), and printed in Holland, where it hath gained an universal applause. It is now at last translated for the benefit of the English reader, from the generality of whom it hopes for a favourable reception." Fol. A3v.

6. Reprint of 1548 edition with new title, as in subsequent reprints.

Naples 1806	Lollio, Alberto, trans.	*La scelta della moglie*. Napoli: Presso Vincenzio Orsino, 1806.
Berlin 1933	Gothein, Percy, trans.	*Das Buch von der Ehe: De re uxoria*. Berlin: Verlag die Runde, 1933.
Milan 1952 (partial)	Garin, Eugenio, trans.	"La elezion della moglie, prefazione/ De re uxoria liber, praefatio" (bilingual Latin/Italian version of the dedication to Lorenzo de' Medici). In *Prosatori latini del Quattrocento* (Milan: Ricciardi, 1952), 103–37.
Philadelphia 1978 (partial)	Kohl, Benjamin G., trans.	"On Wifely Duties" (Part Two of *De re uxoria* with dedication to Lorenzo de' Medici). In Benjamin G. Kohl and Ronald G. Witt, eds., *The Earthly Republic: Italian Humanists on Government and Society* (Philadelphia: University of Pennsylvania Press, 1978), 189–228.

Adaptation:

Nuremberg 1472	Von Eyb, Albrecht	Nürnberg: Offizin Anton Koberger, 1472.[7]

Other Primary Sources

Alberti, Leon Battista. *The Albertis of Florence: Leon Battista Alberti's Della famiglia*. Edited and translated by Guido A. Guarino. Lewisburg, PA: Bucknell University Press, 1971.

───────. *The Family in Renaissance Florence*. Translated by Renée Neu Watkins. Columbia: University of South Carolina Press, 1969. Reprint, Lake Grove, IL: Waveland Press, 2004.

───────. *I libri della famiglia*. Edited by Ruggiero Romano and Alberto Tenenti. Turin: G. Einaudi, 1969. 2nd ed., with additional editor Francesco Furlan. Turin: G. Einaudi, 1994.

7. Utilizes Barbaro's *De re uxoria* along with fragments of other humanistic and classical texts; reprinted 10 more times through 1540. For von Eyb, see especially *Das Ehebüchlein*, ed. and trans. Hiram Kümper, a bilingual edition with modern German facing the Middle High German original from the 1472 incunable; and discussion above, Introduction, note 77.

_____. *Opere volgari*. Edited by Cecil Grayson. 3 vols. Bari: G. Laterza, 1960–1973.

_____. *On Painting*. Edited and translated by Rocco Sinisgalli. Cambridge: Cambridge University Press, 2011.

Barbaro, Francesco. *Das Buch von der Ehe: De re uxoria*. Edited and translated by Percy Gothein. Berlin: Verlag die Runde, 1933.

_____. *Epistolario*. Edited by Claudio Griggio. 2 vols. Florence: L.S. Olschki, 1991, 1999. Vol. 2: http://digital.casalini.it/8822247892.

_____. *De re uxoria liber, in partes duas*. Edited by Attilio Gnesotto. *Atti e Memorie della R. Accademia di Scienze, Lettere ed Arti in Padova*, n.s. 32 (1915–1916), 6–105. Offprint, Padua: Tipografia Giov. Batt. Randi, 1915.

Baron, Hans, ed. and trans. *Leonardo Bruni Aretino: Humanistisch-philosophische Schriften mit einer Chronologie seiner Werke und Briefe*. Leipzig: B.G.Teubner, 1928. Reprint, Wiesbaden: Dr. Martin Sändig, 1969.

Boccaccio, Giovanni. *Famous Women*. Edited and translated by Virginia Brown. Cambridge, MA: Harvard University Press, 2003.

Bracciolini, Poggio. *Epistulae*. Edited by Thomas de Tonellis. In vol. 3 of *Opera omnia*, edited by Riccardo Fubini. 4 vols. Turin: Bottega d'Erasmo, 1963–1969.

_____. *Opera omnia*. Edited by Riccardo Fubini. 4 vols. Turin: Bottega d'Erasmo, 1963–1969.

Campano, Giannantonio. *De dignitate matrimonii*. In *Opera selecta: quibus continentur de rebus gestis Andreae Brachii libri sex, cum uita Pii II, pontificis maximi, descriptione Thrasimeni, de ingratitudine fugienda libris tribus, denique de regendo magistratu, et de dignitate matrimonii, libellis singularis*, edited by Friedrich Otto Mencke, 737–57. Lipsiae [Leipzig]: Apud Iacobum Schusterum, 1734.

Comenius, Johann Amos. *The School of Infancy*. Edited and translated by Ernest M. Eller. Chapel Hill: University of North Carolina Press, 1956.

Corfiati, Claudia, ed. *Una disputa umanistica de amore: Guiniforte Barzizza e Giovanni Pontano da Bergamo*. Messina: Centro interdipartimentale di studi umanistici, 2008.

Dolce, Lodovico. *Dialogo della institution delle donne*. In Vinegia [Venice]: Appresso Gabriel Giolito de Ferrari e Fratelli, 1545.

Dominici, Giovanni. *Regola del governo di cura familiare, compilata dal beato Giovanni Dominici, fiorentino*. Edited by Donato Salvi. Florence: A. Garinei, 1860.

_____. *Regola del governo di cura familiare, parte quarta, on the Education of Children*. The fourth part of Dominici's *Regola*, translated by Arthur Basil Coté. Washington, DC: Catholic University of America, 1927.

Donne, John. *Sermons*. Edited by George R. Potter and Evelyn M. Simpson. 10 vols. Berkeley: University of California Press, 1953–1962.

Erasmus, Desiderius. *Dialogus ciceronianus.* Edited by A. H. T. Levi. Vol. 6 of *Literary and Educational Writings,* being vol. 28 of *The Collected Works of Erasmus* [CWE]. Toronto: University of Toronto Press, 1986.

_____. *The Institution of Christian Matrimony / Institutio Christiani Matrimonii.* Edited and translated by Michael J. Heath. In vol. 4 of *Spiritualia and Pastoralia,* edited by John W. O'Malley and Louis A. Perraud, being vol. 69 of *The Collected Works of Erasmus* [CWE], 203–438. Toronto: University of Toronto Press, 1999.

Fonte, Moderata. *The Worth of Women, Wherein is Clearly Revealed their Nobility and their Superiority to Men.* Edited and translated by Virginia Cox. Chicago: University of Chicago Press, 1997.

Froebel, Friedrich. *Friedrich Froebel: A Selection from his Writings.* Edited by Irene M. Lilley. Cambridge: Cambridge University Press, 1967.

Griffiths, Gordon, James Hankins, and David Thompson, ed. and trans. *The Humanism of Leonardo Bruni: Selected Texts.* Binghamton, NY: Medieval and Renaissance Texts and Studies, in conjunction with the Renaissance Society of America, 1987.

Guarino Veronese. *Epistolario di Guarino Veronese.* Edited by Remigio Sabbadini. 3 vols. Venice: A spese della società di storia veneta, 1915–1919.

Justinian I, Emperor. *Codex.* http://www.thelatinlibrary.com/justinian.html.

King, Margaret L., and Albert Rabil, Jr., ed. and trans. *Her Immaculate Hand: Selected Works by and about the Women Humanists of Quattrocento Italy.* Binghamton, NY: Medieval and Renaissance Texts and Studies, 1983; rev. ed. 1992.

Kohl, Benjamin G., and Ronald G. Witt, eds. *The Earthly Republic: Italian Humanists on Government and Society.* Philadelphia: University of Pennsylvania Press, 1978.

Marinella, Lucrezia. *The Nobility and Excellence of Women, and the Defects and Vices of Men.* Edited and translated by Anne Dunhill. Introduction by Letizia Panizza. Chicago: University of Chicago Press, 1999.

Nogarola, Isotta. *Complete Writings: Letterbook, Dialogue on Adam and Eve, Orations.* Edited and translated by Margaret L. King and Diana M. Robin. Chicago: University of Chicago Press, 2004.

Pestalozzi, Johann Heinrich. *Wie Gertrud ihre Kinder lehrt, ein Versuch den Müttern Anleitung zu geben, ihre Kinder selbst zu unterrichten.* Bern: C. Gessner, 1801.

Petrarch, Francis (Francesco Petrarca). *On His Own Ignorance and That of Many Others.* Edited and translated by Hans Nachod. In *The Renaissance Philosophy of Man: Selections in Translation,* edited by Ernst Cassirer, Paul Oskar Kristeller, and John Herman Randall, Jr., 47–133. Chicago: University of Chicago Press, 1948.

Rabil, Albert, Jr., ed. and trans. *Knowledge, Goodness, and Power: The Debate over Nobility among Quattrocento Italian Humanists.* Binghamton, NY: Medieval and Renaissance Texts and Studies, 1991.

Scala, Bartolomeo. *Bartolomeo Scala: Humanistic and Political Writings.* Edited and translated by Alison Brown. Tempe, AZ: Medieval and Renaissance Texts and Studies, 1997.

Traversari, Ambrogio. *Aliorumque ad ipsum, et ad alios de eodem Ambrosio latinae epistolae.* Ordered by Petrus Cannetus. Edited by Laurentius Mehus. 2 vols. Florence: ex typographio Caesareo, 1759. Reprint, Bologna: Forni, 1968.

Valla, Lorenzo. *De falso credita et ementita Constantini donatione.* Edited by Wolfram Setz. Weimar: Böhlau, 1976.

───────. *The Treatise of Lorenzo Valla on the Donation of Constantine.* Edited and translated by Christopher B. Coleman. New Haven: Yale University Press, 1922. Reprint, Toronto: University of Toronto Press in association with the Renaissance Society of America, 1993.

Vegio, Maffeo. *De educatione liberorum et eorum claris moribus, libri sex.* Edited (books 1–3) by Maria Walburg Fanning and (books 4–6) by Anne Stanislaus Sullivan. Washington, DC: Catholic University of America, 1933, 1936.

Vergerio, Pietro Paolo. *The Character and Studies Befitting a Free-Born Youth.* Edited and translated by Craig Kallendorf. In *Humanist Educational Treatises,* edited by Craig Kallendorf, 2–91. Cambridge, MA: Harvard University Press, 2002.

───────. *Epistolario di Pier Paolo Vergerio.* Edited by Leonardo Smith. Rome: Tipografia del Senato, 1934.

───────. *De ingenuis moribus et liberalibus studiis adulescentiae, libellus in partes duas.* Edited by Attilio Gnesotto. *Atti e memorie della R. Accademia di Scienze, Lettere ed Arti in Padova,* n.s. 34, no. 2 (1917–1918): 75–157. Offprint, Padua: Tipografia Giov. Batt. Randi, 1918.

Vives, Juan Luis. *The Education of a Christian Woman: A Sixteenth-Century Manual.* Edited and translated by Charles Fantazzi. Chicago: University of Chicago Press, 2000.

───────. *The Instruction of a Christen Woman.* Edited by Virginia Walcott Beauchamp, Elizabeth H. Hageman, and Margaret Mikesell, with Sheila ffolliott and Betty S. Travitsky. Urbana: University of Illinois Press, 2002.

───────. *De officio mariti: Introduction, Critical Edition, Translation and Notes.* Edited and translated by Charles Fantazzi. Leiden: Brill, 2006.

Von Eyb, Albrecht. *Das Ehebüchlein: Nach dem Inkunabeldruck der Offizin Anton Koberger, Nürnberg 1472.* Edited and translated by Hiram Kümper. Stuttgart: *ibidem*-Verlag, 2008.

Secondary Sources

Allen, Prudence, Sister. *The Concept of Woman*. Vol. 2: *The Early Humanist Reformation, 1250–1500*. Grand Rapids, MI: Wm. B. Eerdmans, 2002.

Atwood, Craig D. *The Theology of the Czech Brethren from Hus to Comenius*. University Park: Pennsylvania State University Press, 2009.

Battista, Giuseppina. *L'educazione dei figli nella regola di Giovanni Dominici, 1355/6–1419*. Florence: Pagnini e Martinelli, 2002.

Bellavitis, Anna. "La dote a Venezia tra medioevo e prima età moderna." In *Spazi, poteri, diritti delle donne a Venezia in età moderna*, edited by Anna Bellavitis, Nadia Maria Filippini, and Tiziana Plebani, 5–20. Verona: QuiEdit, 2012.

_____. "Family and Society." In Dursteler, *A Companion to Venetian History*, 319–52.

Brucker, Gene A. *Renaissance Florence*. New York: John Wiley, 1969. Reprint, Berkeley: University of California Press, 1983.

Burke, Peter. *The Fortunes of the Courtier: The European Reception of Castiglione's Cortegiano*. University Park: Pennsylvania State University Press, 1996.

Cadden, Joan. *Meanings of Sex Difference in the Middle Ages: Medicine, Science, and Culture*. Cambridge: Cambridge University Press, 1993.

Chojnacka, Monica. *Working Women of Early Modern Venice*. Baltimore: Johns Hopkins University Press, 2001.

Chojnacki, Stanley. "Dowries and Kinsmen." In Chojnacki, *Women and Men in Renaissance Venice*, 132–52

_____. "Gender and the Early Renaissance State." In Chojnacki, *Women and Men in Renaissance Venice*, 27–52.

_____. "Getting Back the Dowry." In Chojnacki, *Women and Men in Renaissance Venice*, 95–111.

_____. "Kinship Ties and Young Patricians." In Chojnacki, *Women and Men in Renaissance Venice*, 206–26.

_____. "Marriage Regulation in Venice, 1420–1535." In Chojnacki, *Women and Men in Renaissance Venice*, 53–75.

_____. "Measuring Adulthood: Adolescence and Gender." In Chojnacki, *Women and Men in Renaissance Venice*, 185–205.

_____. "'The Most Serious Duty': Motherhood, Gender, and Patrician Culture." In Chojnacki, *Women and Men in Renaissance Venice*, 169–82.

_____. "Patrician Women in Early Renaissance Venice." In Chojnacki, *Women and Men in Renaissance Venice*, 115–31.

_____. "The Power of Love: Wives and Husbands." In Chojnacki, *Women and Men in Renaissance Venice*, 153–68.

_____. "Subaltern Patriarchs: Patrician Bachelors." In Chojnacki, *Women and Men in Renaissance Venice*, 244–56.

_____. *Women and Men in Renaissance Venice: Twelve Essays on Patrician Society.* Baltimore: Johns Hopkins University Press, 2000.

Cowan, Alexander. "Marriage and Dowry." *Oxford Bibliographies Online: Renaissance and Reformation.* http://www.oxfordbibliographies.com/view/document/obo-9780195399301/obo-9780195399301-0014.xml.

_____. *Marriage, Manners and Mobility in Early Modern Venice.* Aldershot, UK: Ashgate, 2007.

Cristellon, Cecilia. *La carità e l'eros: il matrimonio, la chiesa, i suoi giudici nella Venezia del Rinascimento, 1420–1545.* Bologna: Società Editrice Il Mulino, 2010.

Cristellon, Cecilia, and Silvana Seidel Menchi. "Religious Life." In Dursteler, *A Companion to Venetian History,* 379–420.

Danzi, Massimo. "Fra *oikos* e *polis*: il pensiero familiare di Leon Battista Alberti." In *La memoria e la città: scritture storiche tra Medioevo ed età moderna*, edited by Claudia Bastia and Maria Bolognani, 47–62. Bologna: Il Nove, 1995.

D'Elia, Anthony F. *The Renaissance of Marriage in Fifteenth-Century Italy.* Cambridge, MA: Harvard University Press, 2004.

Dixon, Suzanne. *The Roman Mother.* Norman: University of Oklahoma Press, 1988.

Donati, Claudio. *L'idea di nobiltà in Italia: secoli XIV–XVIII.* Rome: Laterza, 1988.

Dursteler, Eric, ed. *A Companion to Venetian History, 1400–1797.* Leiden: Brill, 2013.

Ferguson, Ronnie. "Venetian Language." In Dursteler, *A Companion to Venetian History,* 929–57.

Ferraro, Joanne M. *Marriage Wars in Late Renaissance Venice.* Oxford: Oxford University Press, 2001.

Fildes, Valerie. *Breasts, Bottles and Babies: A History of Infant Feeding.* Edinburgh: Edinburgh University Press, 1986.

Fletcher, Stella. "The Medici Family." *Oxford Bibliographies Online: Renaissance and Reformation.* http://www.oxfordbibliographies.com/view/document/obo-9780195399301/obo-9780195399301-0260.xml.

Frick, Carole Collier. "The Downcast Eyes of the Women of the Upper Class in Francesco Barbaro's *De re uxoria*." *UCLA Historical Journal* 9 (1989). http://escholarship.org/uc/item/8cm5t90d.

_____. "Francesco Barbaro's *De re uxoria*: A Silent Dialogue for a Young Medici Bride." In *Printed Voices: The Renaissance Culture of Dialogue*, edited by Dorothea B. Heitsch and Jean-François Vallée, 193–205. Toronto: University of Toronto Press, 2004.

Giannetti, Laura. *Lelia's Kiss: Imagining Gender, Sex, and Marriage in Italian Renaissance Comedy.* Toronto: University of Toronto Press, 2009.

Gnesotto, Attilio. "I codici Marciani del 'De re uxoria' di Francesco Barbaro." *Atti e Memorie della R. Accademia di scienze, lettere ed arti in Padova*, n.s. 30 (1913–1914), 105–28.

_____. "Dei Mediceo-Laurenziani e del codice padovano del 'De re uxoria' di Francesco Barbaro." *Atti e Memorie della R. Accademia di scienze, lettere ed arti in Padova*, n.s. 30 (1913–1914), 281–94.

Gordan, Phyllis W. G., ed. and trans. *Two Renaissance Book Hunters: The Letters of Poggius Bracciolini to Nicolaus de Niccolis*. New York: Columbia University Press, 1974.

Gothein, Percy. *Francesco Barbaro: Früh-Humanismus und Staatskunst in Venedig*. Berlin: Verlag die Runde, 1932.

Grafton, Anthony. *Leon Battista Alberti: Master Builder of the Italian Renaissance*. New York: Hill and Wang, 2000.

Grendler, Paul F. *Schooling in Renaissance Italy: Literacy and Learning, 1300–1600*. Baltimore: Johns Hopkins University Press, 1989.

Griggio, Claudio. "Copisti ed editori del *De re uxoria* di Francesco Barbaro." In vol. 2 of *Filologia umanistica per Gianvito Resta*, edited by Vincenzo Fera and Giacomo Ferraú, 1033–55. 3 vols. Padua: Antenore, 1997.

_____. "Senofonte, Guarino, Francesco e Ermolao Barbaro, Alberti." *Filologia e critica* 31 (2006): 161–76.

Gualdo Rosa, Lucia, ed. *Gasparino Barzizza e la Rinascita degli studi classici: fra continuità e rinnovamento: Atti del seminario di studi, Napoli, Palazzo Sforza, 11 Aprile 1997*. Naples: Istituto universitario orientale, 1999.

Hacke, Daniela. *Women, Sex, and Marriage in Early Modern Venice*. Aldershot, UK: Ashgate, 2004.

Hanawalt, Barbara A. *The Wealth of Wives: Women, Law, and Economy in Late Medieval London*. Oxford: Oxford University Press, 2007.

Hurlburt, Holly S. *The Dogaressa of Venice, 1200–1500: Wife and Icon*. New York: Palgrave Macmillan, 2006.

Jacks, Philip Joshua, and William Caferro. *The Spinelli of Florence: Fortunes of a Renaissance Merchant Family*. University Park: Pennsylvania State University Press, 2001.

Jordan, Constance. *Renaissance Feminism: Literary Texts and Political Models*. Ithaca, NY: Cornell University Press, 1990.

Kallendorf, Craig. "Guarino da Verona." *Oxford Bibliographies Online: Renaissance and Reformation*. http://www.oxfordbibliographies.com/view/document/obo-9780195399301/obo-9780195399301-0084.xml.

_____. "Leonardo Bruni." *Oxford Bibliographies Online: Renaissance and Reformation*. http://www.oxfordbibliographies.com/view/document/obo-9780195399301/obo-9780195399301-0069.xml.

_____. "Niccolò Niccoli." *Oxford Bibliographies Online: Renaissance and Reformation.* http://www.oxfordbibliographies.com/view/document/obo-9780195399301/obo-9780195399301-0175.xml.

Katchmer, Michael. *Pier Paolo Vergerio and the Paulus, a Latin Comedy.* New York: P. Lang, 1998.

Kelly-Gadol, Joan. Review of Guido A. Guarino, ed. and trans., *The Albertis of Florence: Leon Battista Alberti's* Della famiglia (Lewisburg, PA: Bucknell University Press, 1971). *Italica* 53, no. 2 (1976): 263–65.

King, Margaret L. "Caldiera and the Barbaros on Marriage and the Family: Humanist Reflections of Venetian Realities." *Journal of Medieval and Renaissance Studies* 6, no. 1 (1976): 19–50. Reprinted in Margaret L. King, *Humanism, Venice, and Women: Essays on the Italian Renaissance,* V. Aldershot, UK: Ashgate, 2005.

_____. *The Death of the Child Valerio Marcello.* Chicago: University of Chicago Press, 1994.

_____. "The School of Infancy: The Emergence of Mother as Teacher in Early Modern Times." In *The Renaissance in the Streets, Schools, and Studies: Essays in Honour of Paul F. Grendler,* edited by Konrad Eisenbichler and Nicholas Terpstra, 41–86. Toronto: Centre for Reformation and Renaissance Studies, 2008.

_____. *Venetian Humanism in an Age of Patrician Dominance.* Princeton: Princeton University Press, 1986.

King, Margaret L. and Albert Rabil, Jr. "The Old Voice and the Other Voice: Introduction to the Series." Reprinted in every volume of the first 60 volumes of the series The Other Voice in Early Modern Europe (University of Chicago Press), 1996–2010. http://www.othervoiceineme.com/othervoice.html.

Kluncker, Karlhans. *Percy Gothein: Humanist und Erzieher, das Ärgernis im George-Kreis.* 2nd ed. Amsterdam: Castrum Peregrini, 1986.

Kohl, Benjamin G. *Culture and Politics in Early Renaissance Padua.* Aldershot, UK: Ashgate, 2001.

Kristeller, Paul Oskar. *Iter Italicum: A Finding List of Uncatalogued or Incompletely Catalogued Humanistic Manuscripts of the Renaissance in Italian and other Libraries.* London: Warburg Institute; Leiden: E.J. Brill, 1963–1992. 7 vols. in 9. Online at Iter Gateway to the Middle Ages and Renaissance (University of Toronto Libraries). http://cf.itergateway.org/italicum/.

Kuehn, Thomas. "Reading between the Patrilines: Leon Battista Alberti's *Della Famiglia* in Light of His Illegitimacy." In *I Tatti Studies: Essays in the Renaissance,* vol. 1, edited by Salvatore Camporeale, Caroline Elam, and F. W. Kent, 161–87. Florence: Villa I Tatti, 1985.

Lentzen, Manfred. "La concezione del matrimonio e della famiglia nel *De re uxoria* (1415) di Francesco Barbaro e nell'*Ehebüchlein* (1472) di Albrecht von

Eyb: struttura e funzione del testo." In *Rapporti e scambi tra Umanesimo italiano ed Umanesimo europeo: l'Europa è uno stato d'animo*, edited by Luisa Rotondi Secchi Tarugi, 167–80. Milan: Nuovi orizzonti, 2001.

_____. "Frühhumanistische Auffassungen über Ehe und Familie (Francesco Barbaro—Matteo Palmieri—Leon Battista Alberti)." In *Saeculum tamquam aureum: Internationales Symposion zur italienischen Renaissance des 14.–16. Jahrhunderts (am 17./18. September 1996 in Mainz)*, edited by Ute Ecker and Clemens Zintzen, 379–94. Hildesheim: G. Olms, 1997.

Lugli, Vittorio. *I trattatisti della famiglia nel Quattrocento*. Bologna: A.F. Formíggini, 1909.

Marsh, David. "Leon Battista Alberti." In *Oxford Bibliographies Online: Renaissance and Reformation*. http://www.oxfordbibliographies .com/view/document/obo- 9780195399301/obo- 9780195399301-0115.xml.

Martellotti, Guido. "Gasperino [sic] Barzizza." In *Dizionario biografico degli italiani* 7 (1970). http://www.treccani.it/enciclopedia/gasperino-barzizza_%28 Dizionario_Biografico%29/.

Martines, Lauro. *The Social World of the Florentine Humanists, 1390–1460*. Princeton: Princeton University Press, 1963. Reprint, Toronto: University of Toronto Press for the Renaissance Society of America, 2011.

Massalin, Paola. "Copistes et lecteurs du *De familia* dans l'entourage d'Alberti." In Paoli, Leclerc, and Dutheillet de Lamorthe, *Les* Livres de la famille *d'Alberti*, 205–44.

McClure, George W. *Sorrow and Consolation in Italian Humanism*. Princeton: Princeton University Press, 1991.

McManamon, John M. *Pierpaolo Vergerio the Elder: The Humanist as Orator*. Tempe, AZ: Medieval and Renaissance Texts and Studies, 1996.

Mercer, R. G. G. *The Teaching of Gasparino Barzizza: With Special Reference to His Place in Paduan Humanism*. London: Modern Humanities Research Association, 1979.

Nardi, Patricia. "Mothers at Home: Their Role in Childrearing and Instruction in Early Modern England." Ph.D. diss., City University of New York, 2007.

Nespoulous, Pierre. "Giovanni Pontano: poète de l'amour conjugale." In *Proceedings of the Acta Conventus Neo-Latini Lovaniensis*, edited by Jozef IJsewijn and Eckhard Kessler, 437–43. Leuven: Leuven University Press, 1973.

Oxford Bibliographies. http://www.oxfordbibliographies.com/.

Paoli, Michel. "La question de la richesse et de l'enrichissement dans les livres *De familia* d'Alberti." In Paoli, Leclerc, and Dutheillet de Lamorthe, *Les* Livres de la famille *d'Alberti*, 121–53.

Paoli, Michel, with Élise Leclerc and Sophie Dutheillet de Lamorthe, eds. *Les* Livres de la famille *d'Alberti: sources, sens et influence*. Paris: Classiques Garnier, 2013.

Ponte, Giovanni. *Leon Battista Alberti, umanista e scrittore*. Genoa: Tilgher, 1981.

Richardson, Brian. "'Amore maritale': Advice on Love and Marriage in the Second Half of the Cinquecento." In *Women in Italian Renaissance Culture and Society*, edited by Letizia Panizza, 194–208. Oxford: Legenda, 2000.

Robey, David. "Humanism and Education in the Early Quattrocento: The *De ingenuis moribus* of Pier Paolo Vergerio." *Bibliothèque d'Humanisme et Renaissance* 42, no. 1 (1980): 27–58.

_____. "Pier Paolo Vergerio the Elder: Republicanism and Civic Values in the Work of an Early Humanist." *Past and Present* 58 (1973): 3–37.

Rollo, Antonio. "Dalla biblioteca di Guarino a quella di Francesco Barbaro." *Studi medievali e umanistici* 3 (2005): 9–40.

Romano, Dennis. *The Likeness of Venice: A Life of Doge Francesco Foscari, 1373–1457*. New Haven: Yale University Press, 2007.

_____. *Patricians and* Popolani: *The Social Foundations of the Venetian Renaissance State*. Baltimore: Johns Hopkins University Press, 1987.

Sabbadini, Remigio. "La gita di Francesco Barbaro a Firenze." In vol. 2 of *Miscellanea di studi in onore di Attilio Hortis*, 615–27. 2 vols. Trieste: Stabilimento artistico tipografico G. Caprin, 1910. Reprinted in Remigio Sabbadini, *Storia e critica di testi latini*, 2nd ed., edited by Eugene and Myriam Billanovich, 25–35. Padua: Antenore, 1971.

_____. *Guariniana*. Reprints of *La vita di Guarino Veronese* (1891) and *La scuola e gli studi di Guarino Veronese* (1896). Edited by Mario Sancipriano. Turin: Bottega d'Erasmo, 1964.

Sberlati, Francesco. "Un lecteur du *De familia* à la fin du XVIe siècle: Bernardino Baldi." In Paoli, Leclerc, and Dutheillet de Lamorthe, Les Livres de la famille d'Alberti, 441–53.

Schutte, Anne Jacobson. "Society and the Sexes in the Venetian Republic." In Dursteler, *A Companion to Venetian History*, 353–78.

Simonetti, Remy. "La conception et l'éducation de l'enfant: médecine et physiognomonie dans le *De familia* d'Alberti." In Paoli, Leclerc, and Dutheillet de Lamorthe, *Les* Livres de la famille d'Alberti, 49–66.

Smith, William. *A Dictionary of Greek and Roman Biography and Mythology*. London: John Murray, 1902. http://www.perseus.tufts.edu/hopper/text?doc=Perseus:text:1999.04.0104:entry=gaius-bio-2.

Soranzo, Matteo. "Poetry and Society in Aragonese Naples: Giovanni Pontano's Elegies of Married Love." In *Marriage in Premodern Europe: Italy and Beyond*, edited by Jacqueline Murray. Toronto: Centre for Reformation and Renaissance Studies, 2012.

Sowards, J. K. "Erasmus and the Education of Women." *Sixteenth Century Journal* 13, no. 4 (1982): 77–89.

Sperling, Jutta Gisela. *Convents and the Body Politic in Late Renaissance Venice.* Chicago: University of Chicago Press, 1999.

Tenenti, Alberto. "La *res uxoria* tra Francesco Barbaro e Leon Battista Alberti." In *Una famiglia veneziana nella storia: i Barbaro: Atti del convegno di studi in occasione del quinto centenario della morte dell'umanista Ermolao, Venezia, 4–6 novembre 1993*, edited by Michela Marangoni and Manlio Pastore Stocchi, 43–66. Venice: Istituto veneto di scienze, lettere ed arti, 1996.

Terpening, Ronnie H. *Lodovico Dolce: Renaissance Man of Letters.* Toronto: University of Toronto Press, 1997.

Vitullo, Juliann. "Fashioning Fatherhood: Leon Battista Alberti's Art of Parenting." In *Childhood in the Middle Ages and the Renaissance: The Results of a Paradigm Shift in the History of Mentality*, edited by Albrecht Classen, 341–53. Berlin: Walter de Gruyter, 2005.

Witt, Ronald G. *In the Footsteps of the Ancients: The Origins of Humanism from Lovato to Bruni.* Leiden: Brill, 2000.

_____. *The Two Latin Cultures and the Foundation of Renaissance Humanism in Medieval Italy.* Cambridge: Cambridge University Press, 2012.

Index

Abradatas, king of Susa, 101
Achilles, Greek hero, 26, 79, 84, 117
adultery, 35, 54, 77, 108, 109, 113
Adusius, Persian general, 69
Aemilius Scaurus, Marcus, Roman statesman, 94
Aeneas, Trojan hero, founder of Rome, 26, 79, 122
Aesop, 87, 89
Afrania, Roman matron, 106
Agamemnon, king of Mycenae, 90
agriculture, as pattern and metaphor for human biological condition, 23–25, 26, 30, 41, 57, 65, 75, 78, 79, 88, 94, 121 (*see also* biology)
Agrippa (Marcus Vipsanius Agrippa), Roman general and statesman, 108
Agrippina, Roman empress, mother of Nero, 81
Ajax, Greek hero, 117
Alber, Erasmus, 15, 45 and n77, 128
Alberti, Adovardo, kinsman of Leon Battista, 48n87, 49
Alberti, Giannozzo, kinsman of Leon Battista, 50, 51n91
Alberti, Leon Battista, 44, 47–53; *Della Famiglia* (On the Family), 47–53
Alberti, Lionardo, kinsman of Leon Battista, 48–50
Alberti, Lorenzo, father of Leon Battista, 48
Alexander the Great, Macedonian conqueror, 66, 69, 74, 85, 86, 97, 98, 115
Alledius Severus, Titus, Roman knight, 81
Amaesia Sentia, Roman matron, 106
Anacreon, 82
Andromache, wife of Hector, 34, 56, 71, 92, 102, 117

animals, as pattern and metaphor for human biology and behavior, 20, 67, 112, 116, 117, 118, 120, 121 (*see also* biology)
Appius Claudius, Gaius, Roman statesman, 94
Archidamus, Spartan king, 81
Ariosto, Ludovico, 59 and n113
Aristotle, 5, 26 and n54, 32, 36, 56, 94, 104n190, 111, 114n245
Armenia, wife of Tigranes, 101, 105
Artabazes, noble Persian, 86
Artemisia, queen of Halicarnassus, 103
Augustine, Saint, 6, 15, 20, 21
Augustus, Roman emperor, 108, 112, 115
Aulus Gellius, 6, 16

Bacchus, god of wine, ecstasy, and madness, 110
Barbaro, Andrea, ancestor of Francesco, 23, 73
Barbaro, Costanza, daughter of Francesco, 58
Barbaro, Francesco, 1–8; and humanism, 2–6, 8, 33, 124–25; and the Medici, 6, 18–20, 65–67; and the *respublica litterarum*, 7, 43 (see also *De re uxoria*; Medici, Lorenzo de'; youth)
Barbaro, Marco, Francesco's kinsman, 73 and n38
Barbaro, Zaccaria, son of Francesco Barbaro, 8
Barbo, Francesca, wife of Giusto Contarini, 23, 73
Barbo, Pantaleone, 23, 73
Barsines, wife of Alexander, 86
Barzizza, Gasparino, 3–4, 18, 52, 54
Barzizza, Guiniforte, son of Gasparino, 54 and n105